Bare Grammar

STANFORD MONOGRAPHS IN LINGUISTICS

The aim of this series is to make exploratory work
that employs new linguistic data, extending the scope or domain
of current theoretical proposals, available to a wide audience.
These monographs will provide an insightful generalization of the
problem and data in question which will be of
interest to people working in a variety of frameworks.

STANFORD MONOGRAPHS IN LINGUISTICS

BARE GRAMMAR
Lectures on
Linguistic Invariants

Edward L. Keenan
&
Edward P. Stabler

CSLI
PUBLICATIONS
Center for the Study of
Language and Information
Stanford, California

Copyright © 2003
CSLI Publications
Center for the Study of Language and Information
Leland Stanford Junior University
Printed in the United States
07 06 05 04 03   1 2 3 4 5

Library of Congress Cataloging-in-Publication Data

Keenan, Edward L. (Edward Louis), 1937–
Bare grammar : lectures on linguistic invariants /
by Edward L. Keenan and Edward P. Stabler.

p. cm. – (Stanford monographs in linguistics)
Includes bibliographical references and index.

ISBN 1-57586-189-5 (alk. paper)
ISBN 1-57586-188-7 (pbk. : alk. paper)

1. Grammar, Comparative and general. 2. Generative grammar.
I. Stabler, Edward P. II. Title. III. Series.

P151 .K397 2003
415′.0182–dc22   2003020066
CIP

The drawing, "Teinture des Gobelins, Service du Couchoir,"
that appears on the cover of the paperback edition of this book is from the
*Encyclopédie ou Dictionnaire Raisonneé des Sciences des Arts et des
Métiers*, edited by Diderot. Première Édition de 1751-1780.

∞ The acid-free paper used in this book meets the minimum requirements
of the American National Standard for Information Sciences—Permanence
of Paper for Printed Library Materials, ANSI Z39.48-1984.

CSLI was founded in 1983 by researchers from Stanford University, SRI
International, and Xerox PARC to further the research and development of
integrated theories of language, information, and computation. CSLI headquarters
and CSLI Publications are located on the campus of Stanford University.

CSLI Publications reports new developments in the study of language,
information, and computation. In addition to lecture notes, our publications
include monographs, working papers, revised dissertations, and conference
proceedings. Our aim is to make new results, ideas, and approaches
available as quickly as possible. Please visit our web site at
http://cslipublications.stanford.edu/
for comments on this and other titles, as well as for changes
and corrections by the author and publisher.

Contents

1

Introduction

> **The structure of a language L is given by the expressions, properties of expressions, relations between expressions,...that are invariant under the structure preserving transformations of L.**

This monograph is an elaboration of this claim, which may seem cryptic at first, but will cease to be so shortly. It is a very simple and surprisingly powerful idea. It has led us to propose several theses and axioms for a theory of language structure, expressed in a very minimal generative framework we call Bare Grammar (BG). All of these theses and axioms are in principle compatible with otherwise rather different specific theories of grammar: Relational Grammar, Arc-Pair Grammar, Categorial Grammar, Lexical Functional Grammar, Head Driven Phrase Structure Grammar, Government Binding Theory/Minimalism, and others. So our proposals are not dependent on any particular claims from any one of these different traditions, but it will be instructive to begin with some comparisons.

As generative grammarians we formulate and study the grammars of particular languages, with the end in mind of finding structural commonalities between them. They represent what is general in human language and may, we hope, give us some insight into the nature of mind. The above mentioned theories do share some very general properties, which thus constitute a (small) first step towards finding structural commonalities. In all those theories, a grammar defines a class (normally infinite) of expressions, and simplex (atomic) expressions are distinguished from complex ones which contain them as constituents. Generally a constituent of an expression also occurs as a constituent of other expressions with essentially the same pronunciation and semantic interpretation. So the *is a constituent of* is a structural relation in all these theories. Furthermore, all the theories partition the expres-

1

sions of a language into *grammatical categories*. Expressions of the same category are assumed to share some distributional properties, and to have some conceptual and notational uniformity across the grammars of different languages.

On this last point, Bare Grammar does not follow the traditional practice: we allow: *Different grammars may have different categories.* The inventory of categories can vary from one language to another, as the lexicon does. Since substantial requirements of categorial uniformity are imposed at the outset, linguistic generalizations about categorial uniformity across languages must be explicit, quantifying over all possible categories, rather than relying on typically implicit and obscure assumptions about the identity of specific categories supposedly common to all languages. Lecture 4 develops this explicit approach, clearly formulating some proposals about the general properties that a system of categories for a natural language should meet. More surprising is that certain fundamental roles of categories are naturally subsumed by the more general notion of linguistic "invariant," as will become clear.

Equally, the mechanisms for defining complex expressions in terms of simple ones can vary as a parameter in Bare Grammars. *Different grammars may have different rules.* In practice, the rules proposed by linguists for different languages share many properties, but in Bare Grammar these common properties are not implicit in the formalism, but rather explicitly formulated. We only take some first steps here, expecting future work to delimit the class of structure building operations from which a natural language grammar can draw.

In principle then, any specific grammar in any of the formalisms above should be representable in BG terms, if only it is clearly formulated, by plugging in the categories and rules that that grammar uses. Lecture 3 of this monograph is concerned with showing how this can be done for certain familiar kinds of grammars. Since almost all universal generalizations offered by specific theories crucially use the categories and generative mechanisms specific to that theory, it might seem that there are few generalizations that do not depend on that choice of category system and generative mechanism. We argue otherwise, by example, but we acknowledge that it is surprising that there is much of substance to say at the level of generality offered by Bare Grammar. Let us begin to say it.

Linguistic Invariants. This is the central notion we use in formulating linguistic generalizations. The notion arises in starting our structural investigation of expressions at a slightly different point than the theories mentioned above. Consider the minimally complex expressions in (1a,b):

(1) a. Trevor laughed

b. Nigel cried

Each of the theories mentioned above asks, and answers, "What is the structure of (1a)?" differently. But the initial query of Bare Grammar is not the essentialist "What is the structure of X?" It is the relational "Do X and Y have the same structure?" A largely pretheoretical argument that (1a,b) have the same structure can be given by claiming first that replacing *Trevor* in (1a) by *Nigel* yielding *Nigel laughed* does not change structure. Then we can replace *laughed* by *cried* without changing structure, yielding (1b). So we argue that (1a,b) have the same structure on the grounds that either can be derived from the other by a succession of structure preserving substitutions. Informally these substitutions are the structure preserving transformations mentioned at the outset of this Lecture.

So given a grammar G, which we think of as a definition of a set of expressions L_G, the *language generated by* G, a structure preserving transformation of G is a function mapping expressions to expressions (functions meeting some natural conditions given in Definition 4 on page 20 just below). Then we say expressions s and t *have the same structure, are isomorphic,* if and only if there is a structure preserving transformation mapping s to t (in which case there is also provably a transformation mapping t to s). The conditions that the transformations are required to meet guarantee that isomorphic expressions are built in the same way (but they guarantee more, so sometimes expressions built in the same way are not isomorphic).

Assuming (1a,b) are built in the same way a grammar for English should admit of a structure preserving transformation h which maps (1a) to (1b). Transformation h will then map *Trevor* to *Nigel* and *laughed* to *cried*. (Despite the orthography, nothing we say here requires that *laughed* and *cried* be simplex.) There will be very many possible values for a structure preserving transformation at *Trevor*; any monomorphemic masculine singular proper noun will do. There will be fewer possibilities, possibly just a few hundred, for *laughed*. But a few other words and morphemes of English are associated directly with certain structure types and do not readily admit of any substitutions preserving structure. Consider the suffix *-ing* in

(2) Pampering herself on Sundays relaxes Olivia.

This whole sentence is isomorphic to many other sentences: consider those that result by replacing *Olivia* by any other monomorphemic feminine singular proper noun; replace *Sunday* by any other weekday name; even replace *Olivia* by *Fred* and *herself* by *himself*, etc. But of the many plausibly structure preserving substitutions we can imagine, none replaces *-ing* with anything. Naively *-ing* plays a structural role here, converting a predicate phrase to a nominal that can function as an argument of *relaxes Olivia*. So we have found a criterion distinguishing "content" words from "function" words (grammatical formatives, grammatical constants): the former typically admit of many structure preserving substitutions whereas the latter do not. This lack of freedom is not an accident. If the role of grammatical formatives is to identify particular syntactic operations then replacing a formative with something else would change the entire syntactic structure. That is, we cannot replace grammatical formatives with other expressions preserving syntactic structure. Informally then, for an arbitrary grammar G for a natural language:

Grammatical Constants Hypothesis: The grammatical formatives of G are lexical items that are always mapped to themselves by the structure preserving transformations on L_G.

So grammatical formatives are morphemes you cannot change without changing structure. To the best of our knowledge this is the first non-stipulative characterization of "function" words. It is given more formally in Lecture 2 and it is later modified in one important way (Lecture 4, page 146), but this formulation captures the basic idea.

Grammatical formatives are a special case of a linguistic invariant, something that doesn't change under the action of structure preserving transformations. The transformations canonically extend to functions mapping sets of expressions to sets of expressions, relations between expressions to relations between expressions, etc. For example, given a structure preserving transformation h on some L_G, h maps any set K of expressions to the set of its values at the elements of K:

$$h(K) =_{df} \{h(s)|\ s \in K\}.$$

And we can ask which sets K of expressions are invariant, that is, which sets K are such that $h(K) = K$ for all structure preserving transformations h? For example, in a grammar of English, will the set of singular proper nouns {Trevor, Nigel, Olivia, Sue,...} be invariant? This would mean, in effect, that every transformation maps each such proper noun to such a proper noun. If so then the property of being a singular proper noun is an invariant, that is, a *structural* property of G: if you replace a proper noun with something else you change structure.

Similarly to say that the *is a constituent of* relation is invariant means that for each structure preserving transformation h, whenever s is a constituent of t then h(s) is a constituent of h(t). We prove shortly that this relation is, in fact, universally invariant - invariant in all grammars G (and not just in grammars of human-like languages). Other constituency relations, like *is a sister of* and *c-commands*, are also universally invariant. These results support the correctness of our proposals, since, pretheoretically, linguists treat constituency relations as structural. Even linguists whose theories focus on non-configurational properties of languages do not doubt that constituency relations are structural, they would just doubt their utility in the analysis of natural language. We define these constituency relations (page 29) on expressions, not, as is more usual, on derivations or tree-like structures representing derivations. As we see in Lecture 2, a variety of linguistic phenomena, from substitution rules to reduplication and second position placement of Latin *-que* 'and' are not naturally representable with standard trees, and constituency is not derivable by segmenting the derived string of expressions. Thus we give our definitions with greater generality than usual so as not to depend on the specific nature of the structure building operations.

We have seen already, albeit informally, that morphemes (grammatical formatives, like *-ing*) may be structural, invariants of the grammar, in exactly the same sense as that in which properties or relations (like *is a constituent of, c-commands*) are structural, So an acceptable structural definition of some phenomenon in some languages is allowed to mention specific morphemes, such as case markers and voice markers, provided they can be shown to be invariant. This we will do explicitly in Lecture 2 in defining the Anaphor-Antecedent relation in (our models of) Korean and Toba Batak, using the provably invariant case markers and voice markers. We consider then that our approach to language structure satisfies one of the basic observations in LFG (Bresnan 2001, pp.6,144) that what is morphological in one language may be syntactic in another - morpheme identity (morphology) and constituency relations may be structural in exactly the same sense: being grammatically invariant.

Invariants and structure dependence. An advantage of our characterization of structural properties as invariants is that it provides a clear criterion for defining conditions on rules or the distribution of expressions (reflexives, negative polarity items, etc). Namely, the condition must be invariant: whenever an expression s satisfies the condition then every expression isomorphic to s also satisfies it. Clearly if this failed, if s had some property P but some t isomorphic to s failed to have P, then we could not determine whether s had P just by checking its structure, so P would not be a structural property. Moreover once our formal definitions are given (page 20), the structure preserving transformations of a grammar are determined, and whether a given condition is invariant is typically provable in standard ways, of which we will see many examples in this monograph.

In contrast, the more usual criteria of "structure dependence" are simply not precise enough to permit a proof or even a definite answer about whether some phenomenon has the property. Chomsky (1965, pp.55-6) says, for example,

> ...grammatical transformations are necessarily "structure-dependent" in that they manipulate substrings only in terms of their assignment to categories...It is impossible...to formulate as a transformation such a simple operation as reflection of an arbitrary string (that is, replacement of any string $a_1 \cdots a_n$, where each a_i is a single symbol, by $a_n \cdots a_1$) or interchange of the $(2n\text{-}1)^{\text{th}}$ word with the $2n^{\text{th}}$ word throughout a string of arbitrary length, or insertion of a symbol in the middle of a string of even length....

This kind of view is sometimes repeated in the research literature (Berwick and Weinberg 1984, 158-159), and even in introductory texts (Radford 1997, 13-15). Chomsky lists a few operations we may not use in grammars of natural language, and lists one permissable condition, namely reference to grammatical categories. But these stipulations are simply not precise or general enough to decide whether other operations or conditions are acceptable. Is an operation like "invert the subject and the Aux in any S with a prime number of NPs" structure dependent? The question is not answerable with the intuitive notion, but is decided by ours. In Lecture 2 we provide a grammar in which Latin *-que* 'and' is positioned around its first conjunct regardless of its category. This operation is provably structural in our grammar, but it might fail to be "structure-dependent" in the sense of the quote above. Again we do not really know how to argue the case.

Syntactic invariants semantically defined. An important conceptual plus for our notion of invariant is that it enables us to assess whether notions defined independently of the syntax are grammatically invariant or not (where the syntax is the lexicon together with structure building operations). For example, is the class of monosyllabic nouns in English invariant? Surely not. We know of no grammatical process or condition that forces us to distinguish *bear* from *beaver*, so we expect that a structure preserving transformation can interchange those two nouns and map all other lexical items to themselves. But this question opens a deeper one: Are grammatical distinctions ever definable in purely phonological terms? Zwicky and Pullum (1983),

Bromberger and Halle (1989), and Fontana (1996) argue for the independence of phonology and syntax, but we do not pursue this difficult issue here.

More pertinent to our concerns is the extent to which semantically defined notions are syntactically invariant. The literature here is often unclear. Semantic notions are often used intuitively without a formal definition, or, worse, the purported definition is actually given in syntactic terms rendering the query vacuous (since the structure preserving transformations are defined as functions that preserve syntactic structure). This monograph will be concerned with several cases of the syntactic characterization of semantically defined notions, so let us begin with some conceptually unproblematic examples.

Consider the class of nouns that denote mammals that live in water. *Whale* and *dolphin* are in this class, *shark* and *barracuda* are not. As we know of no syntactic process or condition that forces us to distinguish *dolphin* from *shark*, we expect that there is a structure preserving transformation of English that interchanges these two nouns and maps all other lexical items to themselves. If so then the class of nouns denoting mammals that live in water is not a grammatically definable class in English (that is, it is not invariant), in accordance with our expectations.

A second example, with somewhat more interesting consequences: define a declarative sentence to be logically true (false) if and only if it is true (false) under every acceptable interpretation of its lexical constituents. So we have semantically defined two classes of sentences, and we can reasonably ask if either is invariant. Thus, is the property of being logically true (false) definable in terms of the grammatical structure of English? Again the answer is no. (3a) is true in some situations and false in others and thus is neither logically true nor logically false. But (3b) is logically false, and its negation, (3c) logically true:

(3)   a. Sue read at least sixty but not more than seventy poems last year

        b. Sue read at least seventy but not more than sixty poems last year

        c. It is not the case that Sue read at least seventy but not more than sixty poems last year

Again, we know of no grammatical conditions that force us to distinguish *sixty* from *seventy*, so we assume a structure preserving transformation h may interchange them, mapping all other lexical items to themselves. Such a transformation h then will map (3b) to (3a), so the property of being logically false is not invariant. Equally, h maps (3c) to the negation of (3a), which is not logically true, so the property of being logically true is not invariant.

These modest observations also show that the entailment relation is not a syntactic invariant of English, where a sentence A *entails* a sentence B if and only if B is interpreted as true in every situation in which A is interpreted as true. So (3b) entails (3a), trivially, but their images under the transformation h mentioned above do not stand in the entailment relation, so this relation is not a structural one in English. Note that these facts are the way they are because the entailments of a sentence depend crucially on the meaning of the sentence, and we can find sentences with identical structures but very different meanings.

These entailment facts are not surprising from the perspective of the logician. It would actually be astounding if we could compute the logically true (false) sentences of English just from a knowledge of English grammar. But these facts are somewhat more interesting from the perspective of current linguistic theory. Many linguists invoke a "level" of structure called LF, intended to represent "syntactically determined aspects of meaning" (May 1985, p.2; Higginbotham 1985, p.549; Hornstein 1995, p.7; Huang 1995, p.128). By our results above we know that a class of structures defined in terms of the lexicon and the structure building operations of English is not rich enough to characterize notions like logical truth and entailment. And in fact, typically, the "aspects of meaning" represented in LF are held not to include these notions (Chomsky 1986, p.205n11).

A more interesting, and more challenging case concerns the grammatically invariant status of DPs (NPs) interpreted by (monotone) decreasing functions. We say that a function F from the subsets of a universe E into the set {True, False} is decreasing if and only if whenever $A \subseteq B$ then F(B) = True implies F(A) = True.[1] Interpreting the rightmost bracketed constituents below as subsets of some domain E of (possibly abstract) objects and interpreting their subjects as functions from subsets of E into {True, False} the validity of the argument in (4) shows that *no athletes* denotes a decreasing function:

(4)　　a.　All poets are vegetarians

　　　　b.　No athletes are vegetarians

　　　　c.　Therefore, no athletes are poets.

Some other decreasing DPs are: *fewer than five students, neither John nor Mary, not more than ten students, at most ten students, no student's doctor, and less than half the students* (Ladusaw 1983, Keenan and Stavi 1986). In contrast, DPs like the following are not decreasing: *some student, each student, most students, more than/at least/exactly ten students, either John or Mary,. . . .*

Now it is meaningful to ask whether the set of decreasing DPs in English is structurally definable (invariant). The class is defined directly in terms of a semantic property, that of denoting a decreasing function, but it could still be that every structure preserving transformation of English mapped a decreasing DP to a decreasing DP. Given the purely semantic nature of the definition this might seem a little surprising, but, as Ladusaw (1983) points out, it seems that decreasing DPs but not others license negative polarity items (NPIs) in the predicate:

(5)   a.   No student here has ever been to Pinsk

      b.   *Some student here has ever been to Pinsk

      c.   *Most students here have ever been to Pinsk.

The NPI *ever* is acceptable in (5a) whose subject is a decreasing DP, and it remains so when *no student* is replaced by other decreasing DPs, but not when it is replaced by non-decreasing DPs. And the syntax of English must include Ss like (5a) and exclude the others, that is, it must give an account of the distribution of NPIs. So quite possibly the class of decreasing DPs might be definable in terms of English grammar. We stop short of asserting this, as the full range of relevant facts is extensive and complicated. Our point is that semantically defined classes may be be syntactically characterizable, and that this syntactic characterization may be quite non-obvious, not in any way part of the original definition.

An even less obvious case, which we do not pursue here, is the claim that the determiners which denote intersective functions are invariant in English, as just those form DPs which occur naturally in "existential there" contexts. Keenan (1987) argues for this, slightly modifying the claim in Keenan (2003). Again the array of relevant facts and judgments is quite complicated. But our concern is to illustrate the claim, not defend it.

A function D taking a pair of sets as arguments is *intersective* if and only if the value it assigns to the pair just depends on their intersection. So $D(A)(B)$ must be the same as $D(X)(Y)$ when $A \cap B = X \cap Y$. Determiners such those in (6a) are intersective, those in (6b) are not. To check whether some As are Bs it suffices to investigate the set $A \cap B$. The claim is true if this set is non-empty, false otherwise. But knowing the members of $A \cap B$ will not enable us to decide the truth of *all As are Bs* or *most As are Bs*. For each of these claims we must know something about the As that are not Bs. So *all* and *most* are not intersective.

(6)   a. some, no, several, at least ten, at most/exactly/more than/ fewer than ten, hardly any, between five and ten, How many?, Which?, no... but John,...

       b. each, every, every... but John, almost all, all but ten, most, the ten, John's,...

And the DPs built from the determiners in (6a) do occur naturally in existential there sentences, while those built from determiners in (6b) are much less natural there:

(7)   a. There are no/several/more than ten students in the next room

       b. Just how many/which students were there at the party anyway?

       c. Was there no student but John in the building?

(8)   a. *? Were there all/most/all but five students at the party?

       b. *? There weren't the ten/John's students at the party

       c. *? Wasn't there every student but John in the building?

Since English grammar must define the class of DPs which occur in these contexts there is at least a chance that the class of intersective determiners in English is invariant. And again the facts that support the invariance claim are fully independent of the semantic conditions used to define the class under study.

Finding the general in the particular. Generalizing over grammars of particular languages creates an empirical tension that generative grammarians are well aware of: the drive for cross-language generality may conflict with the drive for precise and accurate formulations of regularities in particular languages. The latter often involve subclassification of verbs, morphological irregularities, paradigm gaps - none of the specifics of which seem very "universal." But this is only the linguistic manifestation of the general challenge in empirical science, and there is no way to shortcut accurate observation and insightful generalization.

But the generalization task also brings a conceptual problem, one that linguists are less aware of. Namely, how are we to compare grammars of different languages? Within a given language we have reasonable and public criteria for deciding whether one expression is a constituent of another and whether two expressions have the same grammatical category (and thus the same, or comparable, distribution – see

Lecture 4). But how should we argue that two expressions in different languages have the same category? The distributional regularities that evidence sameness of category within a language cannot apply to expressions in different languages, nor is there any realistic hope that grammars of different languages will be isomorphic (which would require the sets of simplex expressions of corresponding categories to have the same cardinality, etc.).[2]

Bare Grammar provides a new perspective on this latter problem. Each linguistic theory mentioned above employs a uniform (or nearly uniform) notation in presenting the grammars of different languages, since that common notation is needed for their generalizations to apply to different languages. But within Bare Grammar we can state generalizations in terms of what is invariant in different grammars even when the grammars themselves are not syntactically comparable. We briefly mention a few cases of this kind that will be discussed later in these lectures.

First, we provide a proper purely semantic definition of "anaphor," one defined in terms of properties of their semantic denotations, quite analogous to our definition of "decreasing DP" earlier. Then we exhibit grammars for fragments of English, Korean, and Toba Batak, and show in each grammar that the set of anaphors is syntactically invariant. In all cases, we allow lexical anaphors like *himself* to coordinate with non-anaphors forming complex expressions such as *both himself and Bill*, as in *Fred criticized both himself and Bill*. So in each of the three languages the set of anaphors is actually infinite. And we claim:

(Anaphor Invariance) In acceptable grammars for natural languages, the set of anaphors is invariant.

We might emphasize here that had we tried to define anaphor directly in syntactic terms, as by enriching the syntax with indices and placing conditions on them, the truth of (Anaphor Invariance) would risk becoming trivial. Quite generally properties and relations defined in terms of the syntax are invariant since structure preserving transformations are required to respect syntactic structure. (Still, each case has to be proved, and we have had some surprises!).

Second, we are interested in studying where antecedents of anaphors may be located relative to the anaphor. Let us refer to the Anaphor-Antecedent relation in a given grammar G informally as the relation given by: s is a possible antecedent for an anaphor t in u. And we claim:

(Anaphor-Antecedent Invariance) In acceptable grammars for natural languages, the Anaphor-Antecedent relation is an invariant of G.

As will be apparent in Lecture 2, the precise syntactic conditions relating anaphors to their antecedents in the different languages we study are not comparable. For example both Korean and Toba but not English allow anaphors to asymmetrically c-command their antecedents in simple clauses. Of course to show this we must give a compositional interpretation of the relevant expressions so we can prove that these expressions have the same truth conditions as their English counterparts. The Anaphor-Antecedent relation has been rather well studied, and in the GB/Minimalist tradition where Binding Theory was first proposed a good deal of notational uniformity is imposed on languages to support their versions of this hypothesis. Advocates of that theory would agree with our hypothesis, but would assert something much stronger, namely, that (at some "level of structure") there is a uniform relation, (asymmetric) c-command, between an antecedent and any anaphors dependent upon it. And indeed in nuclear Ss in English anaphors are normally asymmetrically c-commanded by their antecedents. But this claim is *prima facie* less appealing in the languages cited below, where, plausibly anaphors may c-command their antecedents, sometimes asymmetrically.[3]

Hindi: [Apne   aap-ko   kal   [kis-ne mara]]?
       Self-DAT/ACC yesterday who-ERG struck

       'Who hit himself yesterday?'

Korean: [Caki-casin-ul [(motun) haksayng-TUL-I piphanhayssta]]
        Self-EMPH-ACC (all)   student-PL-NOM criticized
        'All the students criticized themselves'

Tagalog: [[Sinampal ng   babae] ang sarili niya]
         slap-GF   GEN woman TOP self 3POSS
         'The woman slapped herself'

Yatzachi Zapotec: [B-e-xot   [kwiN be?e-na?]]
                   COMP-REP-kill self.of person-that
                   'That person killed himself'

Yalálag Zapotec: [B-a-re'   [kwin be'nn-en]]
                  PERF-REP-see self.of man-DET
                  'The man repeatedly saw himself'

And we note that both LFG (Bresnan 2001, §10) and HPSG (Pollard and Sag 1994, §6) prefer a non-configurational approach to binding based on relational or obliqueness hierarchies (Subject, Object, Secondary Object,...).

As noted, we model the Korean and Toba patterns, showing that it is interpretatively unproblematic for anaphors to be compiled into syntactic structure later than their antecedents. Both languages provide specific morphemes - case markers in Korean, voice markers in Toba – which enable us to provide the relevant semantic interpretations compositionally. (So we do crucially rely on the semantic interpretation of these grammatical morphemes). Once it is seen how easy it is one understandably feels less pressure to "reconstruct" the examples like those above at LF so that anaphors are c-commanded by their antecedents. The upshot of this discussion is that within BG it is quite feasible to state universal generalizations without forcing notational uniformity on the grammatical representations of different languages.

Thirdly, let us note a case of a different sort in which notational uniformity is invoked to express a type of semantic equivalence: *"Identical thematic relationships between items are represented by identical structural relationships between those items"* (Baker 1988, p.46). This is called the "Uniformity of Theta Assignment Hypothesis" (UTAH). It is explicitly a constraint on how things are to be represented, not about how they are. The "thematic relationships" it mentions are the semantic roles (called theta roles), roles that, for example, predicates assign to their arguments. Consider the following, with the theta roles indicated:

(a) John scolded Billy   John=AGENT   Billy=PATIENT
(b) John enjoyed the play   John=EXPERIENCER the play=THEME
(c) John received a prize   John=RECIPIENT   a prize=THEME
(d) Billy was scolded by John   John=AGENT   Billy=PATIENT

So in (a) John is the AGENT of scolding, Billy the PATIENT (= affected by the action), etc. THEME is something of a catch-all theta role often used for a participant that may change location in an event. Much concerning the identification and individuation of theta roles is not well worked out, but the linguist's interest in them is given by:

(Theta Generalization) natural languages present operations which change syntactic form but preserve theta role assignment: Passive, Anti-Passive, Dative Shift, Raising to Object, Possessor Raising, Subject Extraposition, Heavy NP Shift, Topicalization, etc.

In the pair of sentences (a,d) above, an active-passive pair, *John* bears the same theta role, AGENT, in both and so does *Billy* (PATIENT). UTAH requires that (a,d) be derived from a common source, or at least that the syntactic relation of *John* to the verb in both sentences be the same, and similarly for *Billy*.[4]

We return to these questions in the discussion of (10), on page 25 just below. For now it suffices to note that UTAH imposes syntactic identity on expressions that are in some way semantically equivalent: corresponding constituents bear the same theta roles. But the problem is the same again: given an explicit mode of semantic interpretation, it is not only possible, but natural that semantically equivalent expressions be syntactically distinct - they are simply different ways of saying the same thing. The moral of Examples 1-5 is:

The significant properties of objects are invariant under changes of descriptively comparable notation.

Lastly, in Lecture 4 we provide support for the following hypothesis (where a relevant notion of "stability" is introduced):

(Agreement Class Invariance) Agreement classes are (stable) invariants.

Agreement features and classes vary very considerably across languages, with some Bantu languages having up to twenty. But our hypothesis is perfectly compatible with this variation, claiming that, while a language need not have agreement phenomena, when it does the classes it induces are invariant. We provide some non-obvious support for this hypothesis by analyzing a specific problem in Romanian agreement (Corbett 1991, §6) where some nominals trigger "masculine" predicate agreement in the singular and "feminine" in the plural. We show that even adopting just two gender categories, thereby trying to force a two gender analysis, the grammar still yields three invariant agreement classes, the solution advocated by Corbett, without the 'invariance' terminology.

1.1 Language invariants and bare grammar

A grammar provides a definition of a class of expressions (syntax), and a compositional semantic interpretation for these expressions (semantics). We focus here on syntax, though particular syntactic formulations are in part motivated by the need for a compositional interpretation. The following is a formal definition of a bare grammar. The underlying intuition is as simple as it gets: a language is the set of expressions you can build starting from a Lexicon and applying rules from a given set as often as you like. Formally:

Definition 1 A *bare grammar* G has four components,

$$\langle V_G, Cat_G, Lex_G, Rule_G \rangle,$$

where (omitting subscripts) elements of V are called *vocabulary items* and elements of Cat *category symbols* (or just categories). $V^* \times Cat$ is the set of *possible expressions* and for $e = (s, C) \in V^* \times \text{Cat}$, string(e) $=_{df}$ s, its first coordinate, and Cat(e) $=_{df}$ C, its second coordinate. Lex is a subset of $V \times \text{Cat}$, whose elements are called *lexical items*. Rule is a set of partial functions from $(V^* \times \text{Cat})^+$ into $V^* \times \text{Cat}$. Its elements are called *generating or structure building functions*.

L_G, the *language generated by G*, is the closure of Lex under Rule. So L_G is the set of possible expressions we can build starting from those in Lex and applying the functions $F \in$ Rule finitely many times. Formally it is the intersection of the supersets of Lex closed with respect to the $F \in$ Rule. For each $C \in$ Cat,

$$PH(C) =_{df} \{s \in L_G | \; \text{Cat}(s) = C\}, \text{ and}$$
$$\text{Lex}(C) =_{df} \text{Lex} \cap PH(C).$$

Given G, when we refer to an $F \in \text{Rule}_G$, we intend $F \upharpoonright L_G$, that function like F but with its domain restricted to tuples of expressions in L_G. Replacing all $F \in$ Rule by $F \upharpoonright L_G$ results in a grammar with the same derivations, the same expressions, and (as will be clear below) the same automorphisms.

A sample grammar, Eng, illustrates this format. We introduce some notational simplifications that will be used throughout. The category system here is concocted for illustrative purposes, not dictated by any tenets of Bare Grammar. Pn is the category of n-place predicate symbols, with P0 = Sentence (a 0 place predicate). Expressions of category P1/P2 combine with P2s to form P1s, and expressions of category P01/P12 combine with n+1 place predicates to form Pns, n=0 or 1. The order in which expressions combine is determined by the two rules (Merge and Coord), not coded in the category name. Define Eng=$\langle$V, Cat, Lex, Rule$\rangle$, as follows:

V:	laugh, cry, sneeze, praise, criticize, see,
	John, Bill, Sam, himself, and, or, both, either
Cat:	P0, P1, P2, P01/P12, P1/P2, CONJ
Lex:	P1 laughed, cried, sneezed
	P2 praised, criticized, interviewed
	P01/P12 John, Bill, Sam
	P1/P2 himself
	CONJ and, or
Rule:	Merge and Coord, defined below.

We have presented the grammar in this format to make it easy to read, listing *laughed* as a P1 in Lex to indicate that (laughed, P1) $\in$ Lex, etc. The rule Merge applies to pairs of expressions as follows:

Domain	Merge	Value	Conditions
s t A B	$\longmapsto$	s⌢t P0	$A = P01/P12, B = P1$
s t A B	$\longmapsto$	t⌢s P1	$A \in \{P1/P2, P01/P12\}, B = P2$

The first clause of the definition says that the function applies to any expression with string s and category P01/P12, and any expression with string t and category P1, to yield the expression whose string is the result of concatenating s and t with category P0. Note that the domain of Merge is the whole set of pairs $\langle(s, A), (t, B)\rangle$ for any strings $s, t \in V^*$ and any $A, B \in Cat$ satisfying either the first or second conditions. We summarize the argument that (John laughed, P0) is in L_{Eng} using a Function-Argument (FA) tree (in which mother nodes are labeled with the values of the indicated functions applied to the labels on the daughter nodes).

Merge:(John laughed, P0)

(John, P01/P12)　　(laughed, P1)

Linguists more commonly use "standard" trees like this:

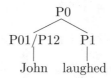

In general we use various styles of trees to represent the argument that a given expression is in the language. Standard trees are of limited utility, only being suitable for grammars whose generating functions are concatenative (derived strings are the concatenation of the argument strings, in order, with insertion of fixed strings like *both, either, nor* in the Coord rule below). They cannot represent string substitution operations for example (see Lecture 4), or reduplication. So this is a clear example of a choice of notation limiting what you can say. The FA tree for *John praised Bill* is this:

Merge:(John praised Bill, P0)

(John, P01/P12)　　Merge:(praised Bill, P1)

(Bill, P01/P12)　　(praised, P2)

We now define the coordination rule Coord. It is convenient to define the set of coordinable categories $cC_{Eng} = Cat - \{CONJ\}$ and the class of nominal categories $nC_{Eng} = \{P1/P2, P01/P12\}$:

Domain			Coord	Value	Conditions
and	s	t	$\longmapsto$	both⌢s ⌢and⌢t	$C \in cC_{Eng}$
CONJ	C	C		C	
or	s	t	$\longmapsto$	either⌢s ⌢or⌢t	$C \in cC_{Eng}$
CONJ	C	C		C	
and	s	t	$\longmapsto$	both⌢s ⌢and⌢t	$C \neq C' \in nC_{Eng}$
CONJ	C	C'		P1/P2	
or	s	t	$\longmapsto$	either⌢s ⌢or⌢t	$C \neq C' \in nC_{Eng}$
CONJ	C	C'		P1/P2	

Here is an FA derivation of (John criticized both himself and Bill, P0):

Merge:(John criticized both himself and Bill, P0)

   (John, P01/P12)   Merge:(criticized both himself and Bill, P1)

      Coord:(both himself and Bill, P1/P2)   (criticized, P2)

   (and, CONJ) (himself, P1/P2)   (Bill, P01/P12)

It is not quite clear how to draw a "standard" derivation tree for this example, since the string order does not correspond exactly to argument order, and since *both* and *either* are syncategorematic – vocabulary items lacking a category and introduced by rule. But we could indicate the derivation with a "standard" tree drawn like this:

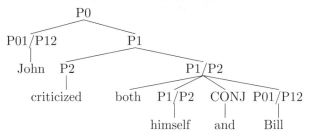

Exercise 1   i. What is the motivation for the last two cases in the definition of Coord?

ii. Exhibit an FA derivation tree for the expression (John both laughed and criticized Bill, P0) and for the expression (John criticized either both himself and Bill or both himself and Sam, P0)

iii. Extend the coordination rule so that the grammar generates (Neither John nor Bill praised Sam, P0)

iv. Suppose that we eliminate *both* from the vocabulary V for Eng, so the Coord rule just combines expressions with *and* and *or* as given, but does not introduce *both*. Then exhibit two derivation trees with distinct constituents for (Either John or Bill and Sam laughed, P0).

Exercise (1.iv) raises the general question: how can we tell whether a grammar is syntactically ambiguous? Early work in generative grammar represented syntactic ambiguity as "derived from two or more deep structures." But that is a notation-dependent representation, and does not survive translation into theories (like most of the current ones) which lack a level of deep structure. Here is a general, notation independent answer:

Definition 2 A grammar G is *ambiguous* iff at least one of the three conditions below is met:

i. One of the generating functions fails to be one to one.

ii. The ranges of two generating functions overlap.

iii. The range of a generating function overlaps with Lex.

In Exercise (1.iv) condition i obtains: when *both* is eliminated, Coord fails to be one to one. Moreover,

Fact 1 *Eng is unambiguous.*

This fact is very useful when we want to define functions, such as semantic interpretations or (shortly) structure preserving transformations on L_{Eng}. It is easy to see that no lexical item can also be derived using Merge or Coord since their values always concatenate at least two lexical strings and no lexical item is such a concatenation. Formally, an induction (on string length and derivational depth) suffice to establish that no expression derived by Merge is also derived by Coord, and finally that both Merge and Coord are one to one. As per Exercise (1.iv), the use of *both* and *either* as "left parentheses" is crucial for Coord being one to one. In fact, we can eliminate the interior *and* and *or* preserving unambiguity, but not, as we have seen, *both* or *either*.

1.2 Some properties of bare grammars

Effability. It is an easy observation that for any sets V and Cat, any subset K of $V^* \times Cat$ is the set L_G for some grammar G. For example, let $Lex_G = K, Rule_G = \emptyset$, or if $K \neq \emptyset$, let $Lex = \{d\}$ for some $d \in K$ and let Rule $= \{F_k| \ k \in K\}$, where F_k maps each possible expression to k. Equally any set of strings is Strings(C) for some G with $C \in Cat_G$. So Bare Grammar does not limit the languages we can define; grammars in any format can be translated into it.

Sameness of structure. We naively argue that *John laughed* has the same structure - whatever it is - as *Bill cried*, on the grounds that we can replace *John* with *Bill* without changing structure and then replace *laughed* with *cried* without changing structure. So the two expressions have the same structure (are isomorphic) since we can derive one from the other by a series of structure preserving substitutions. In general we will say that *s* has the same structure as *t* iff there is a structure preserving map which derives *t* from *s*.

Crucial then to our account of structure is what is to count as a structure (preserving) map. Basically they are substitutions, functions, from L_G to L_G that meet two (standard) conditions: (1) they are bijections (1-1 onto functions), and (2) they do not change how expressions are built up. We explicate these conditions below, then give a formal definition. First, a notational preliminary

Definition 3 An arbitrary function $F : A \rightarrow B$ can be extended to P_F which maps $\wp(A)$, the set of subsets of A, to $\wp(B)$, by setting $P_F(K) = \{F(x)| \ x \in K\}$ for each $K \subseteq A$. In practice we write simply F for P_F. Similarly F extends naturally to F^* which maps A^*, the set of finite sequences of elements of A, to B^*, setting $F^*(s_1, \ldots, s_n) = (F(s_1), \ldots, F(s_n))$. For $s \in A^*$ we write simply F(s) instead of $F^*(s)$. So when R is a relation on A, $F(R) = \{F(s)| \ s \in R\}$ is a relation on B. P_F and F^* are called the *power lift* and *product lift* of F, respectively.

Returning now to structure maps, the bijection condition has two conceptually different parts. First, such functions are onto (surjective). This says that they can't omit anything. Imagine a function f mapping English to English in such a way that no reflexive pronoun (*himself, herself,...*) was the value of f at any expression. This function f does not preserve structure since its set $\{f(s)| \ s \in \text{English}\}$ of values lacks a structurally significant class of expressions, the reflexives. So we require that a structure map h not omit anything: $\{h(s)| \ s \in L_G\} = L_G$, which just says that h is onto.

Second, structure maps should be one to one (injective). A map which sent both *students* and *teachers* to *doctors* might map the natural *more students than teachers laughed* to *more doctors than doctors laughed*, of dubious grammaticality. Similarly a non-injective f might map *Sam neither laughed nor cried* to *Sam neither sneezed nor sneezed*. So maps which are not injective may fail to preserve the property of being grammatical and so are not structure preserving.

Condition (2) says that for h to be a structure map, it must not change how expressions are derived. Using our notation above this just says that h(F) = F for all F ∈ Rule. Note that each such F is a set of sequences of expressions, so h(F) is just the set of h(s) for s ∈ F.

To see that the condition h(F)=F for all F ∈ Rule, implies that an expression u and h(u) are built in the same way let u be derived by applying F to some $(t_1, \ldots, t_n)$. That is, $F(t_1, \ldots, t_n) = u$, which just says that $\langle t_1, \ldots, t_n, u \rangle \in F$. But then $\langle h(t_1), \ldots, h(t_n), h(u) \rangle \in h(F)$, and since h(F)=F we have that $\langle h(t_1), \ldots, h(t_n), h(u) \rangle \in F$, that is, $F(h(t_1), \ldots, h(t_n)) = h(u)$. So if we can derive u by applying some F to a sequence t of arguments then we can derive h(u) by applying that same F to h(t). Formally now we define, using the term "automorphism" for "structure map":[5]

Definition 4 For each grammar G,

1. a map $h : L_G \rightarrow L_G$ is an *automorphism* of G iff h is a bijection and h(F)=F, for all F ∈ Rule$_G$. We write Aut$_G$ for the set of automorphisms of G.

2. For s, t ∈ L$_G$, s is *isomorphic to* t, s ≃ t, iff for some h ∈ Aut$_G$, $h(s) = t$.

With these definitions, we have the following straightforward results:

Fact 2 Aut$_G$ *contains the identity map* id$_G$ *on* L$_G$ *and is closed under inverses and composition, and so is a group.*

Inverses are used extensively in the study of invariants later.

Fact 3 *For* h, h′ ∈ Aut$_G$, h = h′ *iff for all lexical items s*, h(s) = h′(s). *Thus an automorphism can be defined by giving its values (appropriately) on the lexical items.*

This is important, since usually Lex is finite and L$_G$, the domain of an automorphism, is infinite.

Fact 4 *The* ≃ *relation is reflexive* (s ≃ s), *symmetric* (s ≃ t ⇒ t ≃ s), *and transitive* (s ≃ t ∧ t ≃ u ⇒ s ≃ u), *all* s, t, u ∈ L$_G$.

Exercise 2 Prove Facts 2-4.

As usual, we say a function *f fixes* an object *x* in its domain iff $f(x) = x$. Then *x* is called a *fixed point* of *f*. So the automorphisms of a grammar G are the bijections on L$_G$ which fix every F ∈ Rule$_G$.

Since in Eng, both Lex and PH(C) are invariant, the automorphisms of Eng can all be given by functions from Lex to Lex which permute expressions of the same category.

Fact 5 *Let* h *be the function from* Lex$_{\text{Eng}}$ *to* Lex$_{\text{Eng}}$ *which permutes* (praised, P2) *and* (criticized, P2), *fixing all other lexical items. Given the unambiguity of Eng we can extend* h *to a map* h* *on* L$_{\text{Eng}}$ *by setting*

$$\text{h}^*(\text{Merge}(s, t)) = \text{Merge}(\text{h}^*(s), \text{h}^*(t)), \text{ and}$$
$$\text{h}^*(\text{Coord}(s, t, u)) = \text{Coord}(\text{h}^*(s), \text{h}^*(t), \text{h}^*(u)).$$

Exercise 3 Prove Fact 5. (This is a good exercise for the ambitious reader; we prove a very similar fact on page 49.)

Invariants of grammars. A property P of expressions is *invariant*, or *structural* iff whenever an expression s has P then so does every expression with the same structure as s, that is, every h(s), for all h $\in$ Aut$_G$. Clearly if we could find an s with P and a t with the same structure as s that lacked P then P would not be a structural property of G. We could not decide whether s had P just by checking its structure. Moreover the condition that h(s) has P whenever s does just says h(P) $\subseteq$ P, treating P here as the set of expressions with the property. And if this holds for all automorphisms h, then h(P)=P for all automorphisms h:

Theorem 1 *For* A $\subseteq$ L$_G$*, *if* h(A) $\subseteq$ A *for all* h $\in$ Aut$_G$ *then* h(A) = A *for all* h $\in$ Aut$_G$.

Proof. Assume the antecedent and let h be arbitrary in Aut$_G$. We must show that A $\subseteq$ h(A). Since h^{-1} $\in$ Aut$_G$ we know by the assumption that h^{-1}(A) $\subseteq$ A, whence, since automorphisms preserve $\subseteq$, h(h^{-1}(A)) $\subseteq$ h(A), and h(h^{-1}(A)) = A. So for each h $\in$ Aut$_G$, A $\subseteq$ h(A), whence by the assumption, for each such h, h(A) = A. □

Thus a property of expressions is invariant (structural) iff it is a fixed point of the syntactic automorphisms. Similarly a relation R, such as *is a constituent of*, is a structural (invariant) relation if whenever a tuple t $\in$ R then $h(t) \in$ R, for all automorphisms h. And by Theorem 1, this just says that h(R) = R, all h $\in$ Aut$_G$. Succinctly:

Definition 5 The *syntactic invariants* of a grammar G are the fixed points of the automorphisms of G.

By the use of power lifting and product lifting we extend the automorphisms of G to the full type hierarchy generated by L$_G$. So we can consider invariants of any logical type, but so far only four types have naturally arisen: invariant expressions, properties of expressions, relations between expressions, and (partial) functions from expressions to expressions. We consider these in turn.

Invariant expressions. For grammars of natural languages, it seems that the invariant lexical items form a class that has already been noted by linguists:

Thesis 1 *The grammatical formatives of a* L_G *are the lexical items fixed by all* $h \in Aut_G$.[6]

So the "grammatical formatives" or "function words" of a language are those you cannot change without changing structure. To our knowledge this is the first non-stipulative characterization of these items (Keenan 1993, Keenan and Stabler 1996). Note that the sense in which a lexical item (possibly a bound morpheme) is structural is exactly the same as that in which a property (is a Sentence), a relation (c-commands) or a function (the Subject of) are structural. In all cases the structural object is one fixed by all the automorphisms of G. The basic idea that morphology can be directly structural is also central to Lexical-Functional Grammar (see Bresnan 2001, p.6), though the notion of structure there is 'concrete' – particular graph structures, rather than the relationships among expressions induced by generative devices, as here.

As we exhibit grammars to model properties of languages, we should be on the lookout to see how well Thesis 1 is supported. Regarding L_{Eng}, we prove later that in Eng, (himself, P1/P2) is fixed by all automorphisms. This is unsurprising since *himself* has distinctive distributional properties. (Note: we often omit the category coordinate of an expression when it is clear from context). It is for example the only lexical item that combines with P2s to form P1s, but does not combine with P1s to form P0s. It is likely that *himself* is a constant, a function word, in real English, again due to its special distributional properties. Note that if we added (him, P1/P2) to Eng we could find an automorphism that interchanged *him* and *himself*. But further enrichments would reintroduce distributional differences. *Him* can not be grammatically replaced by *himself* in *John thinks that most women like him*.

Invariant properties of expressions. One easy case is L_G itself. Since by definition $h(L_G) = \{h(s) \mid s \in L_G\}$ and h is onto we see that $h(L_G)$ is L_G for an arbitrary automorphism h. Thus the property of being grammatical is a structural property. This is encouraging.

A more challenging case concerns the PH(C), the set of phrases of category C. In §4.2 we exhibit a grammar G in which for some $C \in Cat_G$ some automorphisms map expressions of category C to expressions of other categories, so for that C, PH(C) is not invariant. Prima facie this seems a little surprising, and we consider whether some version of the following should be taken as an axiom for a theory of language structure:

?Axiom: For all C $\in$ Cat$_G$, PH(C) is invariant (that is, the property of being a C is structural).

We will show below that for all C $\in$ Cat$_{Eng}$, PH(C) is invariant. So in L$_{Eng}$, automorphisms always map P1s to P1s, P01/P12s to P01/P12s, etc. (But ultimately, in Lecture 4, we adopt something slightly weaker, "Category Stability.")

Another property we might hope to be invariant is that of being a lexical item. But again it turns out that we can make up grammars G in which Lex$_G$ is not invariant. An automorphism may map a lexical item to a derived expression. But such cases force Lex$_G$ to contain some derived expressions, and we will later show (Theorem 25, page 161) that under certain quite general assumptions the extra lexical items can be eliminated without changing L$_G$ or its automorphisms (and hence its invariants).

?Axiom: For all G for natural languages, Lex$_G$ is invariant.

Eng satisfies this potential axiom. That is, Lex$_{Eng}$ is invariant (proof on p.31, below). Our two possible axioms have the merit of formulating non-trivial structural roles for categories and the lexicon which many natural language grammars will satisfy even if we do not take them as universal. Another natural family of questions about categories draws on specific linguistic theories:

> Within X-bar theoretic grammars, is the property of being a maximal projection invariant? What about the property of being a head? An adjunct? A specifier? A complement?

We expect the answers to all these questions should be Yes, assuming explicit formulation of grammars (and some theory-specific axioms involving these notions).

A fourth, and in some ways the most interesting, class of possible invariant properties concern ones defined semantically. In Eng, for example, certain expressions, such as *himself*, are understood to be referentially dependent on others. If we replace *John* by *Bill* in *John criticized himself*, we change who we understand to have been criticized. By contrast expressions like *Sam* and *John* are referentially autonomous. Let us call the referentially dependent ones anaphors (a proper semantic definition will be given later). Note that the set of anaphors in L$_{Eng}$ is infinite, since expressions like *both himself and John* and *either both himself and John or both himself and Bill* are referentially dependent (due, to be sure, to the presence of *himself* in the expression).

Now it is meaningful to ask of Eng whether the property of being an anaphor is "coded in the grammar," that is, an invariant. In fact in L_{Eng} the anaphors coincide with PH(P1/P2), so the property of being an anaphor in L_{Eng} is invariant (proof on p.36, below). Natural questions like the following become much clearer with these notions:

> Is the set of anaphors in real English invariant?

> Is the set of anaphors in each natural language invariant?

> Are all anaphors in a natural language built from lexical anaphors? Or are there ways of building complex anaphors directly? (We favor the latter option, given Scandinavian *sin*, Latin *suus*, Russian *svoi*, etc., which form referentially dependent expressions such as *sin bok* 'his own book', etc. by modifying nouns as possessive adjectives, not genitive case pronouns).

We return to these later.

Invariant relations and functions. Of course the structure building functions $F \in Rule_G$ are invariant since automorphisms are by definition maps that fix these functions. A more interesting case would be a function $SUBJ_G$ which associates an expression with its "subject" if it has one (in some sense of that notion). For example in real English this function would map *every student left early* to *every student*; but it wouldn't map *every student came early and several students left early* to anything, since coordinate sentences don't have subjects. In Eng we define $SUBJ_{Eng}$ as the partial function from L_{Eng} to L_{Eng} given by:

Domain($SUBJ_{Eng}$) = $\{s \in L_{Eng}|\ Cat(s) = P0\}$ and $s \in Range(Merge)\}$,

$SUBJ_{Eng}(s) = t$ iff for some $u \in PH(P1)$, $s = Merge(t, u)$.

Then, provably, $SUBJ_{Eng}$ is structural, that is, invariant. This is unsurprising, since we have defined $SUBJ_{Eng}$ in terms of the generating functions. More challenging is to specify other properties we associate with subjects, and then see if this definition picks out just the expressions with those properties. For example, anteceding anaphors is a property of subjects: in *John criticized himself* the subject *John* is the antecedent of the anaphor *himself*, and it cannot go the other way: **Himself criticized John*. But also in *John's criticism of himself* we see that the possessor *John* antecedes *himself*, and it cannot go the other way, **himself's criticism of John*. So we would like our definition of $SUBJ_{English}$ to pick out the possessor in possessive constructions as well.

Somewhat analogous to syntactic functions like SUBJ we may consider semantic ones, like theta roles: AGENT, EXPERIENCER, PATIENT, THEME, LOCATION, GOAL, SOURCE, BENEFICIARY, INSTRUMENT,....

Let us look at these a little more closely than we did when we considered UTAH earlier. The fact that *John* is AGENT in (9a) and EXPERIENCER in (9b) is determined by the predicates *produce* and *enjoy* respectively.

(9)   a. John produced the play

        b. John enjoyed the play

So predicates have theta role requirements that must be satisfied by other expressions and we say that they are *theta assigners*. Exactly which types of expressions can be theta assigners is still being worked out, so let's generalize over that issue with the following informal definition:

Definition 6 For all theta roles θ, a pair (s,t) of constituents of u is a θ *domain* (of u) iff (i) s is a constituent of t, (ii) s is assigned θ internal to t, and (iii) no proper constituent t' of t satisfies both (i) and (ii).

Expressions u and u' are *theta equivalent*, $u \equiv u'$, iff for each theta role θ, the θ domains of u, noted $\theta(u)$, match one for one with those of u'

(A definition of "is a proper constituent of" is provided in U8 on page 29 below.) Theta equivalence is a little stronger than meets the eye. In the basic cases of interest an expression will have at most one θ domain for each θ. Below is an example (making common assumptions about the domains in which the theta roles are assigned):

(10)   a. John praised the editor

           AGENT(10a)={(John, John praised the editor)}
           THEME(10a)={(the editor, praised the editor)}
           For all other θ, $\theta(10a)=\emptyset$

        b. The editor criticized John

           AGENT(10b)={(the editor, the editor criticized John)}
           THEME(10b)={(John, criticized John)}
           For all other θ, $\theta(10b)=\emptyset$

        c. John was criticized by the editor

           AGENT(10c)={(the editor, criticized by the editor)}
           THEME(10c)={(John, John was criticized by the editor)}
           For all other θ, $\theta(10c)=\emptyset$

        d. The editor's criticism of John

           AGENT(10d)={(the editor, the editor's criticism of John)}
           THEME(10d)={(John, criticism of John)}
           For all other θ, $\theta(10d)=\emptyset$

One sees then that the four expressions in (10) are theta equivalent. No two, under plausible assumptions about the grammar of English, are isomorphic. Note that an automorphism couldn't map *the editor* to *John* preserving structure, a fact that is even truer when *the editor* is replaced by *the irascible editor* (in case one might think that *John* has some "hidden" structure making it more like *the editor*). Now consider the following possible invariants of natural language:

(Theta Invariance)   For all theta roles θ, all expressions s,t,u, all automorphisms h of G,

1. The map sending each u to $\theta(u)$ is invariant.
   That is, $(s, t) \in \theta(u) \Rightarrow (h(s), h(t)) \in \theta(h(u))$.

2. Theta equivalence is invariant.
   That is, $u \equiv u' \Rightarrow h(u) \equiv h(u')$

The first condition is both weak and far from obvious. It says that whenever u and u′ are isomorphic then their isomorphic constituents bear the same theta roles. So no automorphism could map *John produced the play* to *John enjoyed the play*. The condition is weak because there are many cases of theta equivalent expressions which are not isomorphic.

The second condition says that whenever expressions (isomorphic or not) are theta equivalent then their images under an isomorphism are also theta equivalent. This condition is not as severe as UTAH, as non-isomorphic expressions may be theta equivalent, as in (10).

Lastly, concerning proper relations, consider the AA (Anaphor-Antecedent) relation given informally by: x is a possible antecedent of y in z. Here x and y must be constituents of z, and y must be interpretable as an anaphor. In (11) the possible antecedents for *himself* are underlined:

(11)   a.   <u>John</u> protected Mary from himself

   b.   Mary protected <u>John</u> from himself

   c.   <u>John</u> protected <u>Bill</u> from himself

   d.   John thought that <u>Bill</u> exonerated himself

Though the AA relation may be realized in different ways in different languages, we propose:

Conjecture 2 *For every G for a natural language,* AA_G *is invariant.*

This says that in any grammar, the Anaphor-Antecedent relation is always structurally definable, a claim which almost all generative grammarians would accept. Many linguists believe something much stronger:

that in all natural languages an antecedent of an anaphor stands in a fixed syntactic relation to it, namely it c-commands it. As we have seen, the sort of data we presented on page 12 is problematic for that claim. Indeed, we support the following universal non-uniform invariant (mentioned informally earlier):

(Anaphor-Antecedent Invariance) The AA_G relation is universally invariant but not uniformly so: its structural characterization varies with G. Different Gs draw on different combinations of c-command, linear order, case marking, and voice marking. (See Keenan 1993 and the next lecture.)

In designing grammars for particular languages we always ride two horses at once: empirical adequacy vs. generality, getting the facts of the language right vs. highlighting what is general across languages. The concept of non-uniform invariants provides a new way to reconcile our competing goals. It says that certain semantic relations are always (syntactically) invariant, but different languages effect this in different morphosyntactic ways.

Universal Uniform Invariants. Certain properties and relations are uniformly invariant in all grammars, natural or otherwise, and so not useful in distinguishing natural language grammars from others. But they are useful in proving invariant particular objects in particular grammars. Here is our best list at the moment. It includes a few items already mentioned and it defines several general structural notions useful in the study of natural language structure. For all grammars G,

U1. The language L_G is invariant, as is L_G^n, the set of sequences of n elements of L_G.

Thus the property of being in the language, i.e. grammatical, is structural. In consequence, an operation that derives a possible expression not in L_G from one that is in L_G is not invariant, since it fails to preserve grammaticality.

U2. For any $F \in Rule_G$, F is (trivially) invariant. And for any invariant function F on L_G, Domain(F), the domain of F, and Range(F), the range of F, are invariant.

So if a grammar has a MOVE rule the property of being derived by MOVE is a structural property, in conformity with our informal intuitions. Similarly, the set of sequences of expressions a rule applies to is invariant. For example, let the "subject of" function SUBJ in English map expressions which have subjects to their subjects, mapping for example *Every child was praised* to *every child*. But coordinate sentences don't have subjects, so *Either every child laughed or every child cried* is not in the domain of SUBJ. Thus the property of having a subject is a structural property given that the function SUBJ itself is structurally definable (invariant).

U2 is used extensively, often silently, in what follows, so let us see why it is true. Proof. Let F be an invariant (partial) function on L_G. Let $s = \langle s_1, \ldots, s_n \rangle \in \text{Domain}(F)$, and suppose that F maps s to t. So the sequence $\langle s_1, \ldots, s_n, t \rangle \in F$ and so for h any automorphism, $\langle h(s_1), \ldots, h(s_n), h(t) \rangle \in h(F)$, by the definition of h(F). Since F is invariant, $h(F) = F$ so $\langle h(s_1), \ldots, h(s_n) \rangle \in \text{Domain}(F)$ and $h(t) \in \text{Range}(F)$. Thus $h(\text{Domain}(F)) \subseteq \text{Domain}(F)$ and $h(\text{Range}(F)) \subseteq \text{Range}(F)$. Since h was arbitrary this holds for all h, whence by Theorem 1, $h(\text{Domain}(F)) = \text{Domain}(F)$ and $h(\text{Range}(F)) = \text{Range}(F)$, so Domain(F) and Range(F) are both invariant. □

U3. For any $s \in L_G$, $[s] =_{df} \{h(s)| \ h \in \text{Aut}_G\}$ is invariant; no non-empty proper subset of $[s]$ is invariant. $[s] \neq \emptyset$ since $s \in [s]$, so each $[s]$ is an atomic invariant. For all $s, t \in L_G$, either $[s] = [t]$ or $[s] \cap [t] = \emptyset$, so $\{[s]| \ s \in L_G\}$ is a partition of the set of expressions of L_G.

U4. If Lex_G is invariant, then for all n, Lex_n is invariant, where we define the *complexity hierarchy* Lex_n by the *derivational depth* of an expression: $\text{Lex}_0 = \text{Lex}_G$ and for all $n \geq 0$, $\text{Lex}_{n+1} = \text{Lex}_n \cup \{F(t)| \ F \in \text{Rule}_G, t \in \text{Lex}_n^* \cap \text{Domain}(F)\}$. Note that $L_G = \bigcup_n \text{Lex}_n$ and if for all $F \in \text{Rule}_G$, $\text{Range}(F) \cap \text{Lex}_G = \emptyset$ then Lex_G is invariant.

This last observation is useful, as in many of our model grammars no lexical item is derived, that is, no lexical item $s = F(t)$ for any rule F and any sequence t of expressions. In such a case an automorphism must map lexical items to lexical items since if h mapped s to some F(t) then h^{-1} would map F(t) to the lexical item s, a contradiction since $h^{-1}(F(t)) = F(h^{-1}(t))$ is not in Lex.

U5. If G is category functional and each Lex(C) is invariant then each PH(C) is invariant.

Recall that $\text{Lex}(C) = \text{PH}(C) \cap \text{Lex}$. Grammar G is *category functional* iff the category of a derived expression is a function of the categories of its arguments, i.e. for all $F \in \text{Rule}$, if u,v are n-tuples in Domain(F) and $\text{Cat}(u_i) = \text{Cat}(v_i)$, all $1 \leq i \leq n$ then $\text{Cat}(F(u)) = \text{Cat}(F(v))$. So category functional grammars are ones in which the category of a derived expression s cannot vary merely with the string component of any expression s was derived from.

U6. The set of invariant subsets of L_G is closed under relative complement and arbitrary intersections and unions and thus forms a complete atomic boolean algebra (with the [s] as atoms). So conjunctions, disjunctions, or negations of invariant properties are themselves invariant properties. Comparable claims hold for $R \subseteq L_G{}^n$, all n. Equally cross products of invariant sets are invariant.

So if the property of being a feminine noun is invariant, and the property of being a plural noun is invariant it follows that the property of being a feminine plural noun is invariant, as is the property of being a feminine non-plural noun, etc.

We prove a sample case of U6. Let A, B be invariant subsets of L_G. We show that $A - B$ is invariant. Let $s \in A - B$, and let h be an arbitrary automorphism. Then $h(s) \in h(A) = A$, since A is invariant. And since $s \notin B$, $h(s) \notin B$, otherwise $h^{-1}(h(s)) = s \in h^{-1}(B) = B$, since B is invariant, a contradiction. Thus $h(s) \in A - B$, so $h(A - B) \subseteq A - B$, and since h was arbitrary equality holds by Theorem 1.

U7. The value of an invariant function at an invariant argument is itself invariant.

U8. The is a constituent of relation, CON, is invariant, as are PCON (is a proper constituent of) and ICON (is an immediate constituent of), where for all $s, t \in L_G$ we define:

   i. sICONt iff for some $u_1, \ldots, u_n \in L_G$ and some $F \in Rule_G$, $t = F(u_1, \ldots, u_n)$ and $s = u_i$ for some $1 \leq i \leq n$.

   ii. sPCONt iff for some $n \geq 2$ there is a sequence $\langle v_1, \ldots, v_n \rangle$ such that $v_1 = s, v_n = t$ and for each $1 \leq i < n$, $v_i ICON v_{i+1}$.

   iii. sCONt iff s = t or sPCONt.

It is easy to show the following basic facts:

Theorem 3

a. *For all G, CON is reflexive and transitive. In some G, CON is not antisymmetric.*

b. sICONt $\Rightarrow$ sPCONt $\Rightarrow$ sCONt.

These conform with our pretheoretical notions about constituency.

U9. The *sister of* relation is invariant, where we define: s sister t in u iff some $F(v_1, \ldots, v_n)$ is a constituent of u and for some $i \neq j$, $s = v_i$ and $t = v_j$.

U10. The c-commands relation CC is invariant, where we define: sCCt in u iff for some constituent v of u, s is a sister of v in u and t is a constituent of v.

As noted earlier, U8-U10 define linguistic notions on expressions, not, as is more usual, on derivations or tree-like structures representing derivations. As we see in Lecture 2, a variety of linguistic phenomena, from substitution rules to reduplication and second position placement of Latin -*que* 'and' are not naturally representable with standard trees, and constituency is not derivable from segmenting the derived string of expressions. Our definitions are given with sufficient generality so as not to depend on the nature of the generating functions.

We verify then that ICON is an invariant relation. It suffices to show that whenever sICONt and h is an automorphism, $h(s)ICONh(t)$. By the assumption $t = F(v_1, \ldots, v_n)$ for some generating function F and expressions $v_1, \ldots, v_n$ with $s = v_i$, some $1 \leq i \leq n$. But $h(t) = h(F(v_1, \ldots, v_n)) = F(h(v_1), \ldots, h(v_n))$, so $h(v_i)ICONh(t)$, where $h(v_i) = h(s)$, as was to be shown. The invariance of PCON follows easily from that of ICON, whence CON itself is invariant, observing that equality is a logical invariant ($s = t$ iff $h(s) = h(t)$, all $s, t \in L_G$, all bijections h on L_G).

To see U9, let s sister t in u and show $h(s)$ sister $h(t)$ in $h(u)$ for h an arbitrary automorphism. By the assumption, some $F(v_1, \ldots, v_k)CONu$ with $s = v_i$ and $t = v_j$ for some $i \neq j$. But then by the invariance of CON, $h(F(v_1, \ldots, v_k)) = F(h(v_1), \ldots, h(v_k))CONh(u)$, so $h(v_i) = h(s)$ sister $h(t) = h(v_j)$ in $h(u)$. $\qquad\square$

Exercise 4 Prove U7. Prove U10, given U8 and U9.

Invariance and Definability. For many practical purposes one can think of the invariant objects (expressions, properties, relations, functions) defined on expressions as those that are *definable* in terms of the structure building functions. We do not pursue this perspective here, as it would involve serious study of definability.[7] What is definable depends on the language in which the definitions are given. These languages must allow "logical" operators such as *and, or, not, for all, there exists, equals*, etc., but ultimately what is to count as a logical operator is not independent of what is invariant under automorphisms. See Hodges (1993, pp.27-31) and Keenan (2001). That said, the following may still be useful:

Theorem 4 *For each grammar G, the linguistic objects definable in terms of the F in Rule are invariant (but the converse may fail: there may be invariant objects that are not definable).*

The notions used in the uniform invariants above (except for the antecedents of U4 and U5) are all definable in terms of the functions F in Rule. Here is a proof of some non-trivial (and non-universal) invariants of our grammar Eng:

Theorem 5 *For all* $C \in \text{Cat}_{\text{Eng}}$, *PH(C) is invariant, as is* Lex_{Eng}.

Proof. We begin with some useful preliminary results.

1. Lex_{Eng} is invariant. For each expression s derived by Merge, string(s) is a concatenation of two or more lexical strings. But for $t \in \text{Lex}$, string(t) is just one word long, hence no lexical item is the value of Merge at any arguments. So if an automorphism h mapped a lexical item s to some Merge(a,b) then $s = h^{-1}(h(s)) = h^{-1}(\text{Merge}(a, b)) = \text{Merge}(h^{-1}(a), h^{-1}(b))$, a contradiction. Analogous claims hold if $h(s) = \text{Coord}(a, b, c)$. Hence automorphisms h map lexical items to lexical items. Thus $h(\text{Lex}) \subseteq \text{Lex}$, all automorphisms h, whence equality holds by Theorem 1.

2. PH(CONJ) is invariant. Suppose, leading to a contradiction, that $\text{Cat}(s) = \text{CONJ}$ and that h is an automorphism such that $\text{Cat}(h(s)) \neq \text{CONJ}$. By 1 above, h(s) is a lexical item, and all lexical items except conjunctions coordinate, so the triple

$$\langle(\text{and}, \text{CONJ}), h(s), h(s)\rangle \in \text{Domain}(\text{Coord}),$$

whence the automorphism h^{-1} maps this triple to a triple two of whose coordinates have category CONJ, failing to be in Domain(Coord) in violation of U2. Hence every automorphism h maps s of category CONJ to some t of category CONJ. So $h(\text{PH}(\text{CONJ})) \subseteq \text{PH}(\text{CONJ})$, hence equality holds.

3. If $\text{Cat}(s) = \text{Cat}(t)$, then $\text{Cat}(h(s)) = \text{Cat}(h(t))$ for all automorphisms h. For $\text{Cat}(s) = \text{CONJ}$ we know this is true by 2 above. And if s and t have any other category they can be coordinated; if h mapped them to expressions of different categories h would not preserve the domain of Coord, hence it must map them to expressions of the same category.

4. Note that $\langle(\text{John}, \text{P01/P12}), \text{Merge}((\text{Bill}, \text{P01/P12}), (\text{praised}, \text{P2}))\rangle \in \text{Domain}(\text{Merge})$.

   a. If automorphisms mapped P2s to P1s, then to preserve Domain(Merge), P01/P12s must get mapped to expressions of the same category, whence from 4 we would have a P01/P12, P0 pair in Domain(Merge), which is false. So automorphisms can't map P2s to P1s, and by inverses, can't map P1s to P2s.

b. Automorphisms can't map P01/P12s to P1s (and by inverses can't map P1s to P01/P12s) otherwise by reasoning analogous to (a), Domain(Merge) would contain a (P1,P0) pair, which it doesn't.

c. Automorphisms can't map P1s to P1/P2s, otherwise $\langle(s, P01/P12), (t, P1)\rangle \in$ Domain(Merge) implies that P01/P12s get mapped to P2s to preserve Domain(Merge), whence applying these substitutions in 4 we infer that a (P2,P1) pair is in Domain(Merge), which is false.

But lexical P1s must get mapped to lexical items and so must have category P1, P2, CONJ, P1/P2 or P01/P12, and everything but P1 has been ruled out. Hence automorphisms map lexical P1s to P1s, and by 3, all P1s are mapped to P1s. So PH(P1) is invariant. And since if $\langle(s, C), (t, P1)\rangle \in$ Domain(Merge), C must be P01/P12, so P01/P12s get mapped to P01/P12s, so PH(P01/P12) is invariant. Then looking at 4 again, we infer that P2s must get mapped to P2s to preserve Domain(Merge), so PH(P2) is invariant. Finally P1/P2s must get mapped to P1/P2s, otherwise some lexical item of a different category gets mapped to a P1/P2, and we have just seen that every (s, C) in Lex, $C \neq$ P1/P2, gets mapped to a C. Since automorphisms are onto, something must get mapped to each P1/P2 (there is only one), and for the lexical P1/P2s that something must be in Lex. The only available candidates are other lexical P1/P2s.

This completes the proof. □

We note that in showing the PH(C) above to be invariant we used repeatedly, usually without explicit mention, the fact that automorphisms must preserve Domain(F), for F any generating function in Rule.

On grammaticalization (and degrees thereof). There is a significant literature on the process whereby a content word or class of words becomes "grammaticalized."[8] Proponents of this type of change work with an intuitive notion of grammatical item. We can express that idea more rigorously: a word w becomes grammaticalized if at some time the set [w] of expressions w is isomorphic to is large and over time becomes smaller, ending when it is a unit set; that is, when w is fixed by all automorphisms (later, per note 6, we just require "fixed by all stable automorphisms"). If the size $|[w]|$ of [w] decreases slowly the grammaticalization is gradual, a property often taken to be central to the notion, but merely allowed, not required, by our characterization.

We can represent the degree of grammaticalization of an expression w by $|[w]|$, the number of items w is isomorphic to: the smaller $|[w]|$

the more grammatical w. And it makes sense to say that an item u, say a coordinate conjunction or a preposition, is more grammaticalized than an item v, say a proper, or common, noun, if $\|[u]\|$ is much smaller than $\|[v]\|$ even if $\|[u]\| > 1.$[9] Another merit of this conceptualization of grammaticalization: the literature often talks about the item w as changing (becoming grammaticalized), but thinking of the change as shrinkage of [w] we see that it could happen that w does not change at all, but rather that its "competitors," the other members of [w], die out.

Caveat Lector: To say that s is isomorphic to t does *not* say that string(s) and string(t) are intersubstitutable preserving grammaticality. Rather, it says there is an automorphism mapping one to the other. An automorphism mapping s to t might have to map s' to t' as well. Automorphisms can in fact interchange (and, CONJ) and (or, CONJ) in Eng, but we cannot simply replace the string *and* with *or* preserving grammaticality. That would map *both laughed and cried* to the ungrammatical *both laughed or cried*.

Semantic Invariants. Our notion of invariant applies to any mathematical structure, not just grammars. In particular it applies to the sets in which expressions of a language take their denotations, whence it will make sense to ask whether syntactic invariants always denote semantic invariants.

Definition 7 A *mathematical structure* $\mathcal{A}$ is a pair $(A, \mathcal{R})$, where A is a set, the domain of $\mathcal{A}$, and $\mathcal{R}$ is a set of relations over A. So each $R \in \mathcal{R}$ is a set of sequences of elements of A. If the set is functional, R is called a function; if each sequence is unary, R is called a property (in effect just a subset of A). If R is required to be a unit set, it is called an individual constant.

An *automorphism* of $(A, \mathcal{R})$ is a permutation of A (a bijection from A to A) which fixes each $R \in \mathcal{R}$. An object over $(A, \mathcal{R})$ - an element of A, a subset of A, a relation or function on A, etc., is *invariant* iff it is fixed by all automorphisms of $(A, \mathcal{R})$. An expression will be called *semantically invariant* if it always denotes an invariant object.

We tentatively propose:

Thesis 2 *Syntactically invariant expressions (in a natural language) denote semantically invariant objects*

So, according to this Thesis, the grammatical words in a language have a special semantic status: they denote semantically invariant objects. This perspective differs considerably from the one common in the linguistic literature which holds that grammatical words are meaningless.[10] The common view recognizes a semantic difference between content words and function words, but lacks the conceptual apparatus to characterize either, opting instead for a view which, pushed to the extreme, says that content words are meaningful and constants, function words, are not. On our view function words may have very rich meanings, but they have a "logical" character to them, namely they are semantically invariant.

Below we consider how well Thesis 2 fares for Eng. As with our study of syntactic invariants we first consider some general features of semantic invariants, then give a semantic interpretation for L_{Eng} and show that indeed *himself* does denote an invariant object.

On general invariants of mathematical structures. A detailed study here would be a dissertation in itself. And in general the automorphisms and hence the invariants of a structure $(A, \mathcal{R})$ depend on the choice of relations in $\mathcal{R}$, those relations we agree to hold fixed. For our semantic purposes we are interested in two cases.

The first is fully general: what objects over A must be fixed by all permutations of A - objects we call *permutation invariant* (PI). Since PI objects are fixed by all bijections on A they are invariants of any structure $(A, \mathcal{R})$, whose automorphisms meet additional requirements, and are thus a subset of the permutations of A. For example, assuming A has at least two elements (to avoid degenerate cases) A itself has no PI elements, as any $a \in A$ can be transposed with some other $b \in A$ holding the other elements fixed, so a is not fixed. At the level of $\wp(A)$ there are just two subsets of A which are PI: $\emptyset$ and A itself. For K any non-empty proper subset of A, a permutation h can transpose an element $a \in K$ with a $b \notin K$ holding everything else constant, so K is not fixed by all permutations. At the level of binary relations there are exactly four PI objects: $\emptyset, A \times A, ID = \{(a, a) | a \in A\}$, and $\neg ID = (A \times A) - ID$. More generally the PI n-ary relations (over an A with at least n elements) are given by the sets of equivalence relations over an n-element set. The set of PI n-ary relations of a given arity are closed under the boolean operations (intersection,...).[11]

Our second case of concern is specifically the set $\{0,1\}$ of truth values, equipped with its usual $\wedge$ (meet) and $\vee$ (join) functions given by the standard truth tables for conjunction and disjunction:

x	y	$x \wedge y$	$x \vee y$
1	1	1	1
1	0	0	1
0	1	0	1
0	0	0	0

Treating $\wedge$ above as a functional three place relation, it consists of the set of triples given in the first three columns. And of the two permutations of $\{0,1\}$, the identity map and the complement function, only the identity maps this set of triples to itself, that is, fixes $\wedge$. (If we run through this set of triples replacing each 1 by 0 and each 0 by 1 we do not obtain the same set). So the only automorphism of $(0, 1, \wedge, \vee)$ is the identity map. For the record:

Fact 6 The automorphisms of the truth value lattice map each value to itself.

A semantic interpretation of L_{Eng}. First some notation and definitions:

$[A \rightarrow B]$ is the set of functions from A into B.

A *lattice* is a triple $(L, \wedge, \vee)$ where $\wedge$ (meet) and $\vee$ (join) are binary functions on L which are commutative, associative and satisfy absorption:

$$x \wedge (x \vee y) = x, \text{ and } x \vee (x \wedge y) = x.$$

Given a non-empty set E, we write R_0 for $\{0, 1\}$ or $\{\emptyset, \{\emptyset\}\}$, and R_{n+1} for $[E \rightarrow R_n]$. R_n is the set of n-ary relations over E. We also treat R_1 as $\wp(E)$ and R_2 as $\wp(E \times E)$ with which they are isomorphic.

Type 1 is the set of functions mapping n+1-ary relations to n-ary ones (so their domain is the union of the R_{n+1}, their codomain the union of the R_n).

For each $b \in E$, I_b, the *individual generated by b*, is the following Type 1 function:

$$I_b(R) = R(b).$$

We now provide for Eng a definition of interpretation in a model, in terms of which the basic semantic relation, entailment ($\models$) is defined. Then we show that *himself* is semantically invariant.

Definition 8 $\mathcal{M} = (E, m)$ is a model for *Eng* iff E is a non-empty set and m is a map whose domain is Lex, satisfying the following conditions:

1. $m(s, C) \in Den_E(C)$, the latter defined as follows (for all n):

$\mathrm{Den_E}(\mathrm{P0})$ $= \{0,1\}$, a lattice with $\wedge$ and $\vee$ defined by the standard truth tables

$\mathrm{Den_E}(\mathrm{Pn}+1)$ $= [\mathrm{E} \to \mathrm{Den_E}(\mathrm{Pn})]$, with $\wedge$ and $\vee$ defined pointwise, that is:

$(f \wedge g)(b) =_{\mathrm{df}} f(b) \wedge g(b)$ and
$(f \vee g)(b) =_{\mathrm{df}} f(b) \vee g(b)$

$\mathrm{Den_E}(\mathrm{P1/P2})$ $= [\mathrm{Den_E}(\mathrm{P2}) \to \mathrm{Den_E}(\mathrm{P1})]$ with $\wedge$ and $\vee$ defined pointwise again

$\mathrm{Den_E}(\mathrm{P01/P12})$ $=$ Type 1

$\mathrm{Den_E}(\mathrm{CONJ})$ $= \{f \in [\mathrm{B} \times \mathrm{B} \to \mathrm{B}] \mid \mathrm{B} \in \mathrm{Den_E}(\mathrm{x}), \mathrm{x} \in c\mathrm{C_{Eng}}\}$

2. $\mathrm{m}(\mathrm{s}, \mathrm{P01/P12}) \in \{\mathrm{I_b} \mid \mathrm{b} \in \mathrm{E}\}$

   $\mathrm{m}(\text{himself}, \mathrm{P1/P2}) = \mathrm{SELF}$, where $\mathrm{SELF} : \mathrm{Den_E}(\mathrm{P2}) \to \mathrm{Den_E}(\mathrm{P1})$ is given by $\mathrm{SELF}(\mathrm{R})(\mathrm{a}) = (\mathrm{R}(\mathrm{a}))(\mathrm{a})$

   $\mathrm{m}(\text{and}, \mathrm{CONJ})$ maps (x, y) in $\mathrm{Den_E}(\mathrm{C})^2$, for $\mathrm{C} \in c\mathrm{C_{Eng}}$, to $\mathrm{x} \wedge \mathrm{y}$

   $\mathrm{m}(\text{or}, \mathrm{CONJ})$ maps (x, y) in $\mathrm{Den_E}(\mathrm{C})^2$, for $\mathrm{C} \in c\mathrm{C_{Eng}}$, to $\mathrm{x} \vee \mathrm{y}$

3. For each model $\mathcal{M} = (\mathrm{E}, \mathrm{m})$ an interpretation m^* of $\mathrm{L_{Eng}}$ is a function which extends m and satisfies:

   a. $\mathrm{m}^*(\mathrm{Merge}(\mathrm{s}, \mathrm{t})) = \mathrm{m}^*(\mathrm{s})(\mathrm{m}^*(\mathrm{t}))$, and

   b. $\mathrm{m}^*(\mathrm{Coord}(\mathrm{s}, \mathrm{t}, \mathrm{u})) = \mathrm{m}(\mathrm{s})(\mathrm{m}^*(\mathrm{t}), \mathrm{m}^*(\mathrm{u}))$

Definition 9 For all $\mathrm{s}, \mathrm{t} \in \mathrm{PH}(\mathrm{C})$, $\mathrm{C} \neq \mathrm{CONJ}$, $\mathrm{s} \models \mathrm{t}$ iff for all models $\mathcal{M}$, $\mathrm{m}^*(\mathrm{s}) \leq \mathrm{m}^*(\mathrm{t})$, where by definition $x \leq y$ iff $x \wedge y = x$.

Theorem 6 *In* $\mathrm{L_{Eng}}$, $(\text{himself}, \mathrm{P1/P2})$ *is semantically invariant.*

<u>Proof.</u> In every model $\mathcal{M} = (\mathrm{E}, \mathrm{m})$ for Eng, $\mathrm{m}^*(\text{himself}, \mathrm{P1/P2})$ is invariant. Note that $\mathrm{m}^*(\text{himself}, \mathrm{P1/P2}) = \mathrm{m}(\text{himself}, \mathrm{P1/P2}) = \mathrm{SELF}$. So we must show that SELF is invariant. Let h be an arbitrary permutation of E. We must show that $\mathrm{h}(\mathrm{SELF}) = \mathrm{SELF}$. For R and a arbitrary,

$\mathrm{SELF}(\mathrm{hR})(\mathrm{ha})$	$= (\mathrm{hR})(\mathrm{ha})(\mathrm{ha})$	Def SELF
	$= \mathrm{h}(\mathrm{R}(\mathrm{a}))(\mathrm{ha})$	Def 3
	$= \mathrm{h}((\mathrm{R}(\mathrm{a})(\mathrm{a}))$	Def 3
	$= (\mathrm{R}(\mathrm{a}))(\mathrm{a})$	h fixes truth values
	$= \mathrm{SELF}(\mathrm{R})(\mathrm{a})$	Def SELF
	$= \mathrm{h}(\mathrm{SELF}(\mathrm{R})(\mathrm{a}))$	h fixes truth values
	$= \mathrm{h}(\mathrm{SELF}(\mathrm{R}))(\mathrm{ha})$	Def 3
	$= \mathrm{h}(\mathrm{SELF})(\mathrm{hR})(\mathrm{ha})$	Def 3

Since h is onto, SELF and h(SELF) take the same values at any binary relation and object, so $\mathrm{SELF} = \mathrm{h}(\mathrm{SELF})$, as was to be shown. $\square$

Let's conclude by generalizing the essential anaphor property built into the denotation SELF of *himself*. We will provide a universal semantic definition of anaphor, whence we can non-circularly ask whether the property of being an anaphor is (syntactically) invariant in all natural languages. We limit ourselves, for the nonce to what we consider cross linguistically the core case of anaphors, namely objects of transitive verb phrases (P2s). Referentially dependent expressions like *himself* in English occur in a wider range of contexts than that, but our restricted example will suffice to illustrate how semantically defined properties may be syntactically invariant. (See note 12 on page 40 for the needed generalization.)

We treat P2s informally as denoting binary relations over a universe E. For compatibility with Eng we represent them as functions from E into $[E \to \{0, 1\}]$. Of course ordinary NPs, such *John, most of John's friends*, etc. also map P2 denotations into $[E \to \{0, 1\}]$. The difference in the two cases concerns what the values of the functions depend on. Compare:

(12)   a. Sam criticized most of John's students

      b. Sam criticized himself

In (12a) whether the denotation of *criticized most of John's students* holds of Sam is decided just by checking the set of objects that Sam criticized. If that set includes a majority of John's students then (12a) is true. We don't need to know who Sam is. If Bill praised exactly the people that Sam criticized then (12a) and *Bill praised most of John's students* must have the same truth value. In contrast however it might be that the individuals Sam criticized are just those that Bill praised but (12b) and *Bill praised himself* have different truth values. Formally, for R a binary relation over E and $x \in E$, $xR =_{df} \{y \in E| (R(y))(x) = 1\}$. Then we define:

The Accusative Extensions Condition (AEC): For F a map from binary relations to properties, F satisfies the AEC iff for all $a, b \in E$, all binary relations R,S over E, if $aR = bS$ then $F(R)(a) = F(S)(b)$

The Accusative Anaphor Condition (AAC): For F a map from binary relations to properties, F satisfies the AAC iff for all $a \in E$, all binary relations R,S over E, if $aR = aS$ then $F(R)(a) = F(S)(a)$

Definition 10 Now let D be an expression which combines with P2s to form P1s. Then D is *autonomously referring* iff all interpretations of D satisfy the AEC. D is a *proper accusative anaphor* iff all non-trivial interpretations of D satisfy the AAC but fail the AEC.[12]

Fact 7 In L_{Eng} the proper accusative anaphors are just PH(P1/P2), and thus anaphors, semantically defined in Definition 10, are syntactically invariant in Eng.[13]

A closing note on "Levels of Structure" and Klein's Erlangen Program. The notion of structure we are using was initiated by the mathematician Felix Klein in his dissertation at Erlangen in 1872. He used "preservation under transformations" to characterize different types of geometries. For example, the objects studied by Euclidean geometry were those invariant under rotations, translations and reflections (i.e. rotation around an axis through 2-space). The major invariant was the distance between two points. Different types of geometries are characterized by different classes of permutations of the domain.

We speculate that different "levels" of linguistic structure can be enlighteningly characterized in terms of different classes of permutations.[14] We have already distinguished "syntactic transformations" (automorphisms) and semantic ones. But syntactic automorphisms need not preserve syllable structure, for example, whereas expressions with different syllable structure are plausibly not considered phonologically equivalent. "Phonological automorphisms" would preserve syllable structure and doubtless much else. So the phonological properties of a language would be those preserved by the phonological transformations just as its syntactic properties are those preserved by its syntactic transformations. In this way, the linguist's "level of structure" are plausibly reconstructed as domains preserved by different transformations.

We have, in this lecture, focussed heavily on the notion of "invariants of grammar." It is of some reassurance to note that scientists in other fields have also found the notion of invariant fundamental. It is used in various areas of modern physics (quantum mechanics), as reflected in the following passage from Weyl (1952, p.132):

> We found that objectivity means invariance with respect to the group of automorphisms.

Perhaps a little closer to our interests is the use of invariants in computational studies of perspective and the recognition of three dimensional objects from their projections onto a (two dimensional) plane (Mundy and Zisserman 1992).

Notes

[1] These definitions can be generalized, the crucial factor being that the domain and range sets each carry a partial order.

[2] Indeed, as far as we know, current theories find no *structural* property that characterizes even the category *sentence*. In practice, we rely on semantic criteria: a sentence in a language L is an expression whose translation into English is a sentence. A little less ethnocentrically we might take sentences to be expressions that "express complete thoughts," or "are true or false." But is there no structural property unique to sentences? In the early days of generative grammar there was at least a candidate: *all recursion goes through S,* meaning that whenever u is a proper constituent of v, where u and v have the same category, then there is a sentence w such that u is a (not necessarily proper) constituent of w and w is a constituent of v. Today however linguists find it natural to treat expressions like *John's father's sister* as a DP with two properly embedded DPs and no intervening Ss. So we leave the reader the following gedanken experiment: imagine we are given a sound and complete grammar of an unknown language, in which all category labels have been renamed (with numbers for example). If no information is provided about the meanings of the expressions, can we tell which category is S? If so, how?

[3] Yatzachi Zapotec examples from Butler (1976) and Black (1996). Yalálag Zapotec examples from Avelino (2004).

[4] One of the most recent GB treatments of Passive, Baker et al. (1989), does not quite satisfy the condition of underlying structural identity. In passives the passive morphology *-en* is treated as a separate morpheme of category I0 and bears the AGENT theta role. But subjects in actives are sisters to I1 (Specifiers).

[5] Note that our defining condition on automorphisms, $h(F)=F$, comes down to the traditional "h commutes with F." That is, given any partial function $F : A \rightarrow A$ and any bijection $h : A \rightarrow A$, $h(F) = F$ iff (i) $h(\text{Domain}(F)) = \text{Domain}(F)$ and (ii) $\forall \sigma \in A, F(h(\sigma)) = h(F(\sigma))$. The commuting functions of condition (ii) are often depicted with a diagram like this:

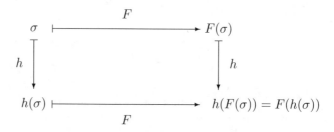

But it is important to remember condition (i) too. Since in the present setting most of our generating functions are partial, it is essential to be careful about the requirement that $h(\text{Domain}(F)) = \text{Domain}(F)$ before concluding $h(F) = F$. Our definition of automorphism fits neatly with the definition of invariant given just below, and we have found it helpful on its own given the importance of condition (i) when the functions F are partial.

[6]We later weaken this to "fixed by all stable automorphisms" when the notion of stability is defined (in Lecture 4, page 145). For most of the grammars we exhibit, all the automorphisms are stable.

[7]See e.g. Enderton (1972, pp.88,89,154-56) for initial discussion.

[8]For example, Hopper and Traugott (1993), Lehmann (1985), Traugott and Heine (1991), Wischer and Diewald (2002).

[9]See Corver and Van Riemsdijk (2001) for some discussion.

[10]Emonds (1985, p.165) considers the idea that "closed class items" cannot be differentiated by any purely semantic features. Chomsky (1995, pp.277-279) suggests that "Case features" are "-interpretable," contrasting them with agreement features, for example. Such views are similar to the rather antique philosophical suggestion that "logical constants do not represent" (Wittgenstein 1922, §4.0312). But we now say: logical constants have semantic values, but these values differ from the values of individual constants in that they are invariant with respect to automorphisms of the semantic domain. Much more on this idea and its extension to grammatical constants below, including a discussion in Lecture 4 of a contrast between case and agreement.

[11]For a much more detailed study of permutation invariance see van Benthem (1989), Keenan (2001).

[12]This way of interpreting *himself* can be criticized as being insuffi-

ciently general (see for example, Heim and Kratzer 1988, p.204), since it only interprets *himself* when it denotes an argument of a binary relation, though the relation-denoting expression itself may be complex. L_{Eng} has expressions like *John both praised and criticized himself*, as well as booleanly more complex ones like *John either praised or criticized both himself and Sam.*

Generalizing our interpretation of *himself* to account for its occurrences as the third argument of a ditransitive verb and more generally the n'th argument of an n-place predicate, $n > 1$, is unproblematic. We define for all $n > 0$, all non-empty E, and all $1 \leq i \leq n$: $SELF_i$ is that map from n+1-ary relations to n-ary ones given by: $SELF_i(R)(a_n)\ldots(a_1) = R(a_i)(a_n)\ldots(a_1)$. Then treating PROTECT-FROM as a three place predicate (due to the naturalness of the example) we have distinct interpretations for *Mary protected John from himself* and *Mary protected John from herself*:

$$SELF_2(\text{PROTECT-FROM})(j)(m)=(\text{PROTECT-FROM})(j)(j)(m)$$
$$SELF_1(\text{PROTECT-FROM})(j)(m)=(\text{PROTECT-FROM})(m)(j)(m)$$

Then in analogy with the Accusative Extensions and the Accusative Anaphor Conditions of page 37, we introduce the following notions (omitting 'Accusative'). A map F from n+1-ary relations to n-ary ones over a universe E satisfies

The Extensions Condition (EC): For F a map from n+1-ary relations to n-ary ones, F satisfies the EC iff for all $a,b \in E^n$, all n-ary relations R,S over E^n, if $\lambda x.R(x)(a_n)\ldots(a_1) = \lambda x.S(x)(a_n)\ldots(a_1)$ then $F(R)(a_n)\ldots(a_1) = F(S)(a_n)\ldots(a_1)$.

The i'th Anaphor Condition (AC_i): For F a map from n+1-ary relations to n-ary ones, F satisfies the AC iff for all $a,b \in E^n$ with $a_i = b_i$, if $\lambda x.R(x)(a_n)\ldots(a_1) = \lambda x.S(x)(a_n)\ldots(a_1)$ then $F(R)(a_n)\ldots(a_1) = F(S)(a_n)\ldots(a_1)$.

Anaphors are now defined to be expressions whose non-trivial interpretations fail the EC but satisfy one or another of the AC_i. One checks, for example, that $SELF_i$ satisfies AC_i and fails the EC (in a universe with enough elements so that the relevant n-tuples can all have distinct coordinates). Finally, to generalize to the case where *himself* may occur as an object of a Preposition it is a straightforward matter semantically to observe that Prepositions which take NP arguments to build predicate modifiers can be treated up to isomorphism as predicate extensors (Keenan and Faltz 1985), in which case *himself* is just interpreted as some $SELF_i$ as already given. We observe that for P a possible Preposition denotation (a map from entities to maps from n-ary relations to n-ary relations) and R an n-ary relation, P(R) is that n+1-ary relation given by:

$$P(R)(x)(a_n) \ldots (a_1) = (P(x)(R))(a_n) \ldots (a_1).$$

Then we interpret a reflexive object of a Preposition which builds an n-place predicate modifier as the n+1st argument of the corresponding n+1 place predicate, so for example, *John talks to himself* takes the value

$$TO(SELF_1)(TALK)(j) = SELF_1(TO(TALK))(j).$$

[13]It is assumed here that the universe E of interpretation always has at least two elements. The non-triviality condition is intended for cases like *at least two of the ten students besides himself*, which requires for non-triviality that E contains at least ten students.

[14]Thanks to Graham Katz for discussion.

2

Some case studies

We exhibit three and a half grammars designed to model certain structure types in natural language. In §2.1 we consider verb final languages with free order of case marked arguments preverbally (Korean, Malayalam, Basque). In §2.2 – the "half" – we present a free word order variant of our verb final language, one in which "second position" is invariant and recursively defined. Our analysis supports that "second position" is another universal non-uniform invariant. §2.3 presents a verb initial language with structural voice morphology (Toba Batak, Sumatra; Tagalog and other Philippine languages; Balinese; Malagasy, Madagascar). These first language types show how certain morphemes - case markers in Korean, voice markers in Toba – are directly structural, in the same sense that c-command and other constituency relations are. And these grammars instantiate our claim that the anaphor-antecedent relation is invariant but not uniform across languages: in Korean case marking is decisive, in Toba, voice marking is. Lastly, §2.4 models some complex and well studied "extraction" phenomena, showing that many of the classical "movement" constraints can be represented by limiting the domains of the generating functions.

2.1 A case marking language

We present a grammar, Kor, designed to model certain properties of Korean, specifically the role of case marking and its relation to the distribution of anaphors.[1] In Kor, the case markers, the lexical anaphor and the AA (anaphor-antecedent) relation are invariant.

The pragmatically least marked word order in simple Korean sentences is verb final. Subject and object in transitive sentences carry distinct postpositions (suffixal case markers). The relative order of subject and object is quite free preverbally. Topicalization is effected by the use of a different postposition, $-(n)un$, not "fronting" of the constituent.

(1)   a. John-i   Mary-lul   piphanhayssta
          John-NOM Mary-ACC criticized

      'John criticized Mary'

      b. Mary-lul   John-i   piphanhayssta
          Mary-ACC John-NOM criticized

      'John criticized Mary'

The same word order freedom obtains when the object is an anaphor:

(2)   a. John-i   caki-casin-ul   piphanhayssta
          John-NOM self-EMPH-ACC criticized

      'John criticized himself'

      b. Caki-casin-ul   John-i   piphanhayssta
          self-EMPH-ACC John-NOM criticized

      'John criticized himself'

Note that -NOM has the shape -*i* on consonant final NPs and -*ka* otherwise. Comparable conditioning holds for the accusative marker -*ul/-lul* and the topic marker -*un/-nun*. This word order freedom, even with anaphors, is preserved when the subject is non-referential:

(3)   a. Nwukwunka(-ka) caki-casin-ul   piphanhayssta
          someone-NOM   self-EMPH-ACC criticized

      'Someone criticized himself'

      b. Caki-casin-ul   nwukwunka(-ka) piphanhayssta
          self-EMPH-ACC someone-NOM   criticized

      'Someone criticized himself'

(4)   a. (Motun) haksayng-tul-i caki-casin-ul   piphanhayssta
          (all)   student-pl-NOM self-EMPH-ACC criticized

      '(All) the students criticized themselves'

      b. Caki-casin-ul   (motun) haksayng-tul-i piphanhayssta
          self-EMPH-ACC (all)   student-pl-NOM criticized

      '(All) the students criticized themselves'

(5)   a. Nwuka caki-casin-ul   piphanhayss-ni
          who   self-EMPH-ACC criticized?

      'Who criticized himself?'

      b. Caki-casin-ul   nwuka piphanhayss-ni
          self-EMPH-ACC who   criticized?

      'Who criticized himself?'

Note that Topicalization of reflexives in these contexts in English varies from marginal to bad:

(6)   a.   *? Himself$_i$ someone$_i$ criticized

      b.   * Himself$_i$ who$_i$ criticized?

Note too that the reflexive first order in English, while sometimes acceptable (7b), is largely limited to root clauses and disallowed in properly subordinate ones. Compare:

(7)   a.   Himself$_i$ John$_i$ criticized at the meeting

      b.   * the meeting at which himself$_i$ John$_i$ criticized

But in Korean the reflexive first order is fully natural in relative clauses:

(8)   a.   Caki-casin-ul   John-i   hoyuy-eyse   piphanhayssta
           self-EMPH-ACC John-NOM meeting-LOC criticized

           'John criticized himself at the meeting'

      b.   Caki-casin-ul   John-i   piphanhay-n
           self-EMPH-ACC John-NOM criticize-PRENOM-PAST
           hoyuy-ka   ecey   iss-ess-ta
           meeting-NOM yesterday exist-past-decl

           'there was a meeting yesterday at which John criticized himself'

Finally note that merely placing an NP in clause initial position does not force contrast or emphasis. Rather to contrast an NP denotation we use the morphological resources of the language, marking the NP with the "topic" marker -$(n)un$. And the immediate preverbal position for the topic marked NP is at least as natural as clause initial position.

(9)   John-i   Mary-nun piphanhayssta
      John-NOM Mary-TOP criticized

      'John criticized MARY (not someone else)'

We see then that the relative order of anaphor and antecedent preverbally is quite free, fronting not having the topicalizing or emphasizing effect it does in English. What does not naturally vary among anaphors and their antecedents however is their relative case marking (O'Grady 1987, Park 1986, Keenan 1988). A -NOM (-i/-ka) or topic marked (-un/-nun) NP can antecede an -ACC (-lul/-ul) (or -DAT -eke, not considered here) one, but we do not in general find -ACC marked NPs interpreted as antecedents of -NOM marked reflexives (even if they precede them). Thus the expressions in (10) with -NOM or -TOP marked anaphors and -ACC or -DAT marked antecedents are generally bad, but interchanging the postpositions produces fully grammatical Ss.

(10)   a. * (Motun) haksayng-tul-ul caki-casin-i   piphanhayssta
              (all)   student-pl-ACC self-EMPH-NOM criticized

           '(All) the students criticized themselves'

      b. * Nwukwu-lul caki-casin-i   pinanhayss-ni
          who-ACC   self-EMPH-NOM criticized?

          'Who criticized himself?'

      c. * Caki-casin-i   piphanha-n   haksayng-ul
          self-EMPH-NOM criticized-ADNOM student-ACC
          manna-ss-ta
          meet-PAST-DECL?

          'I met the student who criticized himself?'

      d. ?* John-ul   caki-casin-i   piphanhayssta
          John-ACC self-EMPH-NOM criticized

          'John criticized himself'

Finally our grammar Kor allows subjects to combine directly with a P2 to form a kind of P1. (11b) provides support for this constituency structure:

(11)   a. Caki-casin-ul [John-i   piphanhayssta]
           self-EMPH-ACC John-NOM criticized

          'John criticized himself'

      b. Caki-casin-ul [John-i   piphanha-ko Bill-i
          self-EMPH-ACC John-NOM criticized-and Bill-NOM
          chingchanhayssta
          praised

          'John criticized himself and Bill praised himself'

(Our speaker's preference was to use the topic marker -*un* instead of NOM -*i* both times in the coordinate expression, but the mere nominative marker -*i* was also acceptable).

The grammar for Kor models the basic case marking and word order properties of Korean noted above. Define $\text{Kor}=\langle V, \text{Cat}, \text{Lex}, \text{Rule}\rangle$, as follows:

V: laughed, cried, sneezed, praised, criticized, saw, -nom, -acc, John, Bill, Sam, himself, and, or, nor, both, either, neither

Cat: NP, NP_{refl}, Ka, Kn, KPa, KPn, P0, P1a, P1n, P2, CONJ

Lex:
Kn	-nom
Ka	-acc
P1n	laughed, cried, sneezed
P2	praised, criticized, interviewed
NP	John, Bill, Sam
NP_{refl}	himself
CONJ	and, or, nor

Rule: CM (case mark), PA (predicate-argument) and Coord.

We now define the functions in Rule. Kor has a Case Marking Rule, as follows:

Domain		CM	Value	Conditions
-nom	t		t⌢-nom	
Kn	NP	$\longmapsto$	KPn	$t \neq$ himself
-acc	t		t⌢-acc	
Ka	NP	$\longmapsto$	KPa	none

For example, $\text{CM}((\text{-acc}, \text{Ka}),(\text{John}, \text{NP}))=(\text{John-acc}, \text{KPa})$.

And Kor has a familiar-looking merge rule for combining predicates and arguments, but this one cares about case marking:

Domain		PA	Value
s	t		s⌢t
KPn	P1n	$\longmapsto$	S
s	t		s⌢t
KPa	P1a	$\longmapsto$	S
s	t		s⌢t
KPn	P2	$\longmapsto$	P1a
s	t		s⌢t
KPa	P2	$\longmapsto$	P1n

For example, we have:

$\text{PA}((\text{John-nom}, \text{KPn}),(\text{praised}, \text{P2}))=(\text{John-nom praised}, \text{P1a})$

Notice how, in this definition of PA, we have "dissimilated" the P1 categories so that once a KP in a certain case combines with a P2 then no KP in that same case can combine with the resulting P1.

Coordination is accomplished with the generating function Coord, which yields coordinations of expressions in certain categories.[2] It is convenient to define the set of coordinable categories $cC_{Kor} = Cat - \{CONJ, Ka, Kn, KPa, KPn\}$ and the class of nominal categories $nC_{Kor} = \{NP, NP_{refl}\}$:

Domain			Coord	Value	Conditions
and	s	t		both⌢s ⌢and⌢t	
CONJ	C	C	$\longmapsto$	C	$C \in cC_{Kor}$
or	s	t		either⌢s ⌢or⌢t	
CONJ	C	C	$\longmapsto$	C	$C \in cC_{Kor}$
nor	s	t		neither⌢s ⌢nor⌢t	
CONJ	C	C	$\longmapsto$	C	$C \in cC_{Kor}$
and	s	t		both⌢s ⌢and⌢t	
CONJ	C	C'	$\longmapsto$	NP_{refl}	$C \neq C' \in nC_{Kor}$
or	s	t		either⌢s ⌢or⌢t	
CONJ	C	C'	$\longmapsto$	NP_{refl}	$C \neq C' \in nC_{Kor}$
nor	s	t		neither⌢s ⌢or⌢t	
CONJ	C	C'	$\longmapsto$	NP_{refl}	$C \neq C' \in nC_{Kor}$

As usual, the language L_{Kor} is the whole set of expressions obtained by applying these rules to lexical items. Here is an FA tree representing the argument that $(\text{himself-acc John-nom praised}, S) \in L_{Kor}$:

PA:(himself -acc John -nom praised, P0)

CM:(himself -acc, KPa)   PA:(John -nom praised, P1a)

(-acc, Ka)   (himself, NP_{refl})   CM:(John -nom, KPn)   (praised, P2)

(-nom, Kn)   (John, NP)

Note that, in this derivation, the anaphor (himself, NP_{refl}) asymmetrically c-commands its antecedent (John-nom, KPn). This is perhaps more visible, or at least more familiar looking, in a "standard" tree representation:

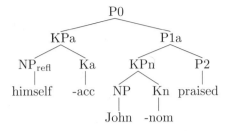

Exercise 5 a. Exhibit an FA tree for (John-nom himself-acc praised, S). Our semantics will shortly tell us that this sentence and the one depicted just above are logically equivalent.

b. Explain why (himself-nom laughed, P0) is not in L_{Kor}.

c. Provide an FA tree for a Kor 'translation' of the English *John praised both himself and Bill.*

2.1.1 Some invariants of Kor

Fact 1 *Kor is unambiguous, and so Lex is invariant. Furthermore, by U4, each n, Lex$_n$ is invariant.*

In Lecture 4 we will see grammars G in which Lex_G is not invariant.

Fact 2 *(-nom, Kn) and (-acc, Ka) are both invariants (grammatical constants).*

Pretheoretically case markers are grammatical constants, so the fact that they are provably invariants in Kor supports that our formal notion of invariant in fact picks out expressions independently judged to be grammatical in nature. So no automorphism can interchange (-nom, Kn) and (-acc, Ka).

Fact 3 *(Bill, NP) is not invariant.*

Proof. Consider the map f : V → V that interchanges *John* and *Bill*, fixing everything else. Extend f with its "product lift" (defined on page 19) so that it applies to arbitrary sequences $f : V^* \to V^*$. Now define the total function h : $L_{Kor} \to L_{Kor}$ as the function such that, for any (s, C) ∈ L_{Kor}, h(s, C) = (f(s), C). This function maps (Bill, NP) to (John, NP). We show that h ∈ Aut_{Kor}.

We leave the proof that h is 1-1 and onto as an exercise. Then we must show just that h fixes every element of Rule={CM, PA, Coord}. (See note 5 on page 39.)

1. To show CM=h(CM), we first show Domain(CM)=h(Domain(CM)). To show ⊆, consider arbitrary ⟨a, b⟩ ∈ Domain(CM). By the definition of CM, either Cat_a = Kn and string(b) ≠ *himself* or

Cat_a = Ka. All expressions of category Ka and Kn are fixed by h, and *himself* is fixed by h, so $\langle h(a), h(b) \rangle \in$ Domain(CM). Now to show $\supseteq$, assume $\langle a, b \rangle \in$ h(Domain(CM)), and reason similarly. Finally, we show that for any $\langle a, b \rangle \in$ Domain(CM), h(CM(a, b)) = CM(h(a), h(b)). Either Cat_a = Ka or Cat_a = Kn. When Cat_a = Ka, we can see that h commutes with CM as follows:

$$
\begin{aligned}
h(CM(a,b)) \quad &= h(CM((\text{-acc}, Ka), (t, NP))) && \text{Def Domain(CM)} \\
&= h((t^\frown\text{-acc}, KPa)) && \text{Def CM} \\
&= (f(t)^\frown\text{-acc}, KPa)) && \text{Def h,f} \\
&= CM((\text{-acc}, Ka), (f(t), NP)) && \text{Def CM} \\
&= CM(h((\text{-acc}, Ka)), h((t, NP))) && \text{Def h,f}
\end{aligned}
$$

The case where Cat_a = Kn is handled similarly.

2-3. The arguments showing PA=h(PA) and Coord=h(Coord) are similar to this one.

□

Exercise 6 Extend the previous result to show that interchanging (and, CONJ) and (or, CONJ), leaving everything else fixed, also yields an automorphism, even though the language has *both* and *either*. For the even more ambitious reader: show that all category-preserving permutations of the lexicon extend to automorphisms.

Fact 4 (himself, NP_{refl}) *is invariant.*

Fact 5 *For all* $C \in$ Cat, *PH(C) is invariant.*

Are the PH(C) always invariant in a natural language grammar? No. In Lecture 4 we offer a model of Spanish in which some PH(C) are not invariant. In general agreement phenomena and allomorphy provide cases where automorphisms can change category.

Semantic interpretation for L_{Kor}. We now provide L_{Kor} with a compositional semantics which shows that Ss with reflexives are interpreted correctly in all cases. Those willing to take our word for this can move directly to the next section. We assume a modest familiarity with standard model theoretic semantics (and we use the notation introduced in the previous lecture – see especially page 35).

Definition 11 $\mathcal{M} = (E, m)$ is a model for *Kor* iff E is a non-empty set and m is a map whose domain is Lex, satisfying the following conditions:

1. $m(s, C) \in Den_E(C)$, the latter defined as follows:

$\text{Den}_E(\text{NP}) = \text{Type 1}$

$\text{Den}_E(\text{NP}_{\text{refl}}) = \{f \in \text{Type 1}|\ \text{if nontrivial, f satisfies AAC and fails AEC}\}$

$\text{Den}_E(\text{P0}) = R_0 = \{0, 1\}$

$\text{Den}_E(\text{P1n}) = R_1 = [E \rightarrow R_0]$

$\text{Den}_E(\text{P1a}) = [\text{Type1} \rightarrow R_1]$

$\text{Den}_E(\text{P2}) = R_2 = [E \rightarrow R_1]$

$\text{Den}_E(\text{KPa}) = \text{Type1}$

$\text{Den}_E(\text{KPn}) = \{\text{NOM}(f)|\ f \in \text{Type1}\}$, where for any $f \in \text{Type1}$, NOM is the function with domain $R_1 \cup R_2$ such that for $P \in R_1$, $\text{NOM}(f)(P) = f(P)$ and for $R \in R_2, h \in \text{Type1}$, $\text{NOM}(f)(R)(h) = f(h(R))$

$\text{Den}_E(\text{CONJ}) = \{f \in [B \times B \rightarrow B]|\ B \in \text{Den}_E(x), x \in cC_{\text{Kor}}\}$

2. $m(s, \text{NP}) \in \{I_b|\ b \in E\}$

    $m(\text{-acc}, \text{Ka})$ is the identity map on Type1

    $m(\text{-nom}, \text{Ka})$ is the function NOM defined above

    $m(\text{himself}, \text{NP}_{\text{refl}}) = \text{SELF}$, where $\text{SELF} : R_2 \rightarrow R_1$
    given by $\text{SELF}(R)(a) = (R(a))(a)$

    $m(\text{and}, \text{CONJ})$ maps each (x, y) in $\text{Den}_E(C)^2$, for $C \in cC_{\text{Kor}}$, to $x \wedge y$

    $m(\text{or}, \text{CONJ})$ maps each (x, y) in $\text{Den}_E(C)^2$, for $C \in cC_{\text{Kor}}$, to $x \vee y$

    $m(\text{nor}, \text{CONJ})$ maps each (x, y) in $\text{Den}_E(C)^2$, $C \in cC_{\text{Kor}}$, to $\neg(x \vee y)$

3. For each model $\mathcal{M} = (E, m)$ an interpretation m^* of L_{Kor} is a function which extends m and satisfies:

    $m^*(\text{CM}(s, t)) = m^*(s)(m^*(t))$,

    $$m^*(\text{PA}(s, t)) = \begin{cases} m^*(s)(m^*(t)) & \text{if Cat(s)=KPn and Cat(t)=P1n} \\ m^*(t)(m^*(s)) & \text{otherwise} \end{cases}$$

    $m^*(\text{Coord}(s, t, u)) = m(s)(m^*(t), m^*(u))$

Using these definitions, it is easy to compute that (12a,b) are logically equivalent (always interpreted the same), supporting that argument identification is done by case marking rather than c-command. For all models $\mathcal{M} = (E, m)$, $m^*(12a) = m^*(12b)$.

(12)   a. (John-nom Bill-acc praised, P0)

        b. (Bill-acc John-nom praised)

PA:(John -nom Bill -acc praised, P0)

CM:(John -nom, KPn)   PA:(Bill -acc praised, P1n)

(-nom, Kn)   (John, NP)   CM:(Bill -acc, KPa)   (praised, P2)

(-acc, Ka)   (Bill, NP)

PA:(Bill -acc John -nom praised, P0)

CM:(Bill -acc, KPa)   PA:(John -nom praised, P1a)

(-acc, Ka)   (Bill, NP)   CM:(John -nom, KPn)   (praised, P2)

(-nom, Kn)   (John, NP)

The logical equivalence of (12a,b) relies crucially on the interpretation of (-nom,Kn). When the KP it derives looks at a P2 it knows to wait until the next KP denotation comes along. So the interpretation of bound morphology here is critical. Moreover the same reasoning shows that the result of replacing (bill, NP) by (himself, NP_{refl}) in (12a,b) are also logically equivalent:

(13) m^*(John-nom himself-acc criticized, P0)

   $= m^*$(himself-acc John-nom criticized, P0)

Thus the interpretation of *himself* as an anaphor does not depend on it being c-commanded by its antecedent. We note that these Ss, like (12a,b), have isomorphic derivation trees (standard or FA). But the expressions are not isomorphic in L_{Kor} since automorphisms can't map KPn's to KPa's, P1n's to P1a's, etc. So,

Lovers of Trees Beware!

Now we are in a position to see,

Fact 6 *(-nom, Kn), (-acc, Ka), and* (himself, NP_{refl}) *are all semantically invariant.*

Recall that semantic invariance was defined on page 33. Semantic invariance is discussed further in Lecture 4.

Our semantic definitions also make the following syntactic definition natural:

Definition 12 s co-argument t in u iff for some v of category P2, PA(s, PA(t, v)) or PA(t, PA(s, v)) is a constituent of u.

Fact 7 *The co-argument relation is invariant.*

Recall that anaphors are by definition expressions that denote functions satisfying the proper accusative anaphor condition (page 37). So we use the same semantic definition of anaphor in all natural languages, it is only their syntactic characterization that varies. In Kor, the expressions that satisfy this condition are just the elements of PH(KPa) which contain *himself* as constituent.

Fact 8 *For all* $s \in L_{Kor}$ *s is an anaphor iff for some NP u, s =* $CM((\text{-}acc, Ka), u)$ *and* $(himself, NP)CONu$.

Fact 9 *The property* is an anaphor *is invariant.*

Definition 13 (Anaphor-antecedent relation in Kor) $sAA_{Kor}t$ in u iff for some P0 v, vCONu, s co-argument t in v, and t is an anaphor.

So whether s is a possible antecedent of t (in u) depends in part on whether t is an anaphor (obviously) and that in turn is decided in part by its case marking. C-command, and more generally, derivational hierarchy, is not mentioned. In (11), recall, the anaphor asymmetrically c-commands its antecedent.

Fact 10 AA_{Kor} *is invariant.*

2.1.2 Concluding remarks on Kor

It is unproblematic that anaphors asymmetrically c-command their antecedents. The interpretation of case markers guarantees the right semantic interpretation (sentence internally) independent of c-command. (Note that *himself* in Kor has the same interpretation as *himself* in Eng). So linguists who claim that the AA relation in nuclear clauses is decided by c-command at least have an alternative to contrast their analyses with.

Morphology is structural, again independent of c-command relations within the clause. The case markers, (-nom,Kn) and (-acc,Ka), are invariant even though the KPs they build do not have fixed structural positions. Specifically a KPa does not always combine with a transitive verb (P2) to form a P1; it also combines with P1s to form P0s (Ss). (See Lecture 4 for consideration of the two forms of accusative (and nominative) case markers).

2.2 Free word order and second position

As we have seen, Korean (and L_{Kor}) has free word order of arguments preverbally. Some languages are much freer, allowing all six orders of a transitive verb and two arguments: Malayalam (Mohanan 1982), Warlpiri (Hale 1983), Papago/Pima (Zapeda 1983, Smith 2002), and others. Korean is not so free, but rather than introducing a new language from scratch to illustrate free word order, we will make some small modifications in Kor to yield "Free Word Korean" (FWK). Then we enrich the grammar still further to show how "second position" can be structurally defined. These two phenomena are not independent, and it has in fact proved problematic in current linguistic theories to define "second position" in structural terms, given precisely this word order freedom. We might stress that our definition has no commitment to the existence of "positions" independent of the expressions that "fill" them.

Free Word Order Korean (FWK) differs from Kor just in allowing all orders of KPn, KPa, and P2 in transitive Ss. The relative order of NP and the case markers is unchanged (and in Malayalam and Warlpiri is always suffixal as well), nor does the order of conjunction and their arguments change. Little of the semantic interpretation of FWK differs from that of Kor, since the interpretation of an expression depends on its grammatical category, not its position relative to other expressions.

Syntax of FWK. V, Cat, and Lex are the same as in Kor. Also the Case Mark and Coordination rules are the same. Only the Predicate-Argument rule PA is extended to PA′ as follows: for each pair (s,t) in Domain(PA) we add the pair (t,s) to Domain(PA′). So Domain(PA′) is permutation closed. In all cases the string coordinate of PA′(u, v) is string(u)⌢string(v). Its category is the same that PA would assign to (u,v) or (v,u), whichever is in Domain(PA). For explicitness we list each case (the first 4 classes are unchanged from the definition of PA):

Domain		PA′	Value
s	t		s⌢t
KPn	P1n	$\longmapsto$	S
s	t		s⌢t
KPa	P1a	$\longmapsto$	S
s	t		s⌢t
KPn	P2	$\longmapsto$	P1a
s	t		s⌢t
KPa	P2	$\longmapsto$	P1n
s	t		s⌢t
P1n	KPn	$\longmapsto$	S
s	t		s⌢t
P1a	KPa	$\longmapsto$	S

$$
\begin{array}{ccc}
\begin{array}{ll} \text{s} & \text{t} \\ \text{P2} & \text{KPn} \end{array} & \longmapsto & \begin{array}{l} \text{s}^\frown\text{t} \\ \text{P1a} \end{array} \\
\begin{array}{ll} \text{s} & \text{t} \\ \text{P2} & \text{KPa} \end{array} & \longmapsto & \begin{array}{l} \text{s}^\frown\text{t} \\ \text{P1n} \end{array}
\end{array}
$$

Notice that PA' is a function, as usual, since the word order in the results is determined in every case by the order of the arguments to the function, and each pair of arguments has distinct categories. Here is an FA tree for the derivation of (praised John-nom himself-acc, P0):

PA:(praised John -nom himself -acc, P0)

PA:(praised John -nom, P1a) CM:(himself -acc, KPa)

(praised, P2) CM:(John -nom, KPn) (-acc, Ka) (himself, NP$_{\text{refl}}$)

(-nom, Kn) (John, NP)

One verifies that all six orders of KPn, KPa, and P2 are derived in this grammar. No order is "basic" with others derived from it. All are directly generated. Nor does semantic interpretation introduce any significant complexities, except that there are more expressions to be interpreted.

Semantics of FWK. The definition of model $\mathcal{M} = (\text{E}, \text{m})$ is the same as for Kor, and as the set of categories for the two grammars is the same the denotation sets associated with each $\text{C} \in \text{Cat}$ are the same as well. And as Lex is the same in the two grammars the interpretations of lexical items is the same. The only difference is that the interpretations m^* of L_{FWK} must extend those of L_{Kor} to assign denotations to the new derived expressions. And all we have to do here is make sure that $\text{m}^*(\text{PA}'(\text{u}, \text{v})) = \text{m}^*(\text{PA}'(\text{v}, \text{u}))$. So let's just say it: for all $(\text{u}, \text{v}) \in$ Domain(PA'),

$$
\text{m}^*(\text{PA}'(\text{u}, \text{v})) = \begin{cases} \text{m}^*(\text{PA}(\text{u}, \text{v})) & \text{if } \langle \text{u}, \text{v} \rangle \in \text{Domain}(\text{PA}) \\ \text{m}^*(\text{PA}(\text{v}, \text{u})) & \text{if } \langle \text{u}, \text{v} \rangle \notin \text{Domain}(\text{PA}) \end{cases}
$$

Thus we see that a fairly trivial change to Kor - adding (u,v) to Domain(PA) whenever (v,u) was already there, produced a free word order language, one whose interpretation is again easily given in terms of that for the original language.

However languages, like Warlpiri and Quechua which allow scrambling out of constituents pose a greater syntactic challenge. Thus in (14a) from Quechua (Weber 1989, p.231) we see a normal prenominal

relative clause where the entire NP takes the accusative postposition
-*ta*. But in (14c,d), with the same meaning as (14a,b), the head *runa*
'man' and the restricting clause *maqashan* 'who hit him' are not adjacent, and both carry the accusative -*ta*:

(14) a. [Maqa-sha-n runa]-ta rikaa
          hit-SUB-3   man-ACC see-1

          'I see the man who hit him'

      b. [Runa maqa-sha-n]-ta rikaa
          Man hit-SUB-3-ACC see-1

      c. [Maqa-sha-n]-ta rikaa runa-ta
          hit-SUB-3-ACC   see-1 man-ACC

      d. Runa-ta   rikaa [maqa-sha-n]-ta
          man-ACC see-1 hit-SUB-3-ACC

A case marked element separated from a case marked host carries both
postpositions. In (15b) below, *hatun* 'big' carries a copy of both the
genitive and the accusative postpositions, as it is understood to modify
the genitive *boy* within an accusative phrase. In contrast, in (15c), which
carries only only the accusative marker, the adjective modifies only the
accusative NP: 'the ball of the boy', not 'the boy'. (Here, following
Weber, we show the presumed initial position of the adjective with *e*.)

(15) a. [[hatun wamra]-pa pelota-n]-ta rikaa
          big   boy-GEN   ball-3-ACC see+1

          'I see the ball of the big boy'

      b. [[*e* wamra]-pa pelota-n]-ta rikaa hatun-pa-ta
             boy-GEN   ball-3-ACC see+1 big-GEN-ACC

          'I see the ball of the big boy'

      c. wamra-pa [*e* pelota-n]-ta rikaa hatun-ta
          boy-GEN   ball-3-ACC see+1 big-ACC

          'I see the big ball of the boy'

We do not attempt a grammar for such structures here. The puzzle is
that we want to be able to place the modifier of the noun argument
<u>after</u> building the clause containing it. We will consider some strategies
for allowing this to happen, in effect, in §3.3.3, but there is a first step
we can take here that will illustrate some important properties of Bare
Grammar and the associated notions of structure.

In a Bare Grammar, derivations can be "collapsed" without changing structure (automorphisms, invariants) at all. In effect, this collapse

makes more arguments 'available' to the generating function, and so this can be regarded as a first step toward a kind of structural manipulation we will consider in more detail later. The 'collapse' is achieved simply by closing the generating functions under composition, (where the relevant notion of 'composition' is suitably generalized so that it applies in a reasonable way to partial functions of various arities). We illustrate this with an artificial example.

Let f be a three place function, and g a two place one. Consider a function whose value at a four-tuple (a,b,c,d) is f(a,g(b,c),d). Let us call this 'composed' function $f \circ_2 g$, more formally defined as follows:

(16)
$$\text{Domain}(f \circ_2 g) = \{\langle a, b, c, d \rangle | \ (b, c) \in \text{Domain}(g), \text{ and} \\ \langle a, g(b, c), d \rangle \in \text{Domain}(f)\} \\ (f \circ_2 g)(a, b, c, d) =_{df} f(a, g(b, c), d)$$

The subscript 2 indicates that the value of g at its arguments will be the 2nd argument of f.

Exercise 7 In analogy with the previous definition, define $f \circ_1 g$, and $f \circ_3 g$. Then, for f,g functions of arity n and m respectively and $1 \leq i < n$, define $f \circ_i g$

Suppose now that we enrich FWK by adding $PA' \circ_2 PA'$ to Rule. The new grammar has the same expressions and the same automorphisms as before. It has all the derivations of the previous grammar, but now many new derivations that use the composed rules. The derivations with the composed rules generate expressions in bigger steps, with less deep derivation trees. $PA' \circ_2 PA'$ takes three arguments directly to a P0:

$$(PA' \circ_2 PA')((\text{John-nom, KPn}), (\text{himself-acc, KPa}), (\text{praised, P2})) \\ = (\text{John-nom himself-acc praised, P0})$$

So with this extension to the grammar, we get not only the first tree below, but the second for this same P0:

PA':(John -nom himself -acc praised, P0)

CM:(John -nom, KPn)   PA':(himself -acc praised, P1n)

(-nom, Kn) (John, NP) CM:(himself -acc, KPa)   (praised, P2)

(-acc, Ka)   (himself, NP$_{\text{refl}}$)

$$\text{PA}'\text{o}_2\text{PA}':(\text{John -nom himself -acc praised}, \text{P0})$$

$$\text{CM}:(\text{John -nom}, \text{KPn}) \quad \text{CM}:(\text{himself -acc}, \text{KPa}) \quad (\text{praised}, \text{P2})$$

$$(\text{-nom}, \text{Kn}) \quad (\text{John}, \text{NP}) \quad (\text{-acc}, \text{Ka}) \quad (\text{himself}, \text{NP}_{\text{refl}})$$

So this new grammar introduces some new "flatter" structures. If we added all the compositions of PA' with CM then we get a one step derivation of the P0 above directly from the lexical items occurring in it, the function used to generate it being three compositions.

$$((\text{PA}' \circ_2 \text{PA}') \circ_1 \text{CM}) \circ_2 \text{CM}:(\text{John -nom himself -acc praised}, \text{P0})$$

$$(\text{-nom}, \text{Kn}) \quad (\text{John}, \text{NP}) \quad (\text{-acc}, \text{Ka}) \quad (\text{himself}, \text{NP}_{\text{refl}}) \quad (\text{praised}, \text{P2})$$

And if we close Rule under i-compositions, then every expression in the language has a one step derivation like this one (though the set of generating functions would be infinite). And we reiterate:

Theorem 7 *Given* $G = \langle V, \text{Cat}, \text{Lex}, \text{Rule} \rangle$ *with* $f, g \in$ Rule, *set* Rule$' = $ Rule$\cup \{f \circ_i g | \; 1 \le i < \text{arity}(f)\}$, *and let* $G' = \langle V, \text{Cat}, \text{Lex}, \text{Rule}' \rangle$. *Then*

$$L_G = L_{G'}, \quad \text{and} \quad \text{Aut}_G = \text{Aut}_{G'}.$$

Proof. It is easy to see that $L_G = L_{G'}$. If we only add functions to Rule we generate all the old things just as we did before using the same lexical items and rules. And in the case at hand the new functions we add don't generate anything new, since anything they generate can be generated by iterated application of old functions. To see that $\text{Aut}_G = \text{Aut}_{G'}$, recall that an automorphism h of G' fixes all Domain(F), $F \in \text{Rule}_G$, and it commutes with all those F since they are all among the functions in $\text{Rule}_{G'}$. So $\text{Aut}_{G'} \subseteq \text{Aut}_G$. To see the reverse inclusion consider the hypothetical case of f, g in (16). If $\langle a, b, c, d \rangle$ is in Domain($f \circ_2 g$) then $\langle b, c \rangle \in$ Domain(g) and $\langle a, g(b, c), d \rangle \in$ Domain(f). So for $h \in \text{Aut}_G$, $\langle h(b), h(c) \rangle \in$ Domain(g) and $\langle h(a), h(g(b, c)), h(d) \rangle = \langle h(a), g(h(b), h(c)), h(d) \rangle \in$ Domain(f), so by the definition of $f \circ_2 g$, $\langle h(a), h(b), h(c), h(d) \rangle \in$ Domain($f \circ_2 g$). And

$$
\begin{aligned}
(f \circ_2 g)(h(a), h(b), h(c), h(d)) &= f(h(a), g(h(b), h(c)), h(d)) \\
&= f(h(a), h(g(b, c)), h(d)) \\
&= h(f(a, g(b, c), d)) \\
&= h(f \circ_2 g)(a, b, c, d)
\end{aligned}
$$

so h commutes with $f \circ_2 g$ and is thus in $\text{Aut}_{G'}$. (Of course the proof should be given for $f \circ_i g$ when $f, g \in \text{Aut}_G$, but this illustrates the basic mechanism of the proof). $\square$

Thus adding compositions of functions already present only changes "strong generative capacity," that is, the derivations of expressions. Generalizing,

Theorem 8 *Given a grammar G, let G* be the grammar that results from closing* Rule$_G$ *under i-compositions for arbitrary i. Then,*

$$L_G = L_{G^*}, \quad Aut_G = Aut_{G^*}$$

and every s $\in$ L$_{G^*}$ *has a one step derivation.*

This is another reason to emphasize again:

Lovers of Trees Beware!

The first reason for saying this was that trees depict a single derivation, but our notion of structure is "global" in the sense that two expressions are structurally isomorphic only if, intuitively, they can play the same role in *all* derivations. The new, second reason for the warning is that two grammars can have very different sets of trees and yet have exactly the same automorphisms and invariants – the same "structure" in the sense we are picking out here.

FWK-2: Free Word Order Korean with Second Position. It is interesting to consider one further elaboration of Kor. Languages as typologically diverse as German, Warlpiri, Tagalog, and Serbo-Croatian have in common that certain items, notably auxiliary verbs and various types of clitics, are placed in "second position" (p2). For recent extensive discussion, see Halpern and Zwicky (1996). The domain in which p2 is determined is not always explicitly given, and may even vary within a language. Zec and Inkelas (1990, p367) note that clitics in Serbo-Croatian may be placed either after the first major constituent, (17a), or after the absolutely first constituent, (17b):

(17) a. Taj čovek-joj-ga-je poklonia
          that man-her-it-aux presented

          'That man presented her with it'

      b. Taj-joj-ga-je čovek poklonia
          That-her-it-aux man presented

          'That man presented her with it'

We focus on the second case, which might (at first) seem more difficult to define structurally. We use the example of the postpositive conjunction -*que* in Latin (Gildersleeve and Lodge 1913):

(18) a. Senatus populus-que Romanus (§476)
          Senate people-and Rome

'The senate and people of Rome'

b. Ibi   mortuus sepultus-que Alexander (§476)
   There dies   buried-and   Alexander

'There Alexander died and was buried'

c. Dumnorix qui principatum obtinebat cui-que
   Dumnorix who chieftancy   held   who(dat)-and
   plebs   favebat (§636)
   commons favored

'Dumnorix, who held the chieftancy and whom the commons favored'

The examples show that enclitic -*que* coordinates expressions in different categories and occurs after the first word in the second conjunct, regardless of the category of the conjunct. This renders a structural characterization even more difficult than in (17) since one might claim that second position within S (IP) has a fixed category, say I^0, rendering a "structural characterization" (as this term is used informally) easier. But second position in an arbitrary coordinate structure is not even clearly a position associated with a category at all, much less a fixed category.[3]

But here is one way of structurally defining this sort of second position, one in which the notion is invariant. First,

Definition 14 Given strings s and t,

1. s is a *prefix* of t iff for some (possibly empty) string u, $s^\frown u = t$

2. $t - s \begin{cases} = t & \text{if s is not a prefix of t} \\ = u & \text{if } s^\frown u = t \end{cases}$

3. Now we define (recursively) a function fwd (first word) from L_{FWK} to L_{FWK}. For all $s \in L_{FWK}$,

$$\text{fwd}(s) = \begin{cases} s \text{ if } s \in \text{Lex} \\ s \text{ if } s = \text{CM}(u, v) \\ \text{fwd}(u) \text{ if } s = \text{PA}'(u, v) \\ \text{fwd}(v) \text{ if } s = \text{Coord}(u, v, w) \end{cases}$$

For example, fwd(praised John-nom Bill-acc, P0) = (praised, P2), since

(praised John-nom Bill-acc, P0)
= PA'(PA'((praised, P2), (John-nom, KPn)), (Bill-acc, KPa))

and

$$\text{fwd}(\text{PA}'(\text{PA}'((\text{praised}, \text{P2}), (\text{John-nom}, \text{KPn})), (\text{Bill-acc}, \text{KPa})))$$
$$= \text{fwd}(\text{PA}'((\text{praised}, \text{P2}), (\text{John-nom}, \text{KPn})))$$
$$= \text{fwd}(\text{praised}, \text{P2})$$
$$= (\text{praised}, \text{P2}).$$

Similarly, $\text{fwd}(\text{John-nom Bill-acc praised}, \text{P0}) = (\text{John-nom}, \text{KPn})$ since

$$\text{fwd}(\text{PA}'(\text{CM}((\text{-nom}, \text{Kn}), (\text{John}, \text{NP})), \text{PA}'((\text{Bill-acc}, \text{KPa}), (\text{praised}, \text{P2}))))$$
$$= \text{fwd}(\text{CM}((\text{-nom}, \text{Kn}), (\text{John}, \text{NP})))$$
$$= \text{CM}((\text{-nom}, \text{Kn}), (\text{John}, \text{NP}))$$
$$= (\text{John-nom}, \text{KPn}).$$

The behavior of fwd on coordinate structures is more surprising, but it sets the stage for our extension of the grammar below. It is easy to see that $\text{fwd}(\text{both John-nom and Bill-nom}, \text{KPn}) = (\text{John-nom}, \text{KPn})$ since

$$\text{fwd}(\text{Coord}((\text{and}, \text{CONJ}), (\text{John-nom}, \text{KPn}), (\text{Bill-nom}, \text{KPn})))$$
$$= \text{fwd}(\text{John-nom}, \text{KPn})$$
$$= (\text{John-nom}, \text{KPn}).$$

Here it is clear that we are regarding the *-nom* and *-acc* postpositions as part of the "word," for the present purpose of defining the *-que* placement rule below. So (omitting category designations) the first word of *John-nom Bill-acc praised* is *John-nom*, not *John*. In fact case marking languages vary with regard to whether the lexical items or the whole phrase carry case. In Korean, Basque, and Quechua, there are arguments for taking the scope of a case marker to be the entire NP it governs, not just the head. For example in Korean we coordinate at the NP level, the entire coordination taking a single case marker. In Basque adjectives may follow the head noun and carry the affixal case marker. We do not pursue this further here.

Theorem 9 *The function fwd is invariant.*

Proof. Consider arbitrary $h \in \text{Aut}_{\text{FWK}}$. Domain(fwd) = L_{FWK}, which is fixed by all automorphisms, so in particular by h. For an induction, Let $K = \{s \in L_{\text{FWK}} | h(\text{fwd}(s)) = \text{fwd}(h(s))\}$.

1. For $s \in \text{Lex}$, $h(\text{fwd}(s)) = h(s) = \text{fwd}(h(s))$ since Lex is invariant (its intersection with the ranges of CM, PA′, and Coord is empty)

2. We now show that K is closed under CM, PA′, and Coord.

Let $(s, t) \in \text{Domain}(CM)$. Then

$$
\begin{aligned}
h(\text{fwd}((CM(s, t)))) &= h(CM(s, t)) && \text{Def fwd} \\
&= CM(h(s, t)) && \text{h commutes with CM} \\
&= \text{fwd}(CM(h(s), h(t))) && \text{Def fwd} \\
&= \text{fwd}(h(CM(s, t))) && \text{h commutes with CM}
\end{aligned}
$$

Letting $(s, t) \in \text{Domain}(PA')$. Then

$$
\begin{aligned}
h(\text{fwd}(PA'(s, t))) & \\
&= h(s) && \text{Def fwd} \\
&= \text{fwd}(PA'(h(s), h(t))) && \text{Def fwd; h fixes Domain}(PA') \\
&= \text{fwd}(h(PA'(s, t))) && \text{h commutes with PA}'
\end{aligned}
$$

Let $(s, t) \in \text{Domain}(\text{Coord})$. Then

$$
\begin{aligned}
h(\text{fwd}(\text{Coord}(s, t, u))) & \\
&= h(t) && \text{Def fwd} \\
&= \text{fwd}(\text{Coord}(h(s), h(t), h(u))) && \text{Def fwd; h fix Domain(Coord)} \\
&= \text{fwd}(h(\text{Coord}(s, t, u))) && \text{h commutes with Coord}
\end{aligned}
$$

$\square$

Exercise 8 a. Define a function *last*(s) that maps any $s \in L_{\text{FWK}}$ to its last, single-word constituent, and show that *last* is invariant.

b. Define a function *sec*(s) that maps any $s \in L_{\text{FWK}}$ to its second, single-word constituent, if it has one, and otherwise (if it is just one word long) to its last word. Show that *sec* is invariant.

We now define FWK-2 from FWK by adding (-que, CONJ) to Lex and for u, v coordinable constituents in FWK, and extending the definition of Coord with the following new clauses. Using the abbreviations

$$\text{sf}(t, C) \text{ for string}(\text{fwd}(t, C)) \text{ and}$$
$$\text{sfr}(t, C) \text{ for } t - \text{string}(\text{fwd}(t, C)),$$

and for all C, C' such that either $C \in cC_{\text{Kor}}$ or $C \neq C' \in nC_{\text{Kor}}$:

Domain			Coord	Value
-que	s	t	$\longmapsto$	s ⌢sf(t,C)⌢-que⌢sfr(t,C)
CONJ	C	C		C
-que	s	t	$\longmapsto$	s ⌢sf(t,C')⌢-que⌢sfr(t,C')
CONJ	C	C'		NP_{refl}

Note that we have defined the domains of fwd and the extension of Coord so that *-que* can only conjoin expressions in L_{FWK}. If we allowed it to iterate, applying to arbitrary coordinable categories of FWK-2, we would generate expressions like *laughed cried-que sneezed-que* but our Latin sources give us no information on iterated coordination with -*que*.

Here is a derivation of a P1n using this new rule:

Coord:(laughed praised -que Bill -acc, P1n)

(-que, CONJ) (laughed, P1n) PA:(praised Bill -acc, P1n)

(praised, P2) CM:(Bill -acc, KPa)

(-acc, Ka) (Bill, NP)

Combining this P1n with the KPn *John-nom*, we obtain the sentence *John-nom laughed praised-que Bill-acc*.

Notice that it is not clear how a "standard" phrase structure tree could be drawn for this expression. The morphemes in the derived string can be assigned categories, but they do not all group into constituents. Also we see in this example how the rule Coord analyzes its second argument in order to place the coordinator properly. An alternative approach would be to keep some structure in the predicate so that no analysis would be necessary, or to use the tree "flattening" strategy described above in such a way that the "first word" is kept as a separate argument.

As mentioned in Lecture 1 (page 6), generative grammarians often regard putative rules stated in terms of position in the linear string as not "structure dependent," even though numerical position in an order seems like it should be a logical, structural property. We have shown that an operation that identifies the first element in designated constituents is, unsurprisingly, a "structural" operation in our sense, that is, syntactically invariant, as is the operation defining the n'th word (see Exercise 8 above). Clearly, the fwd function is defined on the particular structure building functions of FWK. Had we been working with a different grammar with different functions the fwd map in that language would have looked different. This is the basis for our suggestion that if identifying second position is universally invariant it is not uniformly so, just as we think that the Anaphor-Antecedent relation is universally invariant but not uniformly so. Different languages do it in structurally different ways.

Exercise 9 Substitution Rules. Exhibit a grammar in which *some student praised every teacher* has the derivations depicted in the FA trees below. Montague (1969) presents such a grammar of a fragment of English:

(some student praised every teacher, P0)

(some student, NP)   (praised every teacher, P1)

(praised, P2)   (every teacher, NP)

(some student praised every teacher, P0)

(every teacher, NP)   (some student praised x, P0)

(some student, NP)   (praised x, P1)

(praised, P2)   (x, NP)

In such grammars, the second tree has the "object wide scope" reading, and the first tree, derived by a "lowering" rule (a substitution rule), has the object narrow scope reading. This is a kind of inverse to currently more popular "LF" approaches to scope ambiguity in which such Ss are generated with *every teacher* in situ and then raised out leaving a "trace" at LF. Note again that on the second analysis, the string of lexical items in the P0 cannot be grouped into constituents, so again such analyses are not representable with "standard" trees.

Exercise 10 Below is a bare grammar for reduplication over the alphabet {a,b} (Stabler 2004). Exhibit an FA derivation tree for (bbabbbab, S) and say informally why your expression is not representable by a standard tree:

$V = \{a, b\}$ $Cat = \{S, T, U\}$ $Lex = \{\langle a, U \rangle, \langle b, U \rangle\}$ $Rule = \{F, G, H\}$:

Domain			Value
s	$\xrightarrow{F}$		ss
T			S
s	t	$\xrightarrow{G}$	st
U	T		T
s	$\xrightarrow{H}$		s
U			T

2.3 A voice marking language

We turn now to a language type we might reasonably call the dual of the Korean type. These are natural languages in which verbs are marked for the roles of syntactically identifiable arguments, analogous to the ways arguments are marked in case marking languages. It is tempting to call these languages verbal case marking ones, though we will stick with voice marking.

Voice marking languages are ones in which verbs are marked for "voice" and many major syntactic and interpretative processes, in particular the AA relation, are defined in terms of voice marking, analogous to the role case marking plays in case marking languages. We choose Toba Batak, a dialect of Batak, as our example, relying heavily on Schachter (1984), supplemented with some original consultant work.

Toba Syntax. Like many Austronesian languages Toba is verb initial. Verbal roots combine with one of two voice prefixes, *man(g)-* or *di-*, glossed AF and PF (see below) which decide much about the structure of the clause. (Western Austronesian languages often have 4-7 "voices.") Proper nouns are accompanied by a proper noun article, *si*:

(19)   a. [[Mang-ida si   Ria] si   Torus]
             MANG-see ART Ria ART Torus

          'Torus sees Ria'

   b. [[Di-ida si   Torus] si   Ria]
            DI-see ART Torus ART Ria

          'Torus saw Ria'

(Schachter 1984) gives extensive evidence that with each type of verb the immediate postverbal NP forms a constituent it. We shall refer to the NP that is not part of that constituent, the one that comes last in these examples, as the external NP. 'AF' and 'PF' stand for 'Actor Focus' and 'Patient Focus' respectively, and are designed to show that the two verbs differ with respect to the semantic role of the external NP. It is the Actor (Perceiver in this case) in (19a) and the Theme (object perceived in this case) in (19b). The apparent tense difference (past vs. present) is misleading. In isolation Ss built from *di-* verbs are understood more punctually, but the event does not have to be prior to speaking time. Moreover, the punctual interpretation is easily abandoned when in conflict with syntactic constraints, such as relativization patterns (below).

Evidence for the constituent bracketing in (19a,b) is the following: adverbs, such as *yesterday*, cannot separate the initial V and the following NP. Both types of P1 in (19) are assigned the same Predicate Phrase intonation with a peak on the last stressed syllable. The immediate postverbal NP in both cases is not subject to discourse or controlled deletion and cannot be moved or extracted, as in Wh-question or Relative Clause Formation. In contrast the external NP is subject to discourse deletion, it is the missing argument in control constructions, it can be relativized and questioned by movement and can be separated from its P1s by sentence adverbs. Here is one illustrative pattern:

(20) a. Mangida turiturian si   Ria
             MANG-see play   ART Ria

             'Ria is seeing a play'

      b. Ise mangida turiturian
           who MANG-see play

             'Who is seeing a play?'

      c. *Aha mangida si   Ria
           what MANG-see ART Ria

             'What is Ria seeing?'

(21) a. Diida si   Ria turiturian i
             DI-see ART Ria play   ART

             'Ria saw the play'

      b. Aha diida si   Ria
           what DI-see ART Ria

             'What is Ria watching?'

      c. *Ise diida turiturian i
           who DI-see play   ART

             'Who sees the play?'

The only meaning associable with (21c) is 'Who does the play see?' since only the external NP can be fronted so it is the perceived object and *the play* is the perceiver, which is absurd.

The constituency and interpretative pattern illustrated in (19) applies to Ss with reflexive themes unproblematically:

(22) a. [[Mang-ida dirina] si   Torus]
             MANG-see self   ART Torus

             'Torus sees himself'

      b. * Mang-ida si   Torus dirina
             MANG-see ART Torus self

             'self sees Torus'

      c. Di-ida si   Torus dirina
             DI-see ART Torus self

             'Torus saw himself'

d. *Di-ida dirina si   Torus
   DI-see   SELF   ART Torus

'Torus saw himself'

We now design a small model grammar which represents this type of anaphor-voice dependency.

We write Vaf for "actor focus affix" and Vpf for "patient focus affix." NP_{refl} is used like P01/P12 in Eng, and Coordination is treated as in Eng. Then Toba = $\langle V, Cat, Lex, Rule \rangle$ as follows:

V: laughed, cried, sneezed, praised, criticized, saw,
         John, Bill, Sam, self, and, or, both, either, mang-, di-

Cat: Vaf, Vpf, P2, P2a, P2n, P1a, P1n, P0, NP, NP_{refl}, CONJ

Lex:

Vaf	mang-
Vpf	di-
P1n	laughed, cried, sneezed
P2	praised, criticized, saw
NP	John, Bill, Sam
NP_{refl}	self
CONJ	and, or

Rule: VM (verb mark), PA (predicate-argument) and Coord.

We define the elements of Rule as follows. First, a simple verb marking rule, VM:

Domain		VM	Value
mang-	t		mang-$^\frown$t
Vaf	P2	$\longmapsto$	P2a
di-	t		di-$^\frown$t
Vpf	P2	$\longmapsto$	P2n

The predicate-argument rule is similar to earlier ones, but this time it is sensitive to the category of the affixed verb:

Domain		PA	Value	Conditions
s	t		s$^\frown$t	
P2x	NP	$\longmapsto$	P1y	$x \neq y \in \{n, a\}$
s	t		s$^\frown$t	
P1x	NP	$\longmapsto$	P0	$x \in \{n, a\}$
s	t		s$^\frown$t	
P2a	NP_{refl}	$\longmapsto$	P1n	
s	t		s$^\frown$t	
P1a	NP_{refl}	$\longmapsto$	P0	

And we provide a recursive Coord rule that makes the language infinite, letting the coordinable categories $cC_{Toba} = Cat - \{Vaf, Vpf, CONJ, P2\}$ and the class of nominal categories $nC_{Toba} = \{NP, NP_{refl}\}$:

Domain			Coord	Value	Conditions
and	s	t		both⌢s ⌢and⌢t	
CONJ	C	C	$\longmapsto$	C	$C \in cC_{Toba}$
or	s	t		either⌢s ⌢or⌢t	
CONJ	C	C	$\longmapsto$	C	$C \in cC_{Toba}$
and	s	t		both⌢s ⌢and⌢t	
CONJ	C	C'	$\longmapsto$	NP_{refl}	$C \neq C' \in nC_{Toba}$
or	s	t		either⌢s ⌢or⌢t	
CONJ	C	C'	$\longmapsto$	NP_{refl}	$C \neq C' \in nC_{Toba}$

With these rules, we obtain derivations like this:

(23) a.
$$PA:(mang\text{- see self Bill}, P0)$$
$$PA:(mang\text{- see self}, P1n) \qquad (Bill, NP)$$
$$VM:(mang\text{- see}, P2a) \quad (self, NP_{refl})$$
$$(mang\text{-}, Vaf) \quad (see, P2)$$

b.
$$PA:(di\text{- see Bill self}, P0)$$
$$PA:(di\text{- see Bill}, P1a) \qquad (self, NP_{refl})$$
$$VM:(di\text{- see}, P2n) \quad (Bill, NP)$$
$$(di\text{-}, Vpf) \quad (see, P2)$$

Note that Toba verbs differ morphologically, by prefix, and that in (23a) the anaphor is c-commanded by its antecedent, whereas in (23b) it c-commands its antecedent.

2.3.1 Some invariants of Toba

Fact 1 *Lex is invariant, and so* Lex_n *is invariant, all n.*

Proof. Checking the definitions of the three generating functions, it is easy to see that no element of Lex is in their ranges, so Lex is invariant. And so by U4 (on page 28) every Lex_n is invariant too.   □

Fact 2 *For every* $C \in Cat$, $PH(C)$ *is invariant.*

Proof. We work through $PH(C)$ by cases:

a. PH(CONJ) is invariant. If an automorphism h maps (u, CONJ) to an expression s of category other than Vaf, Vap, P2, or CONJ, then since $\langle(\text{and}, \text{CONJ}), s, s\rangle \in \text{Domain(Coord)}$, h^{-1} must map that triple to one with two conjunctions, failing thus to preserve Domain(Coord). And if a CONJ were mapped to a Vaf, a Vap or a P2 then Domain(Coord) would contain a triple one of whose coordinates was a Vaf, Vap, or P2 and it doesn't. So the only possibility is that (u,CONJ) is mapped by an automorphism to some (u', CONJ).

b. For the other categories it will be helpful to list the category coordinates of tuples that lie in VM and PA:

		Domain		Value
VM tuple categories:	1.	Vaf	P2	P2a
	2.	Vap	P2	P2n
PA tuple categories:	3.	P2a	NP	P1n
	4.	P2n	NP	P1a
	5.	P1a	NP	P0
	6.	P1n	NP	P0
	7.	P2a	NP_{refl}	P1n
	8.	P1a	NP_{refl}	P0

Now consider line 6, with (John, NP) the NP coordinate. Since Domain(PA) must be fixed by all automorphisms, an NP can only be mapped to other expressions which are coordinates in Domain(PA). That is, it must have category NP, NP_{refl}, P1n, P2a, P1a, or P2n. But since lexical items must be mapped to lexical items, the only possibilities are the first three, since the others have no lexical members.[4]

Now suppose, leading to a contradiction, that (John, NP) is mapped by an automorphism to a P1n. But then since

$$\langle(\text{mang-praise}, \text{P2a}), (\text{John}, \text{NP})\rangle \in \text{Domain(PA)},$$

(mang-praise, P2a) must get mapped to an NP. It can't get mapped to a lexical NP since it is not itself lexical. The only derived NPs are coordinations, and no automorphism h can map it to any Coord(s,t,u) since then $h^{-1}(\text{Coord}(s, t, u))$ would contain an *and* or an *or*, and (mang-praise, P2a) does not. So no lexical P1n (and hence no P1n) can get mapped by an automorphism to (John, NP) or any other lexical NP.

Similarly assume that (laughed, P1n) is mapped by an automorphism to (self, NP_{refl}). Then (cried, P1n) cannot be mapped by an automorphism h to an NP_{refl} since *self* is the only one, and h is one to one. Since (cried, P1n) can't get mapped to an NP, it can only get mapped to a P1n. But this means that h applied to $\langle(\text{or}, \text{CONJ}), (\text{laughed}, \text{P1n}), (\text{cried}, \text{P1n})\rangle$ would be a triple with categories CONJ, NP_{refl}, P1n and no such triple lies in Domain(Coord). Thus (laughed, P1n) cannot be mapped to any NP_{refl} and since (laughed, P1n) was arbitrary among the lexical P1n's, all lexical P1n's must get mapped to (lexical) P1n's. But now let (s, P1n) be arbitrary. Since

$$\langle(\text{or}, \text{CONJ}), (\text{cried}, \text{P1n}), (\text{s}, \text{P1n})\rangle \in \text{Domain(Coord)},$$

and any automorphism maps the first coordinate to a CONJ and the second to a P1n, the third must also get mapped to a P1n . Thus PH(P1n) is invariant.

And from line 6 above again, since P1n is fixed, PH(NP) must also be invariant to preserve Domain(PA), since only NPs cooccur with P1n's in Domain(PA). Since P1n and NP are fixed then any P0 derived from them must be mapped to a P0. Coordinating any of those P0's with an arbitrary P0 shows then that PH(P0) is invariant. We can also infer that (self, NP_{refl}) is invaraint, since its only possible images under an automorphism were NPs and P1n's, and they are both unavailable now. Now since P0 is invariant and using (self, NP_{refl}) for the second coordinate in line 8, we infer that PH(P1a) is invariant. And given this, again from line 8, we infer that PH(NP_{refl}) is invariant. Recall that there are complex NP_{refl}, such as (both self and John, NP_{refl}).

From line 7 we infer that PH(P2a) is invariant and given the invariance of PH(NP) and PH(P1a) we infer from line 4 that P2n is invariant. And finally, checking lines 1 and 2, the fixity of P2a and P2n means that an automorphism could not interchange a Vaf with a Vap. Nor could an automorphism h map the Vaf to a P2, for if it did then only one of the lexical P2's can be mapped to (mang-, Vaf) so the other, call it s, must get mapped to itself. But then the pair $\langle(\text{mang-}, \text{Vaf}), \text{t}\rangle \in \text{Domain(VM)}$ gets mapped to a pair of P2s, failing thus to preserve Domain(VM). So (mang-, Vaf) must get mapped to itself, as must, by similar reasoning, (di-, Vap). And thus also Lex(P2) is invariant.

This completes the proof that all PH(C) are invariant in Toba. □

Fact 3 (*mang-*, Vaf), (*di-*, Vap) *and* (self, NP_{refl}) *are all invariant.*

Proof. This follows directly from the invariance of Lex and of all PH(C). □

Definition 15 For all expressions $s, t, u \in L_{Toba}$

a. s is a *co-argument* of t in u iff for some constituent w of u such that for some expression v, $Cat(v) \in \{P2a, P2n\}$ and

$$w \in \{PA(PA(v, s), t), PA(PA(v, t), s)\}.$$

b. s is *a possible antecedent of* t in u, $AA_{Toba}(s,t,u)$ iff s is a co-argument of t in u and $Cat(t) = NP_{refl}$.

Fact 4 *The* AA_{Toba} *relation is invariant.*

Semantic interpretation for L_{Toba}. It is easy to provide L_{Toba} with a simple compositional semantics, showing that Ss with reflexives are interpreted correctly in all cases. (We use the notation and terminology introduced for languages discussed earlier.)

Definition 16 $\mathcal{M} = (E, m)$ is a model for *Toba* iff E is a non-empty set and m is a map whose domain is Lex, satisfying the following conditions:

1. $m(s, C) \in Den_E(C)$, the latter defined as follows:

$Den_E(NP)$ $= Type\ 1$
$Den_E(NP_{refl})$ $= [R_2 \rightarrow R_1]$
$Den_E(P0)$ $= R_0 = \{0, 1\}$
$Den_E(P1n)$ $= R_1 = [E \rightarrow R_0]$
$Den_E(P2)$ $= R_2 = [E \rightarrow R_1]$
$Den_E(P2a)$ $= Den_E(P2n) = [Type1 \rightarrow [Type1 \rightarrow R_0]]$
$Den_E(CONJ)$ $= \{f \in [B \times B \rightarrow B] \mid B \in Den_E(x), x \in cC_{Toba}\}$
$Den_E(Vaf)$ $= \{MANG\}$ and $Den_E(Vpf) = \{DI\}$, where
$\qquad\qquad\qquad MANG(R)(G)(F) = F(G(R))$ and
$\qquad\qquad\qquad DI(R)(H)(K) = H(K(R))$,
$\qquad\qquad$ for all $R \in R_2$, $F, G, H, K \in Type1$

2. $m(s, NP) \in \{I_b \mid b \in E\}$
$m(self, NP_{refl}) = SELF$, where $SELF : R_2 \rightarrow R_1$
$\qquad$ given by $SELF(R)(a) = (R(a))(a)$
$m(and, CONJ)$ maps each (x, y) in $Den_E(C)^2$, for $C \in cC_{Toba}$, to $x \wedge y$
$m(or, CONJ)$ maps each (x, y) in $Den_E(C)^2$, for $C \in cC_{Toba}$, to $x \vee y$

3. For each model $\mathcal{M} = (E, m)$ an interpretation m^* of L_{Toba} is a function which extends m and satisfies:

a. $m^*(VM(s, t)) = m(s)(m(t))$,

b. $m^*(PA(s, t)) = m^*(s)(m^*(t))$,

c. $m^*(Coord(s, t, u)) = m(s)(m^*(t), m^*(u))$

Using these definitions, we compute $m^*(23a)$:

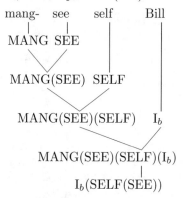

And $m^*(23b)$ is computed similarly:

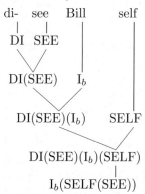

So it follows from these definitions that, for all models $\mathcal{M} = (E, m)$, $m^*(23a) = m^*(23b)$. And using the definitions again,

$$I_b(SELF(SEE)) \quad = T \quad \text{iff } b \in SELF(SEE)$$
$$\text{iff } b \in \{x| \langle x, x \rangle \in SEE\}$$
$$\text{iff } \langle b, b \rangle \in SEE.$$

Thus, as in Kor, the basic semantics for reflexives is correct, with the c-command relations varying.

2.3.2 Concluding remarks on Toba

As in Kor, the bound morphemes of Toba, the voice markers (mang-, Vaf) and (di-, Vap) are invariant, and the distribution of anaphors is determined by which of these affixes the verb carries, independent of c-command relations. In this language, anaphors may asymmetrically c-command their antecedents, unproblematically. And again the AA relation is invariant, though syntactically characterized differently in

Toba, Kor, and Eng.

2.4 A language with relative clauses

We turn finally to the well studied phenomenon of relative clause formation (representative of a larger class of "extraction" phenomena). English, and natural languages quite generally, present a variety of expression types whose semantic interpretation is naturally given using variable binding operators (VBOs), though in these constructions the "variable" is often unpronounced. An example is the relative clause, italicized, below.

(24)   every student *who John saw at the meeting* passed the exam

Syntactically a transitive verb such as *saw* usually requires an NP object, but none is present in (24). Consequently, the expression *John saw at the meeting* is not a grammatical sentence of English; it resembles a sentence which lacks an NP. Semantically, it is distinct from a sentence or question too. The proposal is that it differs semantically from a sentence in the way a sentential form with a variable does. That is, we can regard the meaning of *John saw at the meeting* as rather like *John saw x at the meeting*, where the variable x gets bound by the relative pronoun *who*. So then the semantic value of (24) is the value of the denotation of *every* applied to the set of those students x such that John saw x at the meeting. It is no surprise that linguists who propose "logical forms" for sentences like (24) often put a bound variable in the object position, the "gap."[5] Linguists have been studying the distribution of relative pronouns and the gaps they bind for many years. Here are four standard observations about this distribution in English. For readability we mark gaps with a special, unpronounced, symbol t.

(25)   (Unboundedness) A relative clause gap and its binder may be arbitrarily far apart:

    a. every student who Mary thought that John saw t at the meeting

    b. every student who Bill said that Mary thought that... John saw t at the meeting

(26)   (Coordinate Structure Constraint, CSC) In coordinations each conjunct contains a gap:

    a. every student who John praised t and Bill criticized t

    b. *every student who John praised Sam and Bill criticized t

    c. *every student who John praised t and Bill criticized Sam

(27)   (Complex NP Constraint, CNPC) Relative clause gaps do not occur within expressions that are already relative clauses:[6]

    a. every student who Mary knows t

    b. I interviewed every student who Mary knows t

    c. *a woman who I interviewed every student who t knows t

(28)   (No Vacuous Binding) A relative pronoun requires a gap:

    a. *I interviewed every student who Mary knows Bill

    b. *the teacher who John put it here cries

So gaps do not occur freely, and characterizing precisely where relative clause gaps may occur remains a descriptively challenging problem with non-trivial consequences for linguistic theory. Moreover we find comparable (but not identical) distributions of wh-phrases in wh-questions like,

(29)   Who did John see t at the meeting?

and indirect questions like,

(30)   I don't know who John saw t at the meeting.

We will not undertake a comprehensive treatment, but will begin with a simple English-like grammar which generates relative clauses satisfying the four properties (25-28) The coverage of this grammar overlaps the language Eng from Lecture 1, but rather than simply extending that grammar, we begin again from scratch, introducing a category system with more structure.. Later we consider some extensions of the grammar that capture further regularities.

Define $\text{Eng}_{\text{RC}} = \langle V, \text{Cat}, \text{Lex}, \text{Rule} \rangle$ as follows, together with the associated sets of "basic categories" BCat and "features" Feat:

V: man, woman, student, teacher, doctor, lawyer, John, Bill,
Mary, Sue, friend of, colleague of, every, no, the, a, some,
laughed, cried, fainted, sneezed, spoke, praised, criticized,
interviewed, saw, likes, knows, who, t, and, or

BCat   is the closure of $\{N, NP, S, CONJ\}$ under Slash, where
$$Slash(C,D)=(C/D)$$

Feat $=(BCat \cup \{wh\}) - \{CONJ\}$

Cat $=BCat \cup \{\langle C, f \rangle | \ C \in BCat, f \in Feat\}$

Lex:

N	man, woman, student, teacher, doctor, lawyer
NP	John, Bill, Mary, Sue
N/NP	friend of, colleague of
NP/N	every, no, the, a, some
S/NP	laughed, cried, fainted, sneezed, spoke
P2	praised, criticized, interviewed, saw, likes, knows
$\langle NP, wh \rangle$	who
$\langle NP, NP \rangle$	t
CONJ	and, or

Rule: PSB, PSB_{fp}, RC, and Coord.

As usual, we often omit outermost parentheses from category names
when no confusion will result. And instead of writing $\langle NP, wh \rangle$ as the
category of *who*, we will often write NP[wh] to enhance readability. And
note that the lexicon includes the expression $(t, NP[NP])$, instead of an
expression with the empty string $(\epsilon, NP[NP])$. Again, this is just to
make the structures easier to read in the presentation. Nothing of any
importance in our observations about Eng_{RC} depends on this notational
choice.

We now define the functions in Rule. The primary structure building
rule, PSB, is defined as follows, for all $A, B \in BCat$, $s, t \in V^*$:

Domain		PSB	Value	Conditions
s	t	$\longmapsto$	t⌢s	$A/B \in \{S/NP, N/N\}$
A/B	B		A	
s	t	$\longmapsto$	s⌢t	$A/B \notin \{S/NP, N/N\}$
A/B	B		A	

PSB_{fp} is PSB with feature passing. Exactly one argument of PSB_{fp} is
allowed to have a feature, and that feature is "passed" to the result.
That is, for all features $f \in Feat$, all $A, B \in BCat$,

Domain		PSB$_{fp}$	Value	Conditions
s	t		t⌢s	
(A/B)[f]	B	$\longmapsto$	A[f]	A/B $\in$ {S/NP, N/N}
s	t		s⌢t	
(A/B)[f]	B	$\longmapsto$	A[f]	A/B $\notin$ {S/NP, N/N}
s	t		t⌢s	
A/B	B[f]	$\longmapsto$	A[f]	A/B $\in$ {S/NP, N/N}
s	t		s⌢t	
A/B	B[f]	$\longmapsto$	A[f]	A/B $\notin$ {S/NP, N/N}

The relative clause rule, RC, applies to a pair of expressions with features and "cancels" them, the derived wh-clause lacking both.

Domain		RC	Value
s	t		s⌢t
NP[wh]	S[NP]	$\longmapsto$	N/N

Lastly, the coordination rule, Coord, combines triples to yield expressions, as in the previous grammars. The domain of Coord is the set of triples of possible expressions $\langle (u, CONJ), (s, C), (t, C) \rangle$ satisfying

a. $C \in cC_{Eng_{RC}} = Cat - \{CONJ\}$

b. if $C \in \{NP[wh], NP[NP]\}$ then $(s, C), (t, C) \notin Lex$

Domain			Coord	Value
and	s	t		both⌢s ⌢and⌢t
CONJ	C	C	$\longmapsto$	C
or	s	t		either⌢s ⌢or⌢t
CONJ	C	C	$\longmapsto$	C

The conditions on the domain of Coord serve to block cases like the following:

(31) a. *both or and and

b. *a man both who and who John interviewed t

c. *a woman who both John interviewed t and some friend of t

With this grammar, we get derivations like this:

PSB:(every student who John praised t, NP)

(every, $\overline{NP/N}$)   PSB:(student who John praised t, N)

RC:(who John praised t, N/N)   (student, N)

(who, $\overline{NP[wh]}$)   PSB$_{fp}$:(John praised t, S[NP])

PSB$_{fp}$:(praised t, (S/NP)[NP])   (John, NP)

(praised, (S/NP)/NP)   (t, NP[NP])

As usual, the leaves of this derivation tree are lexical items. The RC rule applies to the lexical item (who, NP[wh]) and the derived expression (John praised t, S[NP]) to derive an expression whose category, N/N, has no features.

It is easy to see that this simple grammar yields infinitely many relative clauses. Consider the following, for example. In addition to "object relative clauses" like the one shown above, we can derive "subject relative clauses" – that is, relative clauses where the gap is in subject position:

PSB:(every student who t knows Mary, NP)

(every, $\overline{NP/N}$)   PSB:(student who t knows Mary, N)

RC:(who t knows Mary, N/N)   (student, N)

(who, $\overline{NP[wh]}$)   PSB$_{fp}$:(t knows Mary, S[NP])

PSB:(knows Mary, S/NP)   (t, NP[NP])

(knows, (S/NP)/NP)   (Mary, NP)

And since this entire expression is a NP it could replace the last NP *Mary*, yielding:

(32)   every student who t knows every student who t knows Mary

And again the last NP could be replaced by (32), yielding

(33)   every student who t knows every student who t knows every student who t knows every student who t knows Mary

Clearly, this can process can be iterated without limit.

The following derivation illustrates an "across the board" coordinate structure, and of course, again, each conjunct could be expanded to another. We show a "standard" tree structure because it is a little smaller and fits onto the page:

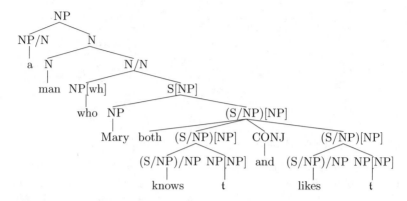

Exercise 11 Exhibit a derivation tree for the following NP:

a doctor both who John likes t and who Mary interviewed t.

It is easy to see that Eng_{RC} has the four properties (25-28) discussed above. First, the CSC (Coordinate Structure Constraint) is satisfied, since Coord requires that its second and third arguments have the same category, and so will not apply to the categories are S and S[NP]. Second, relativization is unbounded in Eng_{RC}. This can be seen using coordinate expressions with arbitrarily many conjuncts as in (34a), or using iterated relational nouns as in (34b)

(34) a. a doctor who Mary likes t and John interviewed t or Sue praised t...

     b. a doctor who Mary interviewed a friend of a friend of a friend of... t

Third, the Complex NP Constraint holds, since to derive something like (35), PSB_{fp} would have to apply to (t, NP[NP]) and (praised t, P1[NP]), both of whose categories have features.

(35) *a doctor who Mary knows every student who t praised t

But the PSB_{fp} rule requires one of its arguments to lie in BCat and thus be featureless. Finally, No Vacuous Binding holds since the RC rule only combines a relative pronoun (who, NP[wh]) with an S[NP], a category all of whose expressions have gaps.

Exercise 12 Exhibit a derivation tree for (i) below and say why (ii) is not generated.

  i. a doctor who Sue interviewed both a colleague of t and a friend of t

ii. *a doctor who we interviewed both a colleague of every lawyer and a friend of t

Semantics for Eng_{RC}**.** Our purpose here is to show that our syntax supports a compositional interpretation. Those who are willing to take our word for this may skip to the next section which extends the class of relative clauses. We assume familiarity with the notion of interpretation in a model relative to an assignment. Assignments, or "contexts," are maps from the "variables" into the universe E of the model. We have only one variable, $(t, \text{NP}[\text{NP}])$, so an assignment a is a function mapping that one object into E. For $b \in E$ we write $a^{t/b}$ for that assignment which is like a except that it maps t to b. The expression $(\text{who}, \text{NP}[\text{wh}])$ is treated as a VBO. Otherwise expressions are interpreted as maps from assignments to their expected denotations. (We use notation introduced for the semantics of previously considered languages.)

Definition 17 $\mathcal{M} = (E, m)$ is a model for Eng_{RC} iff E is a non-empty set and m is a map whose domain is Lex-$\{t, \text{who}\}$, satisfying the following conditions:

1. $m(s, C) \in \text{Den}_E(C)$, the latter defined as follows:

$\text{Den}_E(S)$	$= R_0 = \{0, 1\}$
$\text{Den}_E(N)$	$= R_1 = [E \rightarrow R_0]$
$\text{Den}_E(N/NP)$	$= R_2 = [E \rightarrow R_1]$
$\text{Den}_E(NP)$	$= \{I_b \mid b \in E\}$
$\text{Den}_E(S/NP)$	$= R_1$
$\text{Den}_E((S/NP)/NP)$	$= R_2$
$\text{Den}_E(NP/N)$	$= [R_1 \rightarrow [R_1 \rightarrow R_0]]$
$\text{Den}_E(CONJ)$	$= \{f \in [B \times B \rightarrow B] \mid B \in \text{Den}_E(x), x \in cC_{\text{Eng}_{\text{RC}}}\}$

2. $m(\text{every}, NP/N)(p)(q) = 1$ iff $p(b) = 1$ implies $q(b) = 1$ (all $b \in E$)

   $m(\text{no}, NP/N)(p)(q) = 1$ iff $p(b) = 1$ implies $q(b) = 0$

   $m(\text{the}, NP/N)(p)(q) = 1$ iff $\exists! b \in E$ such that $p(b) = 1$, and $q(b) = 1$

   $m(\text{a}, NP/N)(p)(q) = 1$ iff $\exists b \in E$ such that both $p(b) = 1$ and $q(b) = 1$

   $m(\text{some}, NP/N)(p)(q) = 1$ iff $\exists b \in E$ such that both $p(b) = 1$ and $q(b) = 1$

   $m(\text{and}, CONJ)$ maps each (x, y) in $\text{Den}_E(C)^2$, for $C \in cC_{\text{Eng}_{\text{RC}}}$, to $x \wedge y$

   $m(\text{or}, CONJ)$ maps each (x, y) in $\text{Den}_E(C)^2$, for $C \in cC_{\text{Eng}_{\text{RC}}}$, to $x \vee y$

3. For each model $\mathcal{M} = (E, m)$ an interpretation m^* of $L_{\text{Eng}_{\text{RC}}}$ is a function which relativizes m to assignments, satisfying:

a. for lexical s of category N, N/NP, NP, S/NP, (S/NP)/NP, NP/N, and CONJ,

$$m^*(s)(a) = m(s)(a), \text{ for all assignments a.}$$

b. $m^*(t, NP[NP])(a) = I_{a(t)}$. (Since $a(t) \in E$, $I_{a(t)}$ is an individual.)

c. for $F \in \{PSB, PSB_{fp}\}$, for all $s, t \in Domain(F)$,

$$m^*(F(s,t)) = \begin{cases} m^*(s)(a)(m^*(t)(a)) & \text{if } m^*(t) \in Domain(m^*(s)) \\ m^*(t)(a)(m^*(s)(a)) & \text{otherwise} \end{cases}$$

d. $m^*(Coord(s, t, u)) = m(s)(m^*(t), m^*(u))$

e. $m^*(RC(s, t))(a)(q)(b) = m^*(t)(a^{t/b}) \wedge q(b)$

With a semantics like this, entailment relations between sentences hold in the standard way. Recall the definition of generalized entailment, repeated here from page 35:

Definition 18 For all categories C where $Den_E(C)$ is boolean, $s, t \in PH(C)$, $s \models t$ iff for all models (E, m), all assignments a, $m^*(s)(a) \leq m^*(t)(a)$. Equivalently $m^*(s)(a) \wedge m^*(t)(a) = m^*(s)(a)$.

Now given (E,m) we can recursively compute the interpretation of (man who John saw t, N). To ease readability we omit the category coordinate of expressions, and note the constant interpretation of lexical items in upper case, except the semantic values of proper nouns like *John* are given as individuals like I_j.

1. Since assignment $a^{t/b}$ maps the trace t to an entity $b \in E$, the interpretation of the trace at that assignment is the individual I_b, $m^*(t)(a^{t/b}) = I_b$.

2.

$m^*(\text{John saw } t)(a)$		
$=$	$m^*(\text{John})(a)(m^*(\text{saw } t)(a))$	Def m^* on PSB
$=$	$m(\text{John})(m^*(\text{saw } t)(a))$	Def m^* on Lex
$=$	$I_j(m^*(\text{saw } t)(a))$	Notation
$=$	$I_j(m^*(t)(a)(m^*(\text{saw})(a)))$	Def m^* on PSB_{fp}
$=$	$I_j(m^*(t)(a)(m(\text{saw})))$	Def m^* on Lex
$=$	$I_j(I_{a(t)}(SAW))$	Def $m * (t)(a)$
$=$	T iff $SAW(a(t))(j) = T$	Def individual

3.

$m^*(\text{man who John saw } t)(a)$

$= m^*(\text{who John saw } t)(a)(m^*(\text{man})(a))(b)$	Def m^* on PSB
$= m^*(\text{who John saw } t)(a)(MAN)(b)$	Def m^* on Lex
$= m^*(\text{John saw } t)(a^{t/b}) \wedge MAN(b)$	Def m^* on RC
$= SAW(b)(j) \wedge MAN(b)$	1 and 2 above.

So under any assignment, *man who John saw* t is that property which holds of an entity b iff b is a man and John saw b, the correct interpretation.

This completes our semantic analysis of Eng_{RC}. It provides a compositional interpretation of a language which has expressions containing arbitrarily many instances of relative clause binding, though only one variable is needed. Moreover no length decreasing rules are needed (meaning the length of the string coordinate of any $F(s_1, \ldots, s_n)$ is never less than the sum of the lengths of the strings of its argument expressions s_i.).

The extension of Eng_{RC} to a richer class of relative clauses will be effected by enriching Cat and Lex. Consider our original unbounded dependencies, as in (36):

(36)   a.   a student who John knew t

      b.   a student who Bill thought that John knew t

      c.   a student who Mary said that Bill thought that John knew t,...

In order to get constructions like this, to BCat we add S' (read: "S-bar") and to Lex we add:

Lex: (S/NP)/S'   thought, said, believed
       (S/NP)/S   thought, said, believed
          S'/S   that

Here is a simple S using these categories, followed by a corresponding relative clause:

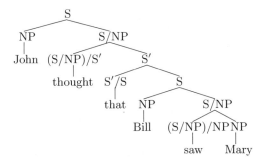

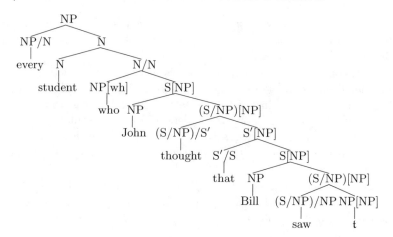

We can insert as many expressions of the form *Mary said that...* between *who* and *John* deriving ever longer expressions of category S[NP], so the *who* and the t can be arbitrarily far apart.

The second categorization for *thought* generates *John thought Bill laughed* without the complementizer *that*. Verbs like *think* exhibit a complication in English known as the *that-trace effect*: a trace t can not immediately follow the complementizer *that*. (37a) is good, but (37b) is not:

(37)   a. no student who John thought passed the exam (did poorly in the course)

   b. *? no student who John thought that passed the exam (did poorly in the course)

We can handle this constraint by limiting what the PSB$_{fp}$ rule applies to. We require,

(38)   When a pair $\langle(s,S'/S), (t, S[NP])\rangle$ is in Domain(PSB$_{fp}$) then no $(t', S/NP)$ is an immediate constituent of $(t, S[NP])$.

The condition in (38) blocks putative relative clauses like:

(39)   a. *a woman who John thought that t interviewed Bill

   b. *a woman who John thought that some colleague of t interviewed Bill

(38) blocks (39a) since the S[NP] which the S'/S *that* combines with has (interviewed Bill, S/NP) as an immediate constituent. Similarly for (39b). Note that in this grammar if an S[NP] is built from a $(v', S/NP)$ then the other immediate constituent(s) must have an NP gap, that is,

be of the form X[NP]. So (38) applies only in a very specific context, blocking relativization into the subject of an S when that S combines with an overt complementizer, such as (that,S'/S).

It is well-known, and not a surprise, that the that-trace effect is language particular. It is not present, for example, in Malagasy, Dutch or Spanish. In Spanish, for example,

(40)   a. Creo   que los niños   juegan en el   parque
           believe-1sg that the children play   in the park

           'I think that the children are playing in the park'

       b. los niños   que creo   que juegan en el   parque
           the children that believe-1sg that play   in the park

           'the children who I think are playing in the park'

The condition in (38) differs from most conditions we place on what tuples may occur in the domain of a generating function F by requiring that we check what one of the arguments of F, the $(v, S[NP])$, is built from. In the case of Eng_{RC} this checking process is finite since the string component of every derived expression is the concatenation of the strings of the arguments of the function (plus adding *both* and *either* in the case of Coord). So there are only finitely many (just four) functions to consider, and for each there are only finitely many sequences of strings whose concatenation is v, so the condition in (38) is well defined.

Relativizing objects of prepositions. Now consider applying RC to objects of prepositions. In English the "wh-PP" may occur at the front of S[NP], so called "pied piping," as in (41a), or we can "strand" the preposition, as in (41b):

(41)   a. the teacher with whom John spoke

       b. the teacher (who) John spoke with

To derive structures like this, we first enrich the lexicon. We give prepositional phrases the category of P1-modifiers, P1/P1, where P1 is the category S/NP, so PPs have the category (S/NP)/(S/NP). Since a PP is formed by a preposition and a NP, we give prepositions the category ((S/NP)/(S/NP))/NP. And we introduce some new relative pronouns, including the empty string which is represented by ϵ. We also introduce the PP trace, with the category PP[PP], which is really ((S/NP)/(S/NP))[(S/NP)/(S/NP)], again using t for readability:

((S/NP)/(S/NP))/NP	to, with, in
NP[wh]	that, ϵ, who, whom, which
((S/NP)/(S/NP))[(S/NP)/(S/NP)]	t

To use these new elements in prepositional phrases, we generalize RC, imposing several conditions on its domain:

Domain		RC	Value	Conditions
s	t		s⌢t	
C[wh]	S[C]	⟼	N/N	i, ii, ii

where category C and the strings s,t are restricted by the three conditions i, ii, and iii:[7]

  i. C ∈ {NP, PP}

 ii. s ≠ whom

iii. if C = NP and s = ε then no (t′, S/NP)ICON(t, S[NP]).

Our grammar now covers PP pied piping, allowing *whom* in this construction:

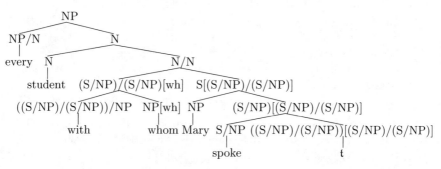

But in preposition stranding constructions, *whom* is not allowed:

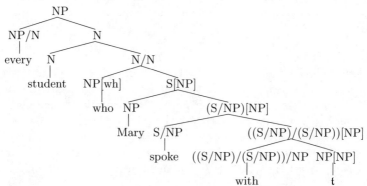

Condition ii in the revised definition of RC blocks *a woman whom t laughed*, and *every man whom John saw* t, but allows *a man with*

whom John spoke t. Condition iii blocks the omission of subject relative pronouns. So we generate

$$(\text{the man John saw } t, \text{NP})$$

but not

$$*(\text{the man } t \text{ saw John}, \text{NP}).$$

Some approaches to relativization have difficulty relativizing on objects when they are not peripheral, as in *a man who John saw* t *with Mary*. Eng_{RC} has no such difficulties:

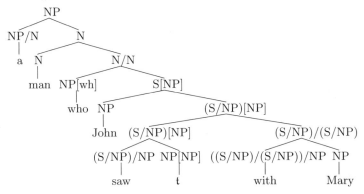

We should note that there are a variety of constraints on the distribution of relative pronouns according to their string coordinates: *who, whom, ϵ,* and *that*. Here is one class: an NP[wh] governed by a preposition cannot be *who, ϵ,* or *that*, but can be *whom* or a more complicated form such as *whose doctor* (below). The "bottom up" format of Bare Grammar allows us to handle such constraints easily as conditions on the domain of PSB_{fp}, which, recall, takes pairs of the form $\langle(s, (A/B)[f]), (t, B)\rangle$ and ones of the form $\langle(s, A/B), (t, B[f])\rangle$ as arguments. To obtain this special restriction, we just require that these coordinates of PSB_{fp} satisfy the following additional constraint:

(42) if $A/B = PP/NP$ and $B[f] = NP[wh]$ then $t \neq who, \epsilon,$ or *that*.

Relativizing possessives. We want to generate relative clauses like (43a,b) but not (43c): (61b)

(43) a. a man whose doctor John praised t   (poss-pied-piping)

     b. a man in whose house John met Mary t (PP pied-piping)

     c. *a student who John saw t's professor   (no poss-stranding!)

To get structures like (43a,b), we need only make the following addition to the lexicon:

Lex: (NP/N)[wh]   whose.

With just this addition, we have derivations like this:

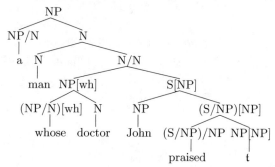

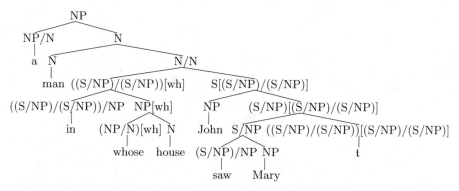

Note that we may coordinate expressions of category C[wh] too, as in the following, for example:

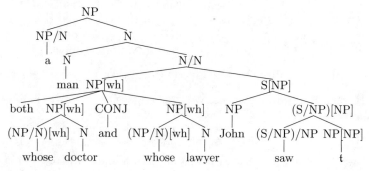

But recall that no conjunct however may be lexical by condition b on page 76:

(44)   *a man who and whose doctor John knows t.

To generate possessive NPs such as *every student's doctor*, we can first add the following lexical item:

Lex: $(NP/N)/NP$'s

Then, to generate e.g. $(John's, NP/N)$ rather than $('s John, NP/N)$ we condition the PSB rule as we did for subjects forcing the NP argument of *'s* to precede it. (See the summary presentation of the revised syntax, just below.) With this modification, the grammar will generate the NPs in (45), and it blocks (46a) but not (46b), as desired:

(45)　a.　every student's doctor

　　　b.　some student's doctor's lawyer

　　　c.　a professor whose doctor and whose doctor's lawyer John interviewed t

(46)　a.　*a student who's doctor John saw t

　　　b.　a student whose doctor's lawyer John interviewed t

We sidestep the problem of deciding just what NPs may host the possessive *'s*, since this problem is not specific to relative clauses.[8]

(47)　a.　*? the woman who John saw t in the garden's lawyer

　　　b.　*? the woman who John saw t's lawyer

　　　c.　a friend of [[the doctor]'s lawyer]

　　　d.　? [a friend of the doctor]'s lawyer
　　　　　(= the lawyer of a friend of the doctor)

Summary of the revised Eng_{RC}. The revised syntax of Eng_{RC} can be given as follows. Define $Eng_{RC} = \langle V, Cat, Lex, Rule \rangle$ as follows:

V: man, woman, student, teacher, doctor, lawyer, John, Bill, Mary, Sue, friend of, colleague of, every, no, the, a, some, laughed, cried, fainted, sneezed, spoke, praised, criticized, interviewed, saw, likes, knows, who, t, and, or, 's

BCat is the closure of $\{N, NP, S, CONJ\}$ under Slash, where
$$Slash(C,D)=C/D$$

Feat $=(BCat \cup \{wh\}) - \{CONJ\}$

Cat $=BCat \cup \{\langle C, f\rangle | \; C \in Cat, f \in Feat\}$

Lex:

N	man, woman, student, teacher, doctor, lawyer
NP	John, Bill, Mary, Sue
N/NP	friend of, colleague of
NP/N	every, no, the, a, some
S/NP	laughed, cried, fainted, sneezed, spoke
P2	praised, criticized, interviewed, saw, likes, knows
NP[NP]	t
CONJ	and, or
(S/NP)/S′	thought, said, believed
(S/NP)/S	thought, said, believed
S′/S	that
((S/NP)/(S/NP))/NP	to, with, in
NP[wh]	that, ϵ, whom, who, which
((S/NP)/(S/NP))[(S/NP)/(S/NP)]	t
(NP/N)[wh]	whose.
(NP/N)/NP	's

Rule: PSB, PSB$_{fp}$, RC, and Coord, defined as follows.

The primary structure building rule, PSB, is revised as follows, for all $A, B \in BCat$, $s, t \in V^*$:

Domain		PSB	Value	Conditions
s	t	$\longmapsto$	t⌢s	i
A/B	B		A	
s	t	$\longmapsto$	s⌢t	¬i
A/B	B		A	

where condition i on PSB is this:

i. one of the following conditions is satisfied

   a. $A \in \{S, (NP/N)/NP\}$ and $B=NP$

b. $A = B = N$, or

c. $A = B = (S/NP)$

Domain		PSB$_{fp}$	Value	Conditions
s	t	$\longmapsto$	$t \widehat{} s$	i
A/B[f]	B		A[f]	
s	t	$\longmapsto$	$s \widehat{} t$	¬i
A/B[f]	B		A[f]	
s	t	$\longmapsto$	$t \widehat{} s$	i
A/B	B[f]		A[f]	
s	t	$\longmapsto$	$s \widehat{} t$	¬i
A/B	B[f]		A[f]	

where condition i on PSB$_{fp}$ is this:

i. all the following conditions are satisfied

   a. if $A/B = PP/NP$ and $B[f] = NP[wh]$ then $t \neq who, \epsilon$, or *that*.

   b. if $A/B = (NP/N)/NP$ then $B[f] \neq NP[NP]$

   c. if $A/B = (NP/N)/NP$ and $B[f] = NP[wh]$ then $(t, B[f]) \notin Lex$

   d. if $A/B = S'/S$ and $B[f] = S[NP]$ then no $(t', S/NP)ICON(t, S[NP])$.

The **coordination rule**, Coord, maps triples of expressions to expressions, as follows:

Domain			Coord	Value	Conditions
and	s	t	$\longmapsto$	both$\widehat{}$s $\widehat{}$and$\widehat{}$t	i, ii, iii
CONJ	C	C		C	
or	s	t	$\longmapsto$	either$\widehat{}$s $\widehat{}$or$\widehat{}$t	i, ii, iii
CONJ	C	C		C	

where the conditions on this rule are the following,

i. neither s nor t are the empty string

ii. $C \in cC_{Eng_{RC}} = Cat - \{CONJ, S'/S, (NP/N)[wh], ((S/NP)/(S/NP))/NP\}$

iii. if $C \in \{NP[wh], NP[NP]\}$ then $(s, C), (t, C) \notin Lex$.

Relative clause formation, RC, combines wh-phrases with Ss having an appropriate gap to form N modifiers, as follows:

Domain		RC	Value	Conditions
s	t		s⌢t	
C[wh]	S[C]	⟼	N/N	i, ii, ii

where category C and the strings s,t for RC are restricted by the following three conditions i, ii, and iii:

i. $C \in \{NP, PP\}$

ii. $s \neq whom$

iii. if $C = NP$ and $s = \epsilon$ then no $(w, S/NP)ICON(u, S[NP])$.

This completes our statement of the grammar.

2.4.1 Some invariants of Eng_{RC}

Fact 1 *For all $F \in$ Rule, $Lex \cap Ran(F) = \emptyset$, whence Lex is invariant; so by U4 on page 28, Lex_n is invariant, for each n.*

Fact 2 *Each $F \in$ Rule is category functional.*

Recalling the definition of "category functional" from page 28, Fact 2 means that we never have distinct tuples d, d' in any Domain(F) with corresponding coordinates having the same category but where F(d) and F(d') have different categories. The various conditions we have placed on the structure building functions either just limit what tuples lie in Domain(F) or they condition how the string components of the arguments combine.

Fact 3 *All PH(C) are invariant.*

Proof. By Fact 2 just above and U5 on page 28, it suffices to show that all Lex(C) are invariant. In the proof we often say "C is fixed" meaning "PH(C) is invariant." We consider one category at a time.

1. Lex(NP[wh]) is fixed. To preserve Domain(RC), (who, NP[wh]) must get mapped to another NP[wh], to a PP[wh] or to an S[C] (allowing Domain(RC) to contain permutations of its arguments) and it can't get mapped to a PP[wh] or an S[NP] by Fact 1, as there aren't any in Lex.

2. PH(S[NP]) is invariant given 1, in order that Domain(RC) be preserved.

3. Lex(N) is invariant. To see this, note that

$$\langle (who, NP[wh]), (t\ laughed, S[NP]), (who\ t\ laughed, N/N) \rangle \in RC$$

and any automorphism fixes the first two categories so it must map (who t laughed, N/N) to an N/N. And since for any $(s, N) \in$ Lex,

$\langle(s, N), (who\ t\ laughed, N/N)\rangle \in Domain(PSB)$ and the second coordinate must get mapped to an N/N, (s, N) must get mapped to some (u, N) or some $(v, X/(N/N))$ to preserve Domain(PSB). But no lexical expression has category $X/(N/N)$ for any $X \in Cat$, hence (s, N) is mapped to an N, and the claim is proven.

4. Lex(NP/N) is invariant to preserve Domain(PSB). For consider any $(s, NP/N), (t, N) \in$ Domain(PSB). Since Lex(N) is fixed, $Cat(h(s, NP/N))$ must be of the form X/N, and NP/N is the only candidate in Lex. It follows that (every woman, NP) is mapped to an NP by all automorphisms since the triple

$$\langle(every, NP/N), (woman, N), (every\ woman, NP)\rangle \in PSB,$$

and the first two coordinates must get mapped to lexical expressions without changing category. Similarly, (some man, NP) must get mapped to an NP.

5. Lex(CONJ) = PH(CONJ) is invariant. For observe, for example, that Domain(Coord) includes

$$\langle(or, CONJ), (every\ woman, NP), (some\ man, NP)\rangle$$

and every automorphism h preserves the category of these NPs, hence to preserve Domain(Coord) the automorphism must map $(s, CONJ)$ to some $(t, CONJ)$, and the only choices are lexical.

6. Lex(NP) is invariant. For observe that Domain(Coord) includes

$$\langle(and, CONJ), (every\ student, NP), (u, NP)\rangle$$

and the categories of the first two coordinates are fixed, so any automorphism h maps (u, NP) to some (u, NP) to preserve Domain(Coord). Hence PH(NP) and so Lex(NP) are invariant.

7. Lex(N/NP) is therefore invariant, to preserve Domain(PSB); similarly with Lex((NP/N)/NP), and so $('s, (NP/N)/NP)$ is also an invariant expression.

8. Lex((S/NP)/NP) is invariant. For notice that Domain(PSB) includes

$$\langle(John, NP), PSB((Bill, NP), (praised, (S/NP)/NP))\rangle.$$

Since NPs are fixed by automorphisms, any automorphism h must map $(praised, (S/NP)/NP))$ to something that combines with an NP. The only lexical categories that do this are N/NP, (NP/N)/NP, S/NP, (P1/P1)/NP, and (S/NP)/NP. The first two are ruled out since they are already fixed. S/NP is out since otherwise

$$h(PSB((Bill, NP), (praised, (S/NP)/NP)))$$

would have category S and would not combine by PSB with h(John, NP). The same holds for (P1/P1)/NP, so the only option left is that a lexical (S/NP)/NP is mapped to a lexical (S/NP)/NP by an arbitrary automorphism.

9. Lex(S/NP) is invariant since

$$\langle(\text{Bill}, \text{NP}), (\text{praised}, (\text{S/NP})/\text{NP})), (\text{praised Bill}, \text{S/NP})\rangle \in \text{PSB}$$

and the first two categories are fixed, so the last one must be as well to preserve PSB. And since for any (u,S/NP) we have

$$\langle(\text{and}, \text{CONJ}), (\text{praised Bill}, \text{S/NP}), (\text{u}, \text{S/NP})\rangle \in \text{Domain(Coord)}$$

and so its image under an automorphism h will consist of a CONJ, a S/NP and h(u,S/NP). So to preserve Domain(Coord), Cat(h(u, S/NP)) must be S/NP. So PH(S/NP) is invariant.

10. PH(S) is invariant. Since

$$\langle(\text{John}, \text{NP}), (\text{laughed}, \text{S/NP}), (\text{John laughed}, \text{S})\rangle \in \text{PSB}$$

and the first two categories are fixed, (John laughed, S) must get mapped to an S by any automorphism. Hence any (u, S) must get mapped to an S since

$$\langle(\text{and}, \text{CONJ}), (\text{John laughed}, \text{S}), (\text{u}, \text{S})\rangle \in \text{Domain(Coord)}.$$

11. Using P1 for S/NP, Lex(((P1/P1)/NP) is invariant. Note that

$$\langle(\text{to}, (\text{P1/P1})/\text{NP}), (\text{s}, \text{NP})\rangle \in \text{Domain(PSB)}$$

and NP is fixed so for any automorphism h, Cat(h(to, (P1/P1)/NP))) must combine with NPs and so have the form (X/NP). But all the other lexical X/NP except (P1/P1)/NP are fixed, so this category must also be fixed.

12. Lex(S'/S) and PH(S') are invariant. Notice that

$$\langle(\text{that}, \text{S'}/S), (\text{John laughed}, \text{S}), (\text{that John laughed}, \text{S'})\rangle \in PSB$$

so since S is fixed, h(that, S'/S) must have category X/S to yield an expression of category X. The only lexical candidates are X = S' or X = S/NP. But if the latter then the triple

$$\langle(\text{that}, \text{S'}/S), (\text{John laughed}, \text{S}), (\text{that John laughed}, \text{S'})\rangle \in \text{PSB}$$

is mapped by h to a triple whose categories are (S/NP)/S, S, S/NP. But then h^{-1} maps an S/NP to an S', contradicting 9. Hence X = S' and Lex(S'/S) is invariant. And since

$$\langle(\text{that}, \text{S'}/S), (\text{John laughed}, \text{S}), (\text{that John laughed}, \text{S'})\rangle \in \text{PSB}$$

and the first two categories are fixed, (that John laughed, S') must get mapped to an S'. And by the use of the Coord function, any

(u, S') may coordinate with it and thus must have category S', so PH(S') is fixed.

13. $\text{Lex}((S/NP)/S')$ and $\text{Lex}((S/NP)/S))$ are invariant. In triples of the form

$$\langle (s, (S/NP)/S'), (u, S'), (s\frown u, S/NP)\rangle \in \text{PSB},$$

the second and third categories are fixed so the first must combine with an S' to yield an S/NP, and the only lexical category with this property is $(S/NP)/S'$. An analogous argument shows that $\text{PH}((S/NP)/S)$ is invariant.

14. $(t, NP[NP])$ and $\text{PH}(S[NP])$ are invariant.

$$\langle (t, NP[NP]), (\text{laughed}, S/NP)\rangle \in \text{Domain}(\text{PSB}_{\text{fp}})$$

and S/NP is fixed so $\text{Cat}(h(t,NP[NP]))$ must be either $NP[NP]$ or some $(X/(S/NP))[NP]$. But no lexical categories have that form, so $\text{Cat}(h(t,NP[NP]))$ must be $NP[NP]$. So $\text{Lex}(NP[NP])$ and $(t,NP[NP])$ are invariant. And since

$$\langle (t, NP[NP]), (\text{laughed}, S/NP), (t\,\text{laughed}, S[NP])\rangle \in \text{PSB}_{\text{fp}}$$

and the first two categories are fixed, $(t\,\text{laughed}, S[NP])$ must get mapped to a $S[NP]$, hence by the familiar coordination argument all $(u, S[NP])$ get mapped to $S[NP]$s, and so $\text{PH}(S[NP])$ is invariant.

15. An analogous argument using $\langle (t, PP[PP]), (\text{laughed}, P1)\rangle$ shows that $\text{Lex}(PP[PP])$ and $(t, PP[PP])$ are invariant.

16. $\text{Lex}((NP/N)[wh])$ is invariant since each one must get mapped to some lexical (u, C), and all the lexical C are fixed except $(NP/N)[wh]$.

That completes the proof of Fact 3. □

Although there are several lexical elements of category $NP[wh]$, notice that the role of *who* is unique. It is the only element that can occur wherever any relative pronoun can. So we have:

Fact 4 $(who, NP[wh])$ *is an invariant expression.*

2.4.2 Concluding remarks on Eng_{RC}

The literature on relative clauses and more generally on "extraction" is enormous, with a burst of activity since the seminal work of Ross (1967) and Chomsky (1973, 1977). Readable typological overviews of the different ways of forming relative clauses are provided by Keenan (1985) and Keenan and Andrews (2004). Lehmann (1979) is more thorough.

This concludes our models of different structure types present in natural languages. In the next lecture we consider modeling other grammatical formalisms in a Bare Grammar format.

Notes

[1]We thank Eun Hee Lee, Seungho Nam, and Chungmin Lee, for consultation on Korean.

[2]In head initial languages (Verb initial, or SVO as in English) framing coordinations follow the English pattern (*both X and Y, either X or Y, neither X nor Y*), though the more typical case is where the conjunctive morphemes are the same, as in French: *et Jean et Marie, ou Jean ou Marie, ni Jean ni Marie.* In head final (Verb final) languages the framing order is the postpositional variant of the head initial order, *John-and Bill-and*, as illustrated below from Tamil (Asher 1985, cited in Corbett 1991, p.269)

(48) raaman-um murukan-um va-nt-aa-ka
      Raman-and Murugan-and come-past-3.pl.rational

      'Raman and Murugan came'

We did not elicit framing conjunctions in Korean, and we use the head initial model to ease readability for English readers. Uniformly head initial or head final framing are equally effective in ensuring non-ambiguity. We systematically include coordinate expressions so that many categories of expression will have infinitely many members, forcing us to avoid non-general definitions by listing cases.

[3]Hale (1996) discusses second position placement of coordinate conjunctions in the Rigveda providing convincing motivation for phonological conditioning. The idea is that the conjunction is dependent on a host to its left, and in clausal level coordinations the initial clause does not itself provide a suitable host so the conjunction flips around the first word of the second conjunct. Such "prosodic flipping" does not take place in cases where the second conjunct is itself phonologically reduced and thus cannot serve as a host. Taylor (1996) likewise discusses prosodically motivated inversion in Ancient Greek. But our examples (18) would seem to lack this motivation. (And even when this motivation is present it is still an open question as to whether the function that identifies where the "flipped" item occurs is invariant or not.)

[4]Here and later we ignore the order in which the arguments of generating functions are given so that claims of invariants will not depend

on that order, as we could usually have given the coordinates in the opposite order just as well.

[5]We are presenting a "standard" kind of analysis of relative clauses, in spite of the problem discussed by Geach (1962, p.118) and Quine (1974, p.90). Geach explicitly rejects this standard analysis on the grounds that *man who owns a donkey* cannot mean exactly the same thing as *donkey-owner*, because the sentence *every man who owns a donkey feeds it* is fine while **every donkey-owner feeds it* is odd. A large literature has grown up around this problem, and many proposals keep to the basics of the "standard analysis" proposed here by, in effect, keeping the pronoun-binding mechanisms and the predicate-argument semantics separate.

[6]The Complex NP Constraint (CNPC) proposed here is actually a special case of Ross's (1967) more general constraint of the same name. Many further generalizations of this idea have been explored too, including Chomsky's (1973, 1977) "subjacency" constraint and its many descendants.

[7]Some speakers claim to have friends who say *a man whom I know*. None of our friends are like that, but if desired we could weaken our condition to allow this.

[8]See for example, Emonds (1985) and Di Sciullo and Williams (1987, p.89).

3

Some familiar grammars

The definitions of example languages in the first lectures use standard notation for sets, sequences and functions. Familiar grammar formalisms, when they are clear, can of course be represented in a standard mathematical notation too. In many cases they are easily subsumed by the "bare grammar" framework, with its notions of structure and invariance. We briefly survey a few to see how this goes, and we discover some structural aspects of the formalisms that are not usually noticed.

Recall that a bare grammar G is given by a vocabulary V, some categories Cat, a lexicon of categorized strings $Lex \subseteq V^* \times Cat$, and some generating functions Rule. The language L_G generated by such a grammar $G = \langle V, Cat, Lex, Rule \rangle$ is the closure of Lex with respect to the functions in Rule. These components are the "bare bones" of any generative grammar. The automorphisms Aut_G of $\langle L_G, Rule \rangle$ are by definition those bijections of L_G that fix the generating functions in Rule. Something in the type hierarchy generated by L_G and $\{0, 1\}$ (an expression, property, relation,. . .) is said to be a structural invariant iff it is fixed by all the automorphisms. And two expressions s, t in the language are isomorphic, $s \simeq t$, just in case some automorphism maps one to the other. Often we are interested in subsets of the language: PH(C) is the set of all expressions with category C, and string(PH(C)) is the set of all the sequences of vocabulary elements of category C in the language.

As mentioned in the first lecture, one of the main goals of the present study is to find appropriate concepts for specifying common properties of grammars, languages, and expressions (without requiring the presumption that related things are derived from a common "underlying" structure, or any such thing). Among the basic properties possessed by some but not all grammars, in this setting we can consider many that are familiar from the earlier literature:

(FinLex) The lexicon is finite; finitely many generators.

(FinCat) Just finitely many categories C are such that $\text{PH}(C) \neq \emptyset$.

(Assoc) For all binary $F \in$ Rule all $s, t, u \in L_G$, if $\langle s, F(t, u)\rangle \in$ Domain(F) then $\langle s, t\rangle \in$ Domain(F) and $\langle F(s, t), u\rangle \in$ Domain(F) and

$$F(s, F(t, u)) = F(F(s, t), u).$$

(Lexic) Language variation is "lexicalized" in the sense that Rule is "universal," the same for all human languages.

(CF) For each $C \in$ Cat, string(PH(C)) is a context free language.

(P) For each $C \in$ Cat, deciding $x \in$ string(PH(C)) can be done in polynomial time.

But we have already drawn attention to some other basic properties that have not been explicitly considered before:

(CatSt) The set of expressions of each category is "structural." That is, each PH(C) is invariant.

(CatFunc) Every $F \in$ Rule is category functional. That is, F_2 is a function, where for any $F \in$ Rule,

$$F_2 = \{\langle\langle C_1, \ldots, C_n\rangle, C\rangle \mid \langle\langle(s_1, C_1), \ldots, (s_n, C_n)\rangle, (s, C)\rangle \in F\}.$$

And it is easy to think of many other basic properties that are structurally relevant. The following properties will be considered in detail in the next lecture, but are easily introduced here. For any sequence σ of length $n > i$ and any expression s, we use $\sigma^{i/s}$ to signify the sequence like σ except that s appears in the i'th position instead of σ_i.

(WFnd) For any $s, t \in L_G$, sPCONt implies $s \neq t$.

(MR) For any $s, t \in L_G$ and $F \in$ Rule, $s \simeq t, s \neq t \Rightarrow F(s) \neq F(t)$.

(SFEq) For any $s \in L_G$ and any $\sigma \in$ Domain(F),

$$\text{Cat}(s) = \text{Cat}(\sigma_i) \text{ implies } \sigma^{i/s} \in \text{Domain(F)}.$$

Which of these properties do all (scientifically respectable) grammars of human languages have, if any? Looking back at the example grammars we have already studied, we find:

	Eng	Kor	FWK	Toba	Eng_{RC}
(FinLex)	1	1	1	1	1
(FinCat)	1	1	1	1	1
(Assoc)	0	0	0	0	0
(Lexic)	0	0	0	0	0
(CF)	1	1	1	1	1
(P)	1	1	1	1	1
(CatSt)	1	1	1	1	1
(CatFunc)	1	1	1	1	1
(WFnd)	1	1	1	1	1
(MR)	1	1	1	1	1
(SFEq)	1	1	1	1	0

Here, we consider which of these properties is guaranteed (or allowed, or prohibited) by some familiar grammatical formalisms.

Exercise 13 a. Prove that Eng_{RC} has the property (FinCat) even though it has infinitely many categories.

b. Prove that Eng lacks the property (Assoc).

c. Prove that Toba has (CF) by constructing a context free grammar G such that, for all $C \in \text{Cat}_{Toba}$, $\text{string}(PH(C)) = \{s \in V^* | \ C \Rightarrow_G^* s\}$.

d. Prove that Kor has the property (MR).

e. Prove that Eng_{RC} has the properties (CatSt) and (CatFunc) but lacks (SFEq).

3.1   Context free grammars

Each rule of a context free grammar rewrites a single category C to some (possibly empty) sequence of category symbols and vocabulary items. A context free grammar $G = \langle V, \text{Cat}, \rightarrow \rangle$ where

V is a finite nonempty set of vocabulary elements,
Cat is a finite nonempty set of categories disjoint from V, and
$(\rightarrow) \subseteq \text{Cat} \times (V \cup \text{Cat})^*$ is a finite, nonempty set of pairs.

Often, a particular category $S \in \text{Cat}$ is chosen as the "start" category. As usual the "immediately derives" relation $\Rightarrow_G \subseteq (V \cup \text{Cat})^* \times (V \cup \text{Cat})^*$ is defined in terms of $\rightarrow$ as follows: $\alpha \Rightarrow_G \beta$ iff for some $A \in \text{Cat}$ and some $\alpha_1, \alpha_2, \beta_1 \in (V \cup \text{Cat})^*$

$$\alpha = \alpha_1 A \alpha_2, \quad A \rightarrow \beta_1, \quad \text{and} \quad \beta = \alpha_1 \beta_1 \alpha_2.$$

That is, $\alpha \Rightarrow_G \beta$ just in case β is the result of rewriting some category A in α according to some rewrite rule in the grammar G. We write $\Rightarrow_G^*$ for the "derives" relation: the reflexive, transitive closure of $\Rightarrow$. So $\alpha \Rightarrow_G^* \beta$ iff β is the result of applying 0 or more rewrite steps to α.

Example CFG1: Mimicking the grammar of Eng on page 15:

>   **V:**   laugh, cry, sneeze, praise, criticize, see
>   John, Bill, Sam, Fred, himself, and, or, both, either
>   **Cat:**   P0, P1, P2, P01/P12, P1/P2

And where → is given as follows:

P0→P01/P12 P1
P1→P2 P01/P12P1→P2 P1/P2
P1→laughed   P1→cried   P1→sneezed
P2→praised   P2→criticized P2→interviewed
P01/P12→John   P01/P12→Bill P01/P12→Sam
P1/P2→himself

P0→both P0 and P0   P0→either P0 or P0
P1→both P1 and P1   P1→either P1 or P1
P2→both P2 and P2   P2→either P2 or P2
P01/12→both P01/12 and P01/12P01/12→either P01/12 or P01/12
P1/2→both P1/2 and P1/2   P1/2→either P1/2 or P1/2
P1/2→both P1/2 and P01/12   P1/2→either P1/2 or P01/12
P1/2→both P01/12 and P1/2   P1/2→either P01/12 or P1/2

Notice that 10 of these rules are "lexical" in the sense that they have only lexical items on the right side, and of the remaining 17, 14 build the different kinds of coordinate structures. With this grammar, P0 can be rewritten to the string *John criticized both himself and Bill*, as shown in the following "standard" rewrite derivation tree:

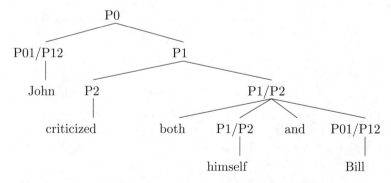

Intuitively, this derivation is done from the top down, first rewriting P0 as the sequence P01/P12 P1, and so on. Compare this derivation to the very similar "bottom up" BG derivation of the Eng expression

(John criticized both himself and Bill, P0),

shown on page 17. (Although both Eng and CFG1 are extremely simple, it is already interesting to consider the question: which provides a more illuminating perspective on the language?)

In traditional treatments of CFGs, G is said to generate the set $L(G) = \{s \in V^* \mid S \Rightarrow^* s\}$, where S is the "start" category of context free grammar G. This perspective is slightly odd because the rules of the grammar, the rewrite rules, do not apply to the elements of $L(G)$ at all, since these strings contain no category symbols in them. So for many analytic purposes, attention immediately shifts to the derivations of these strings, or to special derivation trees of some kind. BG shifts the perspective in a different way. Rather than focusing directly on derivations or derivation trees, BG treats the lexical items and all derivable expressions all as elements of the language, a set of categorized strings explicitly interrelated by the generating functions. This makes explicit the structure we are interested in, the structure defined by the rules of the grammar. We still have derivations and derivation trees, of course, but the rules provide the real structure, not the conventions about representations of derivations.

In fact, it is easy to define a function that maps any CFG to a BG that is "equivalent" in an intuitive sense.

Definition 19 For any context free grammar $G = \langle V, \text{Cat}, \twoheadrightarrow \rangle$, let's say that a rewrite rule r, an element of the relation $\twoheadrightarrow$, is a *lexical* rule iff $r = (C \twoheadrightarrow s)$ for some $s \in V^*$. It is *non-lexical* otherwise.

For any non-lexical rule

$$r = (A \twoheadrightarrow \alpha_0 A_0 \alpha_1 \ldots \alpha_{n-1} A_n \alpha_n)$$

where $n > 0, \alpha_i \in V^*, A_i \in \text{Cat}$, we define a generating function $F_r : (V^* \times \text{Cat})^n \to (V^* \times \text{Cat})$ as follows:

$$\begin{matrix} s_1 & & s_n \\ A_1 & \cdots & A_n \end{matrix} \quad \overset{F_r}{\longmapsto} \quad \begin{matrix} \alpha_0 s_1 \alpha_1 \ldots \alpha_{n-1} s_n \alpha_n \\ A \end{matrix}$$

Definition 20 Define $\text{bg}(G) = \langle V, \text{Cat}, \text{Lex}, \text{Rule} \rangle$ as follows:

$$\text{Lex} = \{\langle s, C \rangle \mid C \twoheadrightarrow s, \ s \in V^*\},$$
$$\text{Rule} = \{F_r \mid r \in (\twoheadrightarrow), \ r \text{ non-lexical}\}.$$

Example bg(CFG1): Applying the function bg to the grammar CFG1 given above, we obtain a bare grammar that has 17 generating functions in Rule, since CFG1 has 17 non-lexical rules:

V: laugh, cry, sneeze, praise, criticize, see,
John, Bill, Sam, Fred, himself, and, or, both, either
Cat: P0, P1, P2, P01/P12, P1/P2
Lex: P1   laughed, cried, sneezed
        P2   praised, criticized, interviewed
        P01/P12   John, Bill, Sam, John
        P1/P2   himself
Rule: F_i for $1 \leq i \leq 17$, as follows:

$$\begin{array}{cc} s & t \\ P01/P12 & P1 \end{array} \xmapsto{\;F_1\;} \begin{array}{c} s{}^\frown t \\ P0 \end{array}$$

$$\begin{array}{cc} s & t \\ P2 & P01/P12 \end{array} \xmapsto{\;F_2\;} \begin{array}{c} s{}^\frown t \\ P1 \end{array}$$

$$\begin{array}{cc} s & t \\ P2 & P1/P2 \end{array} \xmapsto{\;F_3\;} \begin{array}{c} s{}^\frown t \\ P1 \end{array}$$

We list only the first 4 of the 14 coordinate structure rules here:

$$\begin{array}{cc} s & t \\ P0 & P0 \end{array} \xmapsto{\;F_4\;} \begin{array}{c} both{}^\frown s{}^\frown and{}^\frown t \\ P0 \end{array}$$

$$\begin{array}{cc} s & t \\ P0 & P0 \end{array} \xmapsto{\;F_5\;} \begin{array}{c} either{}^\frown s{}^\frown or{}^\frown t \\ P0 \end{array}$$

$$\begin{array}{cc} s & t \\ P1 & P1 \end{array} \xmapsto{\;F_6\;} \begin{array}{c} both{}^\frown s{}^\frown and{}^\frown t \\ P1 \end{array}$$

$$\begin{array}{cc} s & t \\ P1 & P1 \end{array} \xmapsto{\;F_7\;} \begin{array}{c} either{}^\frown s{}^\frown or{}^\frown t \\ P1 \end{array}$$

And so on... It is easy to see what the remaining coordinate structure rules $F_8 - F_{17}$ have to be.

Fact 5 *For any CFG G and any* $C \in Cat, s \in V^*, C \Rightarrow_G^* s$ *iff* $\langle s, C \rangle \in$ $L_{bg(G)}$.

We leave the proof of this first result as an exercise.

Fact 6 *For any CFG* G *and any* C $\in$ Cat *that occurs in the domain or range of* $\twoheadrightarrow$, *PH(C) is invariant in* bg(G).

Proof. If C occurs in the range or (in a tuple in) the domain of some rewrite rule r in some CFG G, then PH(C) must be invariant in bg(G) because by U2 on page 27, any automorphism fixes the domains and ranges of every F_r. $\qquad\square$

For arbitrary CFG G, the invariant expressions of $L_{bg(G)}$ are not simply those that have a unique category. That is,

Fact 7 *It is <u>not</u> the case that* $\langle s, C \rangle \in L_{bg(G)}$ *is invariant iff* $PH(C) = \{\langle s, C \rangle\}$.

Proof. The "if" direction holds by Fact 6, of course, but the "only if" direction fails in many cases. For example, when CFG G has just the following 3 rules, $\langle a, A \rangle$ is invariant in bg(G) even though b has the same category:

$$A \twoheadrightarrow a \qquad A \twoheadrightarrow B \qquad B \twoheadrightarrow b$$

□

Is structural equivalence simply a matter of having the same (or isomorphic) structure building rules and the same trees? No.

Fact 8 *Consider CFGs* G, G' *and a bijection* $h : L_{bg(G')} \to L_{bg(G)}$ *such that* $h(\text{Aut}_{bg(G')}) = \text{Aut}_{bg(G)}$. *It does not follow that for every rule* F_r *of* $bg(G')$, $h(F_r)$ *is a rule of* G.

Proof. A simple example is provided by letting G' be like bg(CFG1) except that we add the rule F_r where r is

$$P0 \twoheadrightarrow P01/P12 \ P2 \ P01/P12$$

Since the automorphisms of a grammar are unchanged by closing Rule under generalized compositions (cf. Theorem 7 on page 58), $L_{bg(CFG1)} = L_{G'}$ and $\text{Aut}_{bg(CFG1)} = \text{Aut}_{G'}$ even though G' has a new rule, and derivation trees that are not isomorphic to any in CFG1. □

It is interesting to reflect on the properties of bare grammars that are images of context free grammars under the function *bg*:

Fact 9 *A bare grammar* $\langle V, \text{Cat}, \text{Lex}, \text{Rule} \rangle$ *is the image of some CFG under bg iff:*

a. *V, Cat, Lex and Rule are finite and nonempty, and*

b. *For each* $F \in \text{Rule}$, *there are* $C_1, \ldots, C_n \in Cat$ *such that* $\text{Domain}(F) = (PH(C_1) \times \ldots \times PH(C_n))$, *and*

c. *Each* $F \in \text{Rule}$ *is category functional:* F_2 *is a function.*

   Given the previous observation, this has the consequence that for each generating function there is a fixed category that every expression in its range has. That is, every F_2 *is a constant function, and*

d. *Each* $F \in \text{Rule}$ *is also string functional:* F_1 *is a function. In particular, for each* $F \in \text{Rule}$ *there is a sequence of strings* $\langle \alpha_0, \alpha_1, \ldots, \alpha_n \rangle \in$

$(V^*)^{n+1}$ *such that for every* $\langle(s_1, C_1) \ldots, (s_n, C_n)\rangle \in \mathrm{Domain}(F_1)$,

$$F_1(s_1, \ldots, s_n) = \alpha_0 s_1 \alpha_1 \ldots \alpha_{n-1} s_n \alpha_n,$$

where for any $F \in \mathrm{Rule}$,

$$F_1 =_{df} \{\langle\langle s_1, \ldots, s_n\rangle, s\rangle|\ \langle\langle(s_1, C_1), \ldots, (s_n, C_n)\rangle, (s, C)\rangle \in F\}.$$

Exercise 14 Write a context free grammar G with a category S such that the strings of category S are $\{a^n b^n|\ n > 0\}$, and compute bg(G). Answer some of our first, basic questions about this grammar: Are all PH(C) invariant? Are any lexical expressions invariant?

Human languages are beyond the power of context free grammars, as can be seen from the "crossing dependencies" in languages like Swiss-German, where the relation between verbs and their objects is signaled not only by word order but also by case marking (Shieber 1985):

	that	we	the children	Hans	the house	let	help	paint
...	das	mer	d'chind	em Hans	es huus	lönd	hälfe	aastriiche

Dutch has similar "crossing" dependencies between subjects and verbs, but the association is not signaled by case, but only by order (Huybregts 1976, Bresnan et al. 1982):

	because	I	Cecilia	Henk	the hippo	saw	help	feed
...	omdat	ik	Cecilia	Henk	de nijlpaarden	zag	helpen	voeren

A simple formal language with these kinds of dependencies, easily shown to be non-context-free, is $\{xx|\ x \in \{a, b\}^*\}$:

a b b a b b

We will consider a grammar that generates this language in §3.3 below.

3.2 Categorial grammars

A categorial grammar is usually regarded as a calculus of types, where the types have strings as members. We can formalize these grammars in the bare grammar framework by regarding the types as categories, and by assuming that all the members of the categories can be given by closure of a finite lexicon under the generative rules (application, composition, etc.). One interesting feature of these grammars is that the set of categories has its own structure, since, like the language, it is generated as a closure. Three varieties of categorial grammars are briefly considered here: classical categorial grammars (CGs), combinatory categorial grammars (CCGs), and pregroup grammars (PGs).

3.2.1 Classical categorial grammars

A (classical) categorial grammar CG can be given as a bare grammar meeting 3 requirements. First, Cat is the closure of some set of basic categories BCat under right and left slashes:

$$\text{Cat} = \text{closure}(\text{BCat}, \{f_/, f_\backslash\})$$

$$\text{where for any } A, B \in (\text{BCat} \cup \{/, \backslash\})^* : \quad \begin{array}{l} f_/(A, B) = (A/B) \\ f_\backslash(A, B) = (A\backslash B) \end{array}$$

(We often leave off outermost parentheses.) Second, Lex is finite. And finally, the only generating function is AP, defined as follows:

Domain		AP	Value
s	t		s⌢t
A/B	B	$\longmapsto$	A
s	t		s⌢t
B	B\A	$\longmapsto$	A

Example CG1.

V:	some, every, tall, short, Albanian, American, doctor, senator, Mary, Sue, coughed, sneezed, praised, criticized, who	
BCat	$=\{N, NP, S, CONJ\}$	
Cat	$=\text{closure}(\text{BCat}, \{f_/, f_\backslash\})$	
Lex:	N	doctor, senator
	NP	Mary, Sue
	NP/N	every, some
	N/N	tall, short, Albanian, American
	NP\S	coughed, sneezed
	(NP\S)/NP)	praised, criticized
	(N\N)/(NP\S)	who
Rule:	AP	

It is clear that L_{CG1} is infinite: we have for example, for all n

(Mary praised some senator (who praised some senator)^n, S) $\in L_{CG1}$.

Derivations can be depicted with "standard" trees like this:

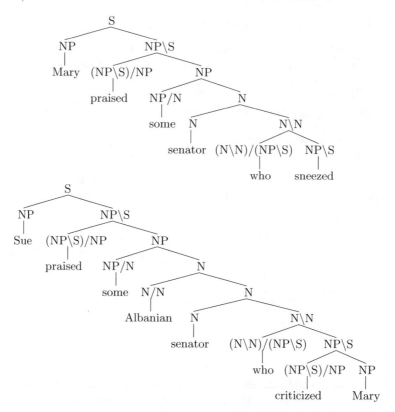

Let's now consider some general properties of categorial grammars, with particular attention to the role category structure, since that is something we do not have in context free and many other grammar formalisms.

Given any bare grammar G, let's say that a category C ∈ Cat is *useful* iff PH(C) ≠ ∅.

Fact 10 *In any categorial grammar, the set of useful categories is finite.*

Proof. Since, by the definition of a categorial grammar, Lex must be finite, and since each application of AP produces categories with strictly fewer slashes than the arguments have, the number of different useful categories is finite. □

And we have this immediate consequence of the definition of the generating function AP:

Fact 11 *Every categorial grammar is category functional.*

So in some cases we will be able to apply the following general fact about bare grammars:

Fact 12 *For any bare grammar G, if G is category functional and for every* s ∈ Lex, $\text{Cat}_s = \text{Cat}_{h(s)}$ *for all* h ∈ Aut_G, *then for any* C ∈ Cat, *PH(C) is invariant.* (Cf. Fact 6 on page 102.)

Fact 13 *In* **CG1**, *every* s ∈ Lex, $\text{Cat}_s = \text{Cat}_{h(s)}$ *for all* h ∈ Aut_{CG}.

This has the immediate consequence that in CG1 every PH(C) is invariant, given the earlier Facts 11 and 12.

Exercise 15 Prove Fact 13.

It is important to notice that the relation between category structure and language structure is not always simple:

Fact 14 *Some automorphisms of some categorial grammars fail to preserve category, even for lexical expressions, even when no derived expression is in the lexicon of the grammar.*

Proof. We present categorial grammar CG2 and define h ∈ Aut_{CG2} such that for certain s ∈ Lex_G, $\text{Cat}_s \neq \text{Cat}_{h(s)}$. Define **CG2** as follows:

V:	Mary, Sue, coughed, sneezed, and	
BCat	={NP, S, A, B}	
Cat	=closure(BCat, {$f_/$, $f_\backslash$})	
Lex:	NP	Mary
	A/B	Sue
	NP\S	coughed
	(A/B)\S	sneezed
	(S/S)/S	and
Rule:	AP	

Only lexical elements have categories NP, A/B, NP\S, and (A/B)\S. There are infinitely many derived expressions but they all have either category S or S/S. Now consider the total function $h^1 : V^* \to V^*$ that interchanges *Mary* and *Sue* wherever they occur, interchanges *coughed* and *sneezed* wherever they occur, and leaves everything else untouched. And consider the total function $h^2 : \text{Cat} \to \text{Cat}$ that interchanges NP and A/B wherever they occur. In terms of these, define:

$$h(s, C) = (h^1(s), h^2(C)), \text{ all } (s, C) \in (V^* \times \text{Cat}).$$

So then h ↾ Lex fixes (and, (S/S)/S) and interchanges these pairs:

$$(\text{Mary}, \text{NP}) \leftrightarrow (\text{Sue}, \text{A/B}) \quad (\text{coughed}, \text{NP}\backslash S) \leftrightarrow (\text{sneezed}, (\text{A/B})\backslash S).$$

Clearly h ↾ L_{CG2} is 1-1 and onto. We show that it fixes Domain(AP). First, to show (⊆), setting K = {s ∈ L_G| ∀t, ⟨s, t⟩ ∈ Domain(AP) ⇒ ⟨h(s), h(t)⟩ ∈ Domain(AP), all h}, we use an induction on structural depth to show that K includes the whole language. First consider arbitrary $s \in$ Lex. When $s = (and, (S/S)/S)$, since S is fixed by h^2, $s \in K$. Otherwise, s is one of the four expressions in one of the exchanged pairs, and the images of any pair under h is in Domain(AP) and so $s \in K$. To show that K is closed with respect to AP, consider AP(s,t) for arbitrary $s, t \in K$. Since everything in the range of AP has category $C \in \{S, S/S\}$, and h^2 fixes these categories, again we see that the images of $h(AP(s, t))$ and anything it combines with are in Domain(AP) and so again $AP(s, t) \in K$. The other direction, $(\supseteq)$ is established by a similar argument.

Finally, we show that for any $\langle a, b \rangle \in$ Domain(AP), $h(AP(a, b)) = AP(h(a), h(b))$. We know that for some $A, B, C \in$ Cat, either (i) a = A/B and b = B or (ii) a = B and b = A\B. Consider case (i):

$$
\begin{array}{ll}
h(AP((s, A/B), (t, B))) & \\
\quad = h((s^\frown t, A)) & \text{Def AP} \\
\quad = (h^1(s^\frown t), h^2(A)) & \text{Def h} \\
\quad = AP((h^1(s), h^2(A/B)), (h^1(t), h^2(B))) & \text{Def AP}, h^1, h^2 \\
\quad = AP(h((s, A/B)), h((t, B))) & \text{Def h}
\end{array}
$$

Case (ii) is similar, and completes the proof. □

Exercise 16 Consider the following grammar CG3:

V:	a, b, c, d, +
BCat	$= \{A, B, C, D, S\}$
Cat	$=$ closure(BCat, $\{f_/, f_\backslash\}$)
Lex:	A/B a
	B b
	D\C c
	D d
	S/A,S/C,S/S +
Rule:	AP

Define a bijection on L_{CG3} that exchanges the following 3 pairs,

$$(a, A/B) \leftrightarrow (d, D) \quad (b, B) \leftrightarrow (c, D\backslash C) \quad (+, S/A) \leftrightarrow (+, C),$$

and show it is an automorphism.

The automorphism defined in the last proof (and the one in the exercise too) not only fails to preserve category, it also fails to preserve the "slash structure" of the categories. To set the stage for saying this more precisely, consider the category structure $\mathcal{C} = (Cat, \{f_/, f_\backslash\})$. Note that $\mathcal{C}$ is especially simple, simpler than many language structures $L = (L_G, Rule)$ in that the generating functions $f_/$ and $f_\backslash$ are 1-1 and total functions on Cat, with ranges disjoint from each other and from BCat. So (by Fact 2 on page 18) there is no ambiguity about how any category is derived, and in this special case, we know that every permutation of BCat extends uniquely to an automorphism, and every automorphism is one of those functions.[1]

In these terms, we can say something about what the automorphisms of the proof and exercise above show us about the relation between language structure:

Fact 15 *There are categorial grammars with automorphisms h such that h_2 does not extend to an automorphism of the category structure*

The automorphism h defined in the last proof is such that h_2 maps NP to A/B, which no automorphism of the category structure $\mathcal{C}$ can do. One expects that a some general positive statement about the relation between L and $\mathcal{C}$ should be possible here, but we leave the problem open.

The string languages definable by CGs are exactly the context free languages (Bar-Hillel et al. 1960, Buszkowski 1988). As noted above, adequate grammars for human languages require more expressive power.

Exercise 17 Write a classical categorial grammar G such that

$$\text{string(PH(S))} = \{a^n b^n | \ n > 0\}.$$

Are all PH(C) in this grammar invariant? Are any lexical expressions invariant?

3.2.2 Combinatory categorial grammars

Classical categorial grammars combine expressions simply by applying functions to arguments, but there are other ways of combining things. In particular, instead of applying x to y, if both are functions, we can compose x and y. In a setting where directionality matters, combinations with things to the left or the right, various kinds of composition could be allowed. Some extensions of this kind allow the definition of languages that are not context free (Vijay-Shanker and Weir 1994). For example, Steedman (2000) proposes extending the structure building rule {AP} with rules like the following, where some of the rules are language-specific:[2]

$$\begin{array}{cc} s & t \\ A/B & B/D \end{array} \quad \overset{>B}{\longmapsto} \quad \begin{array}{c} s\smallfrown t \\ A/D \end{array}$$

$$\begin{array}{cc} s & t \\ D\backslash B & B\backslash A \end{array} \quad \overset{<B}{\longmapsto} \quad \begin{array}{c} s\smallfrown t \\ D\backslash A \end{array}$$

$$\begin{array}{c} s \\ B \end{array} \quad \overset{>T}{\longmapsto} \quad \begin{array}{c} s \\ A/(B\backslash A) \end{array} \qquad \text{if } A=S$$

$$\begin{array}{c} s \\ B \end{array} \quad \overset{<T}{\longmapsto} \quad \begin{array}{c} s \\ (A/B)\backslash A \end{array} \qquad \text{if } A=S$$

$$\begin{array}{cc} s & t \\ A/B & C\backslash B \end{array} \quad \overset{>B_x}{\longmapsto} \quad \begin{array}{c} s\smallfrown t \\ C\backslash A \end{array} \qquad \text{if } B = VP_{-sub}, \text{ Dutch}$$

$$\begin{array}{cc} s & t \\ A/B & D\backslash(C\backslash B) \end{array} \quad \overset{>B_x^2}{\longmapsto} \quad \begin{array}{c} s\smallfrown t \\ D\backslash(C\backslash A) \end{array} \qquad \text{if } B = VP_{-sub}, \text{ Dutch}$$

It is no surprise that when we add these rules to AP, we get more derivations. For example, using the lexicon of CG1 again, instead of just one derivation of (every tall Albanian doctor, NP), we now obtain 5 derivations:

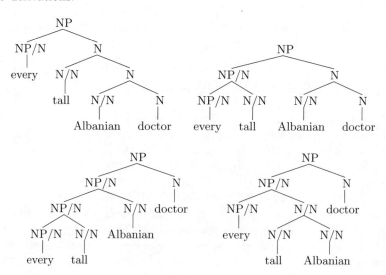

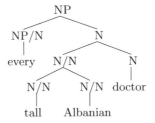

Notice that the last two derivations contain the constituent (tall Albanian, N/N), which may be appropriate since it can be coordinated, as in *every tall Albanian and short American doctor* (although we have not provided coordination in this grammar).

With the slightly frightening "crossed composition" rules $> B_x, > B_x^2$ and with Dutch lexical items of the types indicated, we get derivations of Dutch crossing subject-verb dependencies like the following:

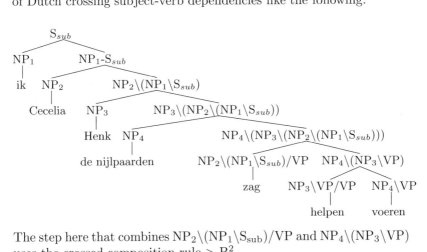

The step here that combines $NP_2\backslash(NP_1\backslash S_{sub})/VP$ and $NP_4\backslash(NP_3\backslash VP)$ uses the crossed composition rule $> B_x^2$.

Like CGs, CCGs are category-functional, and the question of whether each PH(C) is invariant is dependent on the details of each grammar. Lifting rules like $> T, < T$, unless restricted to a finite set of categories (as indicated here), can obviously lead to strings having infinitely many categories, and crossed composition rules, unless restricted to particular categories (as indicated here for Dutch), can lead to overgeneration of unwanted word orders.

Exercise 18 Adding Steedman's generative rules to a a simple classical categorial grammar G defining string(PH(S)) = $\{a^n b^n | \ n > 0\}$ (in the exercise on page 109), are the invariants changed in any way? Are there new derivations for the expressions in this language? Which substrings are constituents?

3.2.3 Pregroup grammars

Lambek (1958) observes that categorial grammars like the ones above have a kind of asymmetry which can be eliminated. CG tells us that if string s has category A/B and string t has category B then $s^\frown t$ has category A. But, for reasons of symmetry (and even for making sense of what the categories mean), we would like to be able to say that when a string $s^\frown t$ has category A and t has category B, then s has category A/B. That is, corresponding to our multiplication of expressions, we should have a kind of division. This addition can be properly specified, rather easily, and takes us to a natural and simple deductive calculus on categories (or "types") that has been explored from both linguistic and logical perspectives (see for example, Moortgat 1996).

In more recent work Lambek has shown how symmetric reasoning about expressions can also be realized in a simpler system called "pregroup grammars." Here, we will leave aside the elegant mathematical foundations[3] and instead just provide a restricted, BG formulation to illustrate the basic idea. In these grammars, a partially ordered set of basic categories (BCat, $\leq$) is provided, and Cat is the set of finite sequences of basic categories and their right and left "adjoints:"

$$\text{Cat} = (\text{closure}(\text{BCat}, \{1\}) \cup \text{closure}(\text{BCat}, \{r\}))^*$$

where, for $A \in \text{BCat}$, $l(A)$ is often written A^l, $l(l(A))$ as $A^{ll}, \ldots$ and similarly for $r(A)$, $r(r(A)), \ldots$. And second, the set of generating functions Rule is always the infinite set

$$\text{Rule} = \begin{array}{l} \{M\} \cup \\ \{\text{CON}_i | \ i > 0\} \cup \\ \{\text{EXP}_{i,A,f} | \ i > 0, A \in \text{BCat}, f \in \{r, l\}\} \cup \\ \{\text{IND}_{i,B} | \ i > 0, B \in \text{BCat}\}, \end{array}$$

where these are defined as follows. First, a simple merge rule just concatenates both strings and categories:

Domain	M	Value
s t		s⌢t
A B	$\longmapsto$	A⌢B

A simple contraction rule "cancels" any adjacent category and right adjunct AA^r or left adjunct and category A^lA. In order to make this contraction rule a generating *function*, we use an index i and require that the first canceled category is the i'th symbol:

Domain	CON_i	Value	Conditions
S $\alpha A^l A \beta$	$\longmapsto$	S $\alpha\beta$	$\|\alpha\| = i - 1$
S $\alpha A A^r \beta$	$\longmapsto$	S $\alpha\beta$	$\|\alpha\| = i - 1$

For each position $i > 0$, each basic category $A \in BCat$ and function $f \in \{l, r\}$, the expand rules insert the category A together with one of its adjoints $f(A)$ as follows:

Domain	$EXP_{i,A,f}$	Value	Conditions
S $\alpha\beta$	$\longmapsto$	S $\alpha A^l A \beta$	$\|\alpha\| = i - 1, f = l$
S $\alpha\beta$	$\longmapsto$	S $\alpha A A^r \beta$	$\|\alpha\| = i - 1, f = r$

Lambek shows that to derive a category of length 1, the rules $EXP_{i,A,f}$ are never needed. They provide a kind of symmetry in the system, but do not add any 'expressive power', and we will not use them in any of the derivations shown here.

Finally, for each $i > 0, B \in BCat$ we have rules which perform substitutions based on the partial order $\leq$:

Domain	$IND_{i,B}$	Value	Conditions
S $\alpha A \beta$	$\longmapsto$	S $\alpha B \beta$	$\|\alpha\| = i - 1, A \leq B$
S $\alpha A^r \beta$	$\longmapsto$	S $\alpha B^r \beta$	$\|\alpha\| = i - 1, B \leq A$
S $\alpha A^l \beta$	$\longmapsto$	S $\alpha B^l \beta$	$\|\alpha\| = i - 1, B \leq A$

Example PG1. This example is designed for comparison with Kor and CG1. We write CON, EXP, IND for the infinite collections of rules just defined, and use D for phrases that can be marked nominative or accusative, R for phrases that can be marked accusative, K for nominative phrase, A for accusative phrase, and as usual, N for noun, S for sentence. For the moment (to avoid some complications beyond our immediate interest) let's assume that the coordinable categories are just the basic categories: $cC_{PG1} = BCat$. Then PG1 is defined as follows:

V:	every, some, tall, short, Asian, American, student, teacher, Sam, John, himself, -nom, -acc, laughed, cried, praised, saw
BCat:	$=\{N, D, R, A, K, S\}$
$\leq$	$=\{\langle x, x \rangle \mid x \in BCat\} \cup \{\langle D, R \rangle\}$
Cat	$=(closure(BCat, \{r\}) \cup closure(BCat, \{l\}))^*$
Lex:	DN^l every, some
	NN^l tall, short, Asian, American
	N student, teacher
	D Sam, John
	R himself
	$D^r K$ -nom
	$R^r A$ -acc
	$K^r S$ laughed, cried
	$K^r A^r S$ praised, saw
	$A^r K^r S$ praised, saw
	$X^r X X^l$ and (for $X \in cC_{PG1}$)
Rule:	M, CON, EXP, IND.

With this grammar, we have derivations like this:

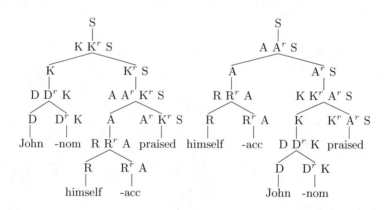

However, as in L_{Kor}, we cannot get SVO order or *nom*- marked reflexive pronouns:

$$(\text{John -nom praised himself -acc}, S) \notin L_{PG1}$$
$$(\text{himself -nom John -acc praised}, S) \notin L_{PG1}$$

Since the only binary rule of combination M is associative, we of course get (many) derivations in which *short American* is a constituent. Notice in the following derivation that we derive the natural expression (short American, N N^l) but we also combine the case marker with the verb before it combines with the subject:

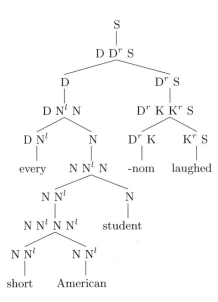

The early combination and feature contraction between the case marker and the verb seems harmless in this case (but some other cases are more troubling – see references in note 3).

We can also get coordination of reflexive and non-reflexive phrases, but where Kor used a special condition on the coordination rule, this grammar uses the general stipulation that any D is an R. Notice the step that changes D to R as we ascend the right branch in the following derivation:

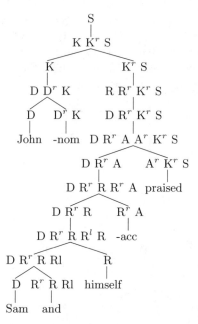

Exercise 19 Write a pregroup grammar G such that $string(PH(S)) = \{a^n b^n \mid n > 0\}$. Does this grammar differ in any significant respects from the similar CG or CCG grammars for the same language? (Consider the properties mentioned in the introduction.)

Pregroup grammars have an appealing simplicity and symmetry, but they define exactly the context free languages (Buszkowski 2001a) and so some extension will be needed to handle human languages. And it is unfortunate that two different type assignments are needed for the transitive verbs to get the alternative word orders (a problem that PGs share with the other varieties of categorial grammar discussed above, since they have similar mechanisms for enforcing order requirements).

3.3 Multiple context free grammars

We now consider briefly the "multiple context free grammars" (MCFGs) of Seki et al. (1991), which allow us to get beyond the context free languages. MCFGs are very similar to the "linear context free rewrite systems" of Weir (1988). These grammars are are also expressively equivalent to "(set local) multiple component tree adjoining grammars," (Weir 1988) and "minimalist grammars" (Stabler 1997, Michaelis 2001, Harkema 2001). and a number of other formalisms. The basic idea is simply this: while CFGs define a finite categorization of strings, MCFGs finitely categorize k-tuples of strings where k has a fixed finite upper bound in each grammar. For example, instead of a string s of category C, (s, X) which we sometimes represent in the "vertical form" $\begin{smallmatrix} s \\ C \end{smallmatrix}$ in our function definitions, an MCFG with $k = 2$ might have a pair of strings s,t with category C, $(\langle s, t \rangle, C)$ which we will sometimes represent with the notation $\begin{smallmatrix} s, t \\ C \end{smallmatrix}$. We could equivalently represent any such expression as a single categorized string by, intuitively, concatenating the elements of the pair and making the length of the first string s part of the category (exempting the "length" parts of the categories from the finiteness requirement). But for readability, it is more convenient to define the grammars in terms of categorized tuples of strings.

MCFGs are like CFGs except that expressions are categorized tuples of strings, and each rewrite rule specifies how the string components of its arguments define the string components of its value. We present an example before the general definition:

Example MCFG1. This 2-MCFG defines categorized tuples of strings where no tuple exceeds length 2. In particular, in this grammar, expressions of category T are pairs of strings, and expressions of category S are single strings. There is just one lexical item of category T, and 3 simple structure building rules:

> **V:** a, b, c, d
> **Cat:** $=\{S,T\}$
> **Lex:** T: $\langle \epsilon, \epsilon \rangle$
> **Rule:** F1, F2, F3, defined as follows.

The function F1 takes an expression of category T with strings s,t and concatenates an a before each component:

$$\begin{smallmatrix} s, t \\ T \end{smallmatrix} \xmapsto{\ F1\ } \begin{smallmatrix} a^\frown s, a^\frown t \\ T \end{smallmatrix}$$

The function F2 is similar but concatenates b:

$$\begin{smallmatrix} s, t \\ T \end{smallmatrix} \xmapsto{\ F2\ } \begin{smallmatrix} b^\frown s, b^\frown t \\ T \end{smallmatrix}$$

And finally, F3 takes an expression of category T with strings s,t as argument to yield as value the expression of category S with the single string $s^\frown t$:

$$\begin{smallmatrix} s, t \\ T \end{smallmatrix} \xmapsto{\ F3\ } \begin{smallmatrix} s^\frown t \\ S \end{smallmatrix}$$

With this grammar, we get derivations like this:

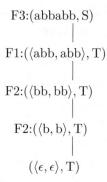

$$F3:(abbabb, S)$$
$$|$$
$$F1:(\langle abb, abb \rangle, T)$$
$$|$$
$$F2:(\langle bb, bb \rangle, T)$$
$$|$$
$$F2:(\langle b, b \rangle, T)$$
$$|$$
$$(\langle \epsilon, \epsilon \rangle, T)$$

Clearly, $string(PH(S)) = \{xx| \ x \in \{a, b\}^*\}$, a non-context free language.

Exercise 20 Write an MCFG that defines the non-context free language $\{a^n b^n c^n d^n e^n| \ n \geq 0\}$. (This can be done with 2 simple rules.)

In Seki et al. (1991), MCFGs are defined as rewrite grammars, but we give a bare grammar formulation directly. Of the four required properties below, notice that the first three are the same as the properties of bare grammar CFGs listed on page 103, and the fourth is more complex but still analogous to the fourth condition on CFGs, now requiring that the string values of each generating function be built in a fixed way from constant strings and string components of the arguments (possibly reordered, without repetitions, possibly leaving some components out).

Definition 21 For each $k > 0$, a *k-MCFG* is a bare grammar with the following properties:

a. V, Cat, Lex and Rule are finite and nonempty.

b. For each $F \in$ Rule, there are $C_1, \ldots, C_n \in$ Cat such that $Domain(F) = (PH(C_1) \times \ldots \times PH(C_n))$.

c. Each $F \in$ Rule is category functional: F_2 is a function.

   Given the previous observation, this has the consequence that for each generating function there is a fixed category that every expression in its range has. That is, every F_2 is a constant function.

d. For each $C \in$ Cat there is a constant $0 < k(C) \leq k$ such that every expression of category C has a $k(C)$-tuple of strings, and each generating function F is string functional: F_1 is a function from tuples of tuples of strings to tuples of strings.

   In particular, for every generating function F with domain

$(\mathrm{PH}(C_1) \times \ldots \times \mathrm{PH}(C_n))$ and range $\mathrm{PH}(C)$, F_1 is a function

$$F_1 : ((V^*)^{k(C_1)} \times \ldots (V^*)^{k(C_n)}) \to (V^*)^{k(C_n)}$$

where, letting the number of string components in the arguments

$$K = k(C_1) + \ldots + k(C_n),$$

the maximum number of constant strings in the values of the function

$$K' = K + k(C),$$

a permutation that specifies a particular reordering of string components,

$$\pi = \text{some permutation of } \{1, 2, \ldots, K\}$$

and an increasing sequence of positive integers with $i_{k(C)} \leq K'$

$$\langle i_1, i_2, \ldots, i_{k(C)} \rangle$$

we require that there are strings

$$\alpha_0, \alpha_1, \ldots, \alpha_{i_{k(C)}} \in V^*$$

such that for every element of in $\mathrm{Domain}(F_1)$,

$$\langle\langle s_1, \ldots, s_{k(C_1)} \rangle, \langle s_{k(C_1)+1}, \ldots, s_{k(C_1)+k(C_2)} \rangle, \ldots, \langle s_{K-k(C_n)}, \ldots, s_K \rangle\rangle$$

the function F_1 takes the value

$$\langle \alpha_0 s_{\pi(1)} \alpha_1 s_{\pi(2)} \alpha_2 \ldots s_{\pi(i_1)} \alpha_{i_1},$$
$$\alpha_{i_1+1} s_{\pi(i_1+1)} \cdots s_{\pi(i_2)} \alpha_{i_2},$$
$$\ldots$$
$$\alpha_{i_{k(C)}-1+1} s_{\pi(i_{k(C)-1}+1)} \cdots s_{\pi(i_{k(C)})} \alpha_{i_{k(C)}} \rangle.$$

The k-MCFGs are a natural extension of CFGs. We see in MCFG1, above, that these grammars can define non-context free sets, but they are of particular interest to linguists because they are rather closely related to certain tree adjoining grammars and even to minimalist grammars inspired by Chomskian syntax, as noted above. Rather than exploring those connections in detail, let's consider another example MCFG which provides some indication of the basis of how MCFGs can mimic these other grammars.

Example MCFG2. Chomsky (1956) pointed out that if we link each verb with the affix it determines on the following verb in English constructions like the following, it is easy to see that the dependencies are crossing:

John will have -∅ be -en eat -ing pie

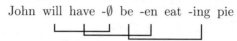

This observation was one motivation behind Chomsky's early claims about the "structure dependence" of human grammars (mentioned on page 6 of Lecture 1): we would like to have grammars that allow a simple treatment of the discontinuous relations between each auxiliary verb and the affix on the next verb. This kind of proposal can be framed in an MCFG using the intuitive idea that a constituent that is going to "move" is kept in a separate string component.[4] Inspired by early proposals, the following 3-MCFG treats verbs, auxiliaries and tense inflection in this way, and so the verbal phrases VP, PerfP, and ProgP will have three components s,t,u, allowing the head t to be kept distinct from any preceding or following material. The English progressive pair ⟨be,-ing⟩ and the perfect ⟨have,-en⟩ are assumed to be lexical items. The fact that *will* is followed by a "bare" verb with no present or past marking is treated differently, partly in order to properly place the adverbs, as will be mentioned again below.

V: the, some, every, student, teacher, actor, film, probably, really, always, sometimes, Sue, Peter, eat, fall, see, bite, be, -ing, have, -en, will, would, can, could, -s, -ed

Cat ={D,DP,N,NP,Adv,AdvP,V,Vt,VP,Prog,ProgP,Perf,PerfP, T,T_{af},TP}

Lex:

D	the, some, every
N	student, teacher, actor, film
DP	Sue, Peter
V	eat, fall
Vt	see, bite, like
Prog	⟨be,-ing⟩
Perf	⟨have,-en⟩, ⟨have,-ed⟩
T	will,would,can,could
Adv	probably, really, always, sometimes
T_{af}	-s,-ed

Rule: F1-F20, as follows.

The first 3 rules F1, F2 and F3 differ only in the choice of X ∈ {N, A, Adv}, in each case building an XP from an X, and so the whole collection could be called "X to XP:"

$$\frac{X}{X} \overset{F1\text{-}3}{\longmapsto} \frac{X}{XP} \qquad \text{for } X \in \{N, A, Adv\} \text{ "X to XP"}$$

$$\frac{x \quad y}{D \quad NP} \overset{F4}{\longmapsto} \frac{xy}{DP} \qquad \text{"D selects NP object"}$$

$$\frac{x \quad y}{Vt \quad DP} \overset{F5}{\longmapsto} \frac{\epsilon, x, y}{VP} \qquad \text{"Vt selects DP object"}$$

$$\frac{x}{V} \overset{F6}{\longmapsto} \frac{\epsilon, x, \epsilon}{VP} \qquad \text{"V to VP"}$$

$$\frac{w \quad x, y, z}{AdvP \quad XP} \overset{F7\text{-}9}{\longmapsto} \frac{wx, y, z}{XP} \qquad \text{for } X \in \{VP, ProgP, PerfP\}$$

$$\frac{x, y \quad v, z, w}{X \quad VP} \overset{F10\text{-}11}{\longmapsto} \frac{\epsilon, x, vzyw}{XP} \qquad \text{for } X \in \{Perf, Prog\} \text{ "selects VP"}$$

$$\frac{x, y \quad v, z, w}{Perf \quad ProgP} \overset{F12}{\longmapsto} \frac{\epsilon, x, vzyw}{PerfP} \qquad \text{"Perf selects ProgP"}$$

$$\frac{x \quad y, z, w}{T \quad X} \overset{F13\text{-}15}{\longmapsto} \frac{x, yzw}{T'} \qquad \text{for } X \in \{VP, ProgP, PerfP\}$$

$$\frac{x \quad y, z, w}{T_{af} \quad VP} \overset{F16}{\longmapsto} \frac{\epsilon, yzxw}{T'} \qquad \text{"Affix Hop"}$$

$$\frac{x \quad w, y, z}{T_{af} \quad X} \overset{F17\text{-}18}{\longmapsto} \frac{yx, wz}{T'} \qquad \text{for } X \in \{ProgP, PerfP\}$$

$$\frac{x \quad y, z}{DP \quad T'} \overset{F19}{\longmapsto} \frac{xyz}{TP} \qquad \text{"S-formation"}$$

$$\frac{x \quad y, z}{DP \quad T'} \overset{F20}{\longmapsto} \frac{yxz}{TP} \qquad \text{"Q-formation"}$$

Notice the rules F16 (Affix Hop) and F17-18 (Auxiliary Raising). These are distinctive to English and we will say more about them in §3.4.3, below. With this grammar, we have derivations like this:

F20:(have -s Sue be -en eat -ing, TP)

   (Sue, DP) F18:(⟨have -s, be -en eat -ing⟩, T′)

      (-s, Taf)   F12:(⟨ϵ, have, be -en eat -ing⟩, ProgP)

           (⟨have, -en⟩, Perf)   F11:(⟨ϵ, be, eat -ing⟩, ProgP)

                 (⟨be, -ing⟩, Prog)   F6:(⟨ϵ, eat, ϵ⟩, VP)

                                       (eat, V)

It is easy to check some of the other examples standardly covered in introductory syntax. The reader is invited to check some of the following:

> (the actor have -s be -en see -ing the film, TP) ∈ L$_{\mathrm{MCFG2}}$
> (have -s the actor be -en see -ing the film, TP) ∈ L$_{\mathrm{MCFG2}}$
> (the actor will have be -en see -ing the film, TP) ∈ L$_{\mathrm{MCFG2}}$
> (will the actor have be -en see -ing the film, TP) ∈ L$_{\mathrm{MCFG2}}$
> (Sue be -s have -en see -ing the film, TP) ∉ L$_{\mathrm{MCFG2}}$
> (be -en Sue have -s see -ing the film, TP) ∉ L$_{\mathrm{MCFG2}}$
> (-s Sue have be -en see -ing the film, TP) ∉ L$_{\mathrm{MCFG2}}$

Since we also have "Auxiliary Raising" constructions like

> (Sue have -s probably see -en the film, TP) ∈ L$_{\mathrm{MCFG2}}$

we check to make sure that we properly get "Affix Hop" constructions which show a different position of the adverb with respect to tense:

F19:(Sue probably like -s the film, TP)

   (Sue, DP) F16:(⟨ϵ, probably like -s the film⟩, T′)

      (-s, Taf)   F7:(⟨probably, like, the film⟩, VP)

         F3:(probably, AdvP) F5:(⟨ϵ, like, the film⟩, VP)

           (probably, Adv)   (like, Vt)   F4:(the film, DP)

                             (the, D)   F1:(film, NP)

                                     (film, N)

In sentences like the one above, with no auxiliary verb, it is impossible for the adverb to follow the tense maker -s:

> (Sue see -s probably the film, TP) ∉ L$_{\mathrm{MCFG2}}$.

Exercise 21 Many of the different rules of MCFG2 are similar to one another, but the MCFG format does not allow a more succinct expression. Define a more succinct bare grammar that generates the exactly same language.

Exercise 22 Which lexical items of L_{MCFG2} are easily shown to be constant? which PH(C)?

3.4 Constraint-based grammars

In BG, the structure maps on a language are determined by the generating functions. Do the structural notions developed in this setting apply in any form to constraint-based grammars? Some constraint-based grammars use some generative mechanisms, but suppose we consider the purely model-theoretic versions of those theories where the expressions of the language are the models of the theories.[5] We briefly consider this question here.

3.4.1 First order grammars

Let's first consider first order theories that have sequences of vocabulary items as their models. A string $s \in V^*$ is standardly regarded as a sequence, a function from a finite initial segment of $\mathbb{N}$ into V. But now we focus on the inverse relation $s^{-1} \subset V \times \mathbb{N}$ which associates each each element of V with the positions where that element occurs. Vocabulary items become properties of numbers. Let a **first order grammar** $G = \langle V, R, \phi \rangle$, where V is a finite set (the vocabulary), now treated as 1-place predicate symbols, R is a set of relation symbols, with fixed interpretations over $\mathbb{N}$, and ϕ is a formula of the standard first order language with equality for R and V.

Example FOG1:

$$V = \{a, b, c, d\} \quad \text{(1-place predicate symbols)}$$
$$R = \{\leq\} \quad \text{(2-place predicate symbol)}$$
$$\phi = \exists x \exists y (\forall z (x \leq z) \wedge a(x) \wedge \forall z (z \leq y) \wedge b(y))$$

Letting $\leq$ receive its standard interpretation over $\mathbb{N}$, we can see that ϕ requires the first position to be a, and the last to be b. So, in a sense we will now make precise, $L_{FOG1} = aV^*b$.

For any $n \in \mathbb{N}$ let $\bar{n} = \{0, 1, \dots, n-1\}$. We can regard any $s \in V^*$ as a function $s : \bar{n} \to V$ for some n, with the associated structure:

$$\underline{s} = (\bar{n}, R^w, V^w)$$

with the convention that the elements of R^w are the restrictions to $\bar{n}$ of specified, standard relations, while for each $a \in V$, $[a]^w = \{x \in \bar{n} | s(x) = a\}$. And for any $G = \langle V, R, \phi \rangle$, $L_G = \{s \in V^* | \underline{s} \models \phi\}$

Fixing any vocabulary V, the **set of languages FO[R]** $= \{L_G | G = \langle V, R, \phi \rangle$ for some $\phi\}$ of course varies with the choice of R. For example, Thomas (1997) shows:

Theorem 10 $\{a^n | n \text{ is even}\} \notin FO[\leq]$

And McNaughton and Papert (1971) show:

Theorem 11 FO[$\leq$] *is a proper subset of the aperiodic regular languages, where $S \subset V^*$ is aperiodic or non-counting iff $\exists n \in \mathbb{N} \; \forall x, y, z \in V^*$, $xy^n z \in S$ implies $xy^{n+1} z \in S$.*

In first order model theory, automorphisms of the models are commonly considered. These are bijections on the domain that fix the relations, semantic automorphisms in the sense defined on page 33. In the case of FOG1 with structures of the form $(\mathbb{N}, a^w, b^w, c^w, d^w, \leq)$, the only automorphism of the domain $\mathbb{N}$ that fixes the relation $\leq$ is the identity $\mathrm{id}_\mathbb{N}$. So this does not provide any useful notion of structural equivalence. The set of models of FOG1 is closed under permutations of $\mathbb{N}$ that fix the sets a^w, b^w, c^w, d^w, but the non-trivial permutations will fail to fix $\leq$.

In bare grammars, the automorphisms are permutations on the language. But here, the language of FOG1 is a set of models, and since the grammar does not explicitly define relations among models, permutations of the set of models are of no particular interest unless we can define an algebraic perspective on the semantic domain.

3.4.2 Monadic second order grammars (MSOGs)

Extending FOL with quantification over monadic predicates, we have MSO logic, in which we can specify relations among sets of expressions. In this logic, $\leq$ can be defined in a language with the successor relation S (and identity). It turns out that MSO[S] is the set of regular languages (Büchi 1960, Elgot 1961). So it is possible to associate any MSOG with a "canonical acceptor," which, via the function bg introduced in §3.1 earlier, induces an algebraic structure.

Theorem 12 *Given any (possibly non-deterministic) finite state acceptor $A = \langle V, Q, I, F, \delta \rangle$, there is a MSO[S] grammar $G = \langle V, R, \phi \rangle$, such that $L_G = L_A$.*

Proof. Consider any acceptor $A = \langle V, Q, I, F, \delta \rangle$ where $V = \{a_1, \ldots, a_n\}$, $Q = \{0, \ldots, k\}$, and $I, F \subseteq Q$. It is easy to construct an MSO grammar $G = \langle V, R, \phi \rangle$ such that $L_G = L_A$. Letting $R = \{\leq\}$, we have already seen that the first and last positions in any model can be distinguished, so for ease of reading let's allow ourselves to use the 1-place predicates first, last. For each state i, we use a monadic second order variable X_i that will be satisfied by the positions in the string that can get us to that state. We construct a formula that, in effect, requires the positions in any model lie along a path from an initial state in I to a final state in F, so we do not allow any position to satisfy two state predicates at once. If $\epsilon \in L_A$ then the following formula has the desired result.

$$\exists X_0 \ldots \exists X_k \quad \bigwedge_{i \neq j} \forall x \neg (X_i(x) \wedge X_j(x))$$
$$\wedge \forall x (\text{first}(x) \rightarrow X_0(x))$$
$$\wedge \forall x \forall y (S(x,y) \rightarrow \bigvee_{\langle i,a,j \rangle \in \delta} (X_i(x) \wedge a(x) \wedge X_j(y)))$$
$$\wedge \forall x (\text{last}(x) \rightarrow \bigvee_{\langle i,a,j \rangle \in \delta \wedge j \in F} (X_i(x) \wedge a(x)))$$

If $\epsilon \notin L_A$ then we add a conjunct like $\exists x(x = x)$ to require the existence of a position. An induction on derivational complexity establishes that $L_G = L_A$. □

A converse to this result is provided by Büchi (1960) and Elgot (1961). The proof is more difficult, and so we will not attempt to provide it here, but will simply observe that it guarantees the existence of an algebraic characterization on the language of any MSOG, though it is not clear that this would be the "right" kind of algebraic characterization for capturing linguistic notions of structure.

Example: Let's look at 4 different ways to define the language L_{FOG1}. First, consider the "right-branching" CFG2 $= \langle V, \text{Cat}, \rightarrow \rangle$:

$$V = \{a, b, c, d\}$$
$$\text{Cat} = \{0, 1, 2\}$$
$$0 \rightarrow a \ 1 \quad 1 \rightarrow a \ 1 \quad 1 \rightarrow b \ 1 \quad 1 \rightarrow c \ 1 \quad 1 \rightarrow d \ 1 \quad 1 \rightarrow b \ 2 \quad 2 \rightarrow \epsilon$$

We have shown that this can be represented as the bare grammar $bg(\text{CFG2}) = \langle V, \text{Cat}, \text{Lex}, \text{Rule} \rangle$:

$$\text{Lex} = \{(\epsilon, 2)\}$$
$$\text{Rule} = \{r1, \ldots, r6\} \text{ defined as follows}$$

Domain		Value	Domain		Value
s 1	$\xrightarrow{r1}$	a⌢s 0	s 1	$\xrightarrow{r4}$	c⌢s 1
s 1	$\xrightarrow{r2}$	a⌢s 1	s 1	$\xrightarrow{r5}$	d⌢s 1
s 1	$\xrightarrow{r3}$	b⌢s 1	s 1	$\xrightarrow{r6}$	b⌢s 2

In this grammar, string(0)$= aV^*b$, string(1)$= V^*b$, string(2)$= \{\epsilon\}$, and each of the phrases of each of these categories is invariant by Fact 6, above. In fact, in this grammar, every expression is invariant.

With 0 as the "start category," these grammars correspond to acceptor $A1 = \langle V, Q, I, F, \delta \rangle$ where

$$V = \{a, b, c, d\}$$
$$Q = \{0, 1, 2\}$$
$$I = \{0\}$$
$$F = \{2\}$$
$$\delta = \{(0, a, 1), (1, a, 1), (1, b, 1), (1, c, 1), (1, d, 1), (1, b, 2)\}$$

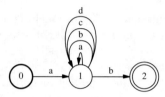

Following the construction used in the previous proof, this acceptor corresponds to the following MSO[S] grammar MSOG1:

$$V = \{a, b, c, d\}$$
$$R = \{\leq\}$$
$$\phi = \exists X_0 \exists X_1 \exists X2$$
$$\forall x \neg (X_0(x) \land X_1(x))$$
$$\land \forall x \neg (X_1(x) \land X_2(x))$$
$$\land \forall x \neg (X_0(x) \land X_2(x))$$
$$\land \forall x (first(x) \rightarrow X_0(x))$$
$$\land \forall x \forall y (S(x, y) \rightarrow ((X_0(x) \land a(x) \land X_1(y))$$
$$\lor (X_1(x) \land a(x) \land X_1(y))$$
$$\lor (X_1(x) \land b(x) \land X_1(y))$$
$$\lor (X_1(x) \land c(x) \land X_1(y))$$
$$\lor (X_1(x) \land d(x) \land X_1(y))$$
$$\lor (X_1(x) \land a(x) \land X_2(y))))$$
$$\land \forall x (last(x) \rightarrow (X_1(x) \land b(x)))$$
$$\land \exists x (x = x)$$

We leave open the question of whether there is a linguistically appropriate way to characterize the notions of structure and isomorphism for MSOGs.

3.4.3 Optimality-theoretic grammars (OTGs)

Some constraint-based grammars for natural languages are quite different from FOGs or MSOGs, deliberately "over-constraining" the languages in the sense that no languages at all satisfy all constraints.

Instead, some notion of "optimal satisfaction" of the constraints is defined. One motivation comes from the idea that different languages have reached different compromises among various conflicting natural tendencies. Rather than defining each particular compromise explicitly, with explicit rules satisfied by that particular language alone (as in every other grammar considered in this text), and rather than characterizing universal properties that every language has, the idea is characterize universals that languages "tend towards having." It is perhaps a surprise that, at least for some "optimality-theoretic grammars" (OTGs) of this kind, there are illuminating ways to apply the notions of structure developed here. In particular, we see first that our notions can apply straightforwardly to the universal basis ("gen"), and that, furthermore, there is a way to identify structure that is induced by the definition of the "optima."

Consider this very simple example used by Vikner (2001) to illustrate the basic idea. (Cf. also Grimshaw 1997.) In English (and embedded clauses in Danish), an inflected main verb follows adverbs like *really*, and we saw in §3.3 that this can be derived by, moving the tense inflection into the verb phrase to attach it to the verb, when combining the tense inflection with the verb phrase:

(1)   a.   The actor t_i really saw$_i$ the film

      b.   *The actor saw really t_i the film

But in French (and embedded clauses in Icelandic), we have the other pattern:

(2)   a.   *L'acteur t_i vraiment voit$_i$ le film

      b.   L'acteur voit$_i$ vraiment t_i le film

The English order satisfies the following constraint, where the "lexical heads" are stipulated to be the verbs, nouns, prepositions, adjectives and adverbs:

LxMv: No movement of a "lexical" head.

While the French (2b) violates LxMv, it satisfies the following constraint,

PrBd: When a constituent moves, it must move to a c-commanding (or "proper binding") position.

The example (2b) satisfies PrBd since the verb has moved "up" from the VP to combine with the tense, while (1a) violates PrBd since the inflection there has moved "down" into the VP. So it seems LxMv is more important than PrBd in English, but the opposite holds in French. So the idea is roughly this: a sentence is admitted in a language only if no other sentence with the same predicates and arguments (and tense and aspect) has fewer violations of the more important constraints.

Let's see how an account like this could be formalized in a little grammar, an elaboration of MCFG2 from page 120. Recall that in MCFG2 we had derivations like this:

F19:(Sue probably see -s the film, TP)

  (Sue, DP) F16:(⟨ϵ, probably see -s the film⟩, T′)

      (-s, T_af)   F7:(⟨probably, see, the film⟩, VP)

         F3:(probably, AdvP) F5:(⟨ϵ, see, the film⟩, VP)

           (probably, Adv)   (see, Vt) F4:(the film, DP)

                         (the, D) F1:(film, NP)

                                  (film, N)

We can easily modify grammar MCFG2 to get the French order instead of the English order, simply by replacing F16 "Affix Hop" with this rule:

$$\frac{\text{x} \quad \text{w, y, z}}{\text{T}_{af} \quad \text{VP}} \overset{F16'}{\longmapsto} \frac{\text{yx, wz}}{\text{T}'}$$

Call this grammar MCFG3. With MCFG3, we have derivations like this:

F19:(Sue see -s probably the film, TP)

  (Sue, DP) F16':(⟨see -s, probably the film⟩, T′)

      (-s, T_af)   F7:(⟨probably, see, the film⟩, VP)

         F3:(probably, AdvP) F5:(⟨ϵ, see, the film⟩, VP)

           (probably, Adv)   (see, Vt) F4:(the film, DP)

                         (the, D) F1:(film, NP)

                                  (film, N)

Notice, first, that this derivation tree and the one above both have the same yields: they combine the same lexical items in the same orders. Furthermore, these yields specify, in a uniform way, the predicates, arguments, tense and aspect. So to determine the "optimal" structures, in a certain sense, we can compare all structures whose derivations have the same yields. Second, notice that if we simply added F16′ to MCFG2 instead of using it to replace F16, then we would derive both the English and the French orders. We use these ideas to define two simple OTGs.

Examples OTG$_{Eng}$ and OTG$_{Fr}$. These grammars are like MCFG1 except they include F16′ and one more rule, either OPT$_{Eng}$ or OPT$_{Fr}$, respectively, as defined below. First, for any possible expression (x, TP), define,

$$
\begin{aligned}
\mathrm{FA(x,TP)} &= \text{the set of FA derivation trees for (x,TP)} \\
\mathrm{ds(x,TP)} &= \text{the set yield(FA(x,TP))} \\
\mathrm{F16(x,TP)} &= \text{the least number of times that F16 is used} \\
&\quad \text{in any d} \in \mathrm{FA(x,TP)} \\
\mathrm{F16'(x,TP)} &= \text{the least number of times that F16' is used} \\
&\quad \text{in any d} \in \mathrm{FA(x,TP)}
\end{aligned}
$$

$$
\mathrm{LxMv{>}PrBd(x,TP)} \begin{cases} = 1 \text{ if } \neg\exists y \text{ such that } \mathrm{ds(y,TP)} = \mathrm{ds(x,TP)} \\ \qquad \text{and } \mathrm{F16(y,TP)} < \mathrm{F16(x,TP)} \\ = 0 \text{ otherwise} \end{cases}
$$

$$
\mathrm{PrBd{>}LxMv(x,TP)} \begin{cases} = 1 \text{ if } \neg\exists y \text{ such that } \mathrm{ds(y,TP)} = \mathrm{ds(x,TP)} \\ \qquad \text{and } \mathrm{F16'(y,TP)} < \mathrm{F16'(x,TP)} \\ = 0 \text{ otherwise} \end{cases}
$$

Finally we define the rules OPT$_{Eng}$ and OPT$_{Fr}$ as follows:

$$
\begin{array}{c} \mathrm{x} \\ \mathrm{TP} \end{array} \xmapsto{\mathrm{OPT_{Eng}}} \begin{array}{c} \mathrm{x} \\ \mathrm{OPT} \end{array} \quad \text{if } \mathrm{LxMv{>}PrBd(x,TP)}
$$

$$
\begin{array}{c} \mathrm{x} \\ \mathrm{TP} \end{array} \xmapsto{\mathrm{OPT_{Fr}}} \begin{array}{c} \mathrm{x} \\ \mathrm{OPT} \end{array} \quad \text{if } \mathrm{PrBd{>}LxMv(x,TP)}
$$

Notice that the conditions on these rules are satisfied only when the argument is "optimal" in one sense or the other. On all other arguments, the functions will be undefined. It is easy to see that with these rules in grammars OTG$_{Eng}$ and OTG$_{Fr}$, respectively, we have

$$
\mathrm{PH(TP)_{Eng}} = \mathrm{PH(TP)_{Fr}}
$$
(Sue probably see -s the film, OPT) $\in \mathrm{L_{OTG_{Eng}}}$
(Sue probably see -s the film, OPT) $\notin \mathrm{L_{OTG_{Fr}}}$
(Sue see -s probably the film, OPT) $\notin \mathrm{L_{OTG_{Eng}}}$
(Sue see -s probably the film, OPT) $\in \mathrm{L_{OTG_{Fr}}}$

Since different rules get used in the derivations of the different orders, it is no surprise that we have:

Fact 16 *In both* OTG_{Eng} *and* OTG_{Fr},

(Sue probably see -*s* the film, TP) $\not\simeq$ (Sue see -*s* probably the film, TP).

However, it is easy to see that rules like OPT can induce structure: no optimal candidate can ever be isomorphic to a non-optimal expression, since any mapping that related such a pair of expressions would fail to preserve the domain of OPT. Although these example grammars are very simple, we see no reason to doubt that this kind of account could be extended to more elaborate proposals of the kind found in Vikner (2001), Grimshaw (1997), and similar work.

3.5   Structure and expressive power

Let's say two bare grammars G1, G2 have *isomorphic invariants* iff there is a bijection $f : L_{G1} \to L_{G2}$ such that $h \in \text{Aut}_{G1}$ iff $f(h) \in \text{Aut}_{G2}$. So then, obviously, if X is an invariant of G1, h(X) is an invariant of G2. You might think that languages with isomorphic invariants would be very similar, and in some sense they are, but it is easy to show that grammars defining languages of very different complexities can have isomorphic invariants. Recall the Chomsky hierarchy of languages:

finite state languages (FSL)

$\subset$

context free languages (CFL)

$\subset$

multiple context free languages (MCFL)

$\subset$

context sensitive languages (CSL)

$\subset$

recursively enumerable languages (RE)

$\subset$

languages, subsets of V^* (L)

Consider the following grammars with the same V, Cat and Lex,

$$V = \{a, b\} \qquad \text{Cat} = \{S\} \qquad \text{Lex} = \{(b, S)\}$$

First, consider the grammar FS with just the rule of the same name:

Domain	FS	Value
s		sa
S	$\longmapsto$	S

Then string(PH(S)) $\in$ FSL. Consider grammar CF with just the rule of the same name:

Domain	CF	Value
s		asa
S	$\longmapsto$	S

Then string(PH(S)) $\in$ CFL $-$ FSL. Slightly fancier, now consider grammar with just this rule:

Domain	MCS	Value	Conditions
s		$a^n b^n a^n$	
S	$\longmapsto$	S	where $n = \lfloor \frac{|s|}{3} \rfloor + 1$

Then string(PH(S)) $\in$ MCFL $-$ CFL. It is easy to get a non-MCS grammar:

Domain	CS	Value
s		ss
S	$\longmapsto$	S

Then string(PH(S)) $\in$ RE $-$ MCFL. Really we can do almost anything:

Domain	XX	Value	Conditions
s		$a^{n+1} b a^{f(n+1)}$	where s= $a^n b a^*$ and f is
S	$\longmapsto$	S	your favorite function on $\mathbb{N}$

In each of these cases, the generating function is 1-1 and its range is disjoint from the lexicon. In fact, there is only 1 expression at each derivational depth, and so the only automorphism is the identity on the language.

3.6 Summary and open questions

In this brief survey we see that many grammars have quite natural bare grammar representations in which our structural notions apply. We can survey, for example, the commitments of various formalisms with respect to the properties mentioned at the beginning of this lecture. In the following table, $\square$ indicates that grammars allowed by the formalism have the property, $\times$ indicates that the property does not hold in grammars allowed by the formalism, and $\diamond$ indicates that the property can but need not hold in grammars allowed by the formalism:

	bg(CFG)	CG	CCG	PG	MCFG	BG
(FinLex)	□	□	□	□	□	◇
(FinCat)	□	□	◇	×	□	◇
(Assoc)	◇	◇	◇	□	◇	◇
(Lexic)	×	□	?	□	×	◇
(CF)	□	□	◇	□	◇	◇
(P)	□	□	□	□	□	◇
(CatSt)	◇	◇	◇	◇	□	◇
(CatFunc)	□	□	□	□	□	◇
(WFnd)	◇	◇	◇	◇	◇	◇
(MR)	□	□	□	□	◇	◇
(SFEq)	□	□	□	□	□	◇

(We have left out FOGs and MSOGs, lacking any satisfactory way to apply our structural notions there, and also OTGs, lacking a general characterization of them.) Many but not all the claims in this table are discussed above. For example, bg(CFG)s only sometimes satisfy (CatSt), since lexical categories that do not appear in any rules need not be preserved. CGs and PGs are "lexicalized" (Lexic) because they have a fixed set of rules that do not vary from one grammar to another. None of these formalisms require (WFnd): they all allow a lexical item to be derived. Only MCFGs and BGs allow deletion rules which can violate (MR). Related matters are discussed in the next Lecture.

Notice that bare grammars (BGs) do not require or prohibit any of these properties, and that BG is the only formalism in the table with this property! As explained in the first lecture, this was our intention. BGs do not determine any significant properties of the languages defined; all of our proposals about significant properties of natural languages are introduced explicitly.

Among the properties that the non-BG formalisms decide, there is little consensus. Consider the properties required by all the formalisms other than BG in the table: (FinLex), (P), (CatFunc) and (SFEq). Of these, only (FinLex) seems to be widely accepted. (P) is controversial: for example, contrast Joshi (1985), Joshi et al. (1991) and Kracht (1998), with Barton et al. (1987) and Ristad (1993). This controversy rests in part on disagreements about the range of phenomena that should be regarded as "syntactic" or "grammatical," but some of the issues are clear and substantial. We will not attempt to resolve them here, and indeed, the results in the previous section suggest that many of them are orthogonal to the structural issues we have been exploring. We have seen an exception to (SFEq) in Eng_{RC}. Some closely related constraints are discussed further in Lecture 4.

Notes

[1]This is what Enderton (1972, p.27) calls the "recursion theorem," a special case of more general and fundamental results about "free algebras" that are presented in almost every algebra text: for example, Birkhoff (1940, §§VI.6-7), Cohn (1965, §III), Grätzer (1968, §4), McKenzie et al. (1987, §4.11).

[2]These rules (and their names) are from Steedman (2000), adapted and simplified slightly, and with categories given in the range-always-on-top slash notation instead of Steedman's range-always-first notation.

[3]For foundations and development, see Lambek (2001,1999,1995), Buszkowski (2001a,b), Casadio (2001) and Casadio and Lambek (2002). To allow an extremely brief exposition, we consider here only right and left adjoints of elements of BCat. This does not restrict our expressive power, since the right or left adjoint of an arbitrary category is always expressible as an element of (closure(BCat, {l}) ∪ closure(BCat, {r}))*, but it hides some of the naturalness of the system, as the cited references make clear.

[4]Chomsky, Joshi and many other linguists use rules that build and modify *trees*, but tuples of strings usually suffice. The relation between MCFGs and tree-transforming grammars is discussed in (Weir 1988, Michaelis 1998, Harkema 2000, Stabler 2001). Example MCFG2 is adapted from (Stabler 2003b).

[5]Some recent treatments of HPSG are model-theoretic (Moshier 1997, Pollard 1999, King et al. 1999, Richter 2000, Mönnich 2001), and some other theories can be construed in this way too (Rogers 1999, Bird 1995).

4

Laws of Language

We are actively searching for "laws of language structure," axioms which collectively identify human languages as opposed to other possible languages. We offer many suggestions here. At this stage of our work the question of their independence is open. More pressing is to test and refine the proposals in light of empirical investigation. It is certain that our proposals for axioms are incomplete: not just any system satisfying these axioms is a possible human grammar.

The axioms we propose cluster around two basic notions: (i) grammatical category, and (ii) constituency and recursion. We conclude with (iii) some constraints relating form and meaning. Throughout G is an arbitrary grammar, while s, t, and u are arbitrary elements of L_G.

4.1 The structural role of grammatical categories

In the structuralist tradition in Linguistics grammatical categories (GCs) were understood as substitution classes: expressions of the same category could be intersubstituted preserving grammaticality. On the other hand, we suggested in Lecture 1 that a distinctive structural role for categories is that the PH(C) are invariant, which just means that automorphisms always map expressions to ones of the same category. Below we investigate the substitution and invariance properties of GCs and adopt appropriately refined statements of each as axiomatic.

Substitution classes. The naive interpretation of substitution preserving grammaticality is a non-starter. Two expressions with the same category cannot in general be intersubstituted:

$$\text{Cat(Sue laughed, S)} = \text{Cat(It rains in Spain, S)}$$
$$\underline{\text{Sue laughed}} \text{ or cried} \Rightarrow *\text{It rains in Spain or cried}$$
$$\text{The boy who kissed } \underline{\text{Sue laughed}} \Rightarrow *\text{The boy who kissed it rains in Spain}$$

One problem here lies in replacing substrings that are not "constituents." We might try (1) as a necessary condition on sameness of category, but it is also not quite precise enough.

(1) If $Cat(s) = Cat(t)$ and sCONu then s can be replaced by t in u preserving grammaticality

One problem with (1) is that constituents cannot in general be measured in terms of observable strings. In Eng, is *and* a constituent of the NP in (2a)?

(2) a. (both John and Bill, NP)

  b. *both John or Bill

In Eng, the answer is yes: (and, CONJ) is in fact a constituent of (2a), and it is also true that *and* and *or* have the same category, namely, CONJ. But obviously substituting the string *or* for *and* yields the ungrammatical (2b). The problem now lies with the notion of substitution, and within Bare Grammar we can offer a more tenable notion: substitute expressions in the domains of the generating functions, not strings in their values. Given a triple $\langle(and, CONJ), s, t\rangle \in$ Domain(Coord) we can indeed replace (and, CONJ) by (or, CONJ) preserving Domain(Coord); the value in the second case will be (either s or t,C) and in the first (both s and t, C), so there is no grammaticality failure. Domain substitution avoids the problem of substituting for non-constituents. But there are other, deeper, problems.

A variety of derivational processes in natural language place identity or non-identity conditions on strings (Stabler 2004). Prominent among these are deletion operations, exemplified in (3).

(3) a. John didn't cry at the wedding but Bill did ~~cry at the wedding~~

  b. Dana gave Sheila flowers and ~~gave~~ Sue chocolates

  c. Frieda read more plays than Bill ~~read~~

These cases may be unconvincing, since there is still controversy surrounding the question of whether there is really deletion under a condition of identity in these constructions. Still there are arguments that deletion gaps are not mere gaps, but are structured in the way that their antecedents are. For example we have seen that relative clause gaps must occur in each conjunct of a coordinate structure, shown in (4a,b). (4c) shows that a VP ellipsis gap satisfies this condition, which would be the case on the structure in (4d).

(4) a. a man John didn't recognize t but Bill did recognize t

  b. *a man John didn't recognize Sam but Bill did recognize t

    c. a man John didn't recognize but Bill did

    d. a man John didn't recognize t but Bill did ~~recognize t~~.

One might argue here that we have derived (4c) just by deleting *recognize* from (4d) leaving the trace, which is independently unpronounced. But this is implausible for at least two reasons. First we cannot independently delete the second verb leaving the object:

(5)   *?John didn't recognize Sam but Bill did Frank

Second, a complex direct object properly containing the relative clause gap cannot remain:

(6)   a. John doesn't have a picture of Marilyn but Bill does have
        a picture of Madonna

      b. *John doesn't have a picture of Marilyn but Bill does a
        picture of Madonna

      c. an actress who John doesn't have a picture of t but Bill
        does ~~have a picture of t~~

      d. *an actress who John doesn't have a picture of t but Bill
        does ~~have~~ a picture of t

For further analysis see Haïk (1987) and Fiengo and May (1995).

    Less problematic are cases in which an expression must be repeated. We present examples from several languages, as they have not played a prominent role in generative grammar. First, Culy (1985) discusses productively formed nominals of the form Noun o Noun in Bambara, where the Nouns flanking the particle o must be identical:

(7)   a. wulu o   wulu
        dog PRT dog

        'whatever dog'

      b. wulu-filèla
        dog-watcher

        'dog watcher'

      c. wulu-filèla   o wulu-filèla
        dog-watcher o dog-watcher

        'whichever dog watcher'

      d. wulu-filèla-filèla   o wulu-filèla-filèla
        dog-watcher-watcher o dog-watcher-watcher

        'whichever watcher of dog watchers'

Interestingly Malagasy (Austronesian; Madagascar) presents a class of copying expressions with comparable meanings. Essentially any interrogative constituent can occur as X in *na X na X*, yielding meanings like whoever, whatever, whenever, wherever, however, whichever student, whatever book,... The phrases on the right of the *na*'s must be identical.

(8) a. Iza no hitanao?
who FOC seen+by+you

'Who did you see?'

b. Na iza na iza hitanao lazao azy mba hiandry ahy
or who or who seen-by-you tell him prt fut-wait me

'Whoever you see, tell him please to wait for me'

c. Na mpianatra iza na mpianatra iza hitanao,...
or student who or student who seen-by-you

'Whichever student you see,...'

d. Ny ratsy vitantsika na tamin'iza na tamin'iza dia
the bad done-by-us or past-to'who or past-to'who PRT
mbola hanontaniana antsika (Rajemisa-Raolison 1971)
still asked us

'The evil done by us to whoever we still will have to pay for'

Also Malagasy intensifies adjectives by copying the adjective on either side of the particle *dia*:

(9) a. Tsara izany
good that

'That's good'

b. Tsara dia tsara izany
good prt good that

'That's very good'

A third class of cases are the A-not-A form of Yes-No questions in Chinese (Stabler 2004), as in (10), where (*,) indicates that a pause is not really acceptable:

(10) a. Zhangsan ai da lanqiu (*,) bu ai da lanqiu
Zhangsan like play basketball (*,) not like play basketball

'Does Zhansan like to play basketball?'

b. Zhangsan ai   da   (*,) bu ai   a   lanqiu
   Zhangsan like play (*,) not like play basketball

'Does Zhangsan like to play basketball?'

We note that if the disjuncts in (10) are not identical, for example replacing *lanqiu* 'basketball' by *paiqiu* 'volleyball', then a pause between
the disjuncts is required, and the resulting expression is not understood
as a question. See Radzinski (1990) and Huang (1991) for further discussion.

English seems poor in such expressions, though Manaster-Ramer
(1986) notes the "X or not X" copy construction:

(11) Politically correct or not politically correct, I'm going to do it
      anyway.

Lastly, as noted earlier, a variety of coordinate and comparative expressions do not naturally accept repetitions, that is, they require non-
identity of strings:

(12)   a. neither every student nor every teacher came to the party

       b. *?neither every student nor every student came to the party

(13)   a. more students than teachers came to the party

       b. *?more students than students came to the party.

These data support that identity and non-identity of string components
of expressions is part of natural language structure. So we take the
notion of substitution that is appropriate here to be one that respects
these logical properties of strings:

Definition 22 For u a sequence of length n, $u^{[s\leftrightarrow t]}$ is that sequence of
length n given by:

$$(u^{[s\leftrightarrow t]})_i =_{df} \begin{cases} s & \text{if } u_i = t \\ t & \text{if } u_i = s, \text{ for all } 1 \leq i \leq n \\ u_i & \text{otherwise} \end{cases}$$

When K is a set of sequences, $K^{[s\leftrightarrow t]} =_{df} \{u^{[s\leftrightarrow t]} \mid u \in K\}$.

So $^{[s\leftrightarrow t]}$ simultaneously replaces all s coordinates by t and all t coordinates by s. It preserves distinctness and identity of expressions, preserving thereby any structure building operations which require such conditions. And it provides the relevant notion of substitution to support
the following plausible universal constraint on grammatical categories
in natural languages:

Axiom 1 If Domain(F) = Domain(F)$^{[s\leftrightarrow t]}$ all F $\in$ Rule$_G$ then Cat(s) = Cat(t).

Axiom 1 is a kind of economy condition. It says that we don't distinguish categories of expression unless the generating functions force us to. It is easy to make up G which fail Axiom 1, but their category systems are misleadingly prolific, using distinct category names for expressions with the same distribution. Axiom 1 also underscores that the role of categories is to constrain what the structure building functions apply to.

But what about the converse of Axiom 1? Here we still find two problems. The first is cooccurrence restrictions of the sort we have seen between *both* and *and*, *either* and *or* and *neither* and *nor*. In Eng, *both*, *either*, and *neither* were introduced syncategorematically as part of the value of the function. But are they syncategorematic in English? They do occur alone, as in *both students, either student*, and *neither student (can do it)*. If we assign them a category, say LC for "Left Conjunct" then we could treat Coord as a four place function:

Domain				Coord	Value
both	and	s	t		both$^\frown$s$^\frown$and$^\frown$t
LC	IC	A	A	$\longmapsto$	A
either	or	s	t		either$^\frown$s$^\frown$or$^\frown$t
LC	IC	A	A	$\longmapsto$	A
neither	nor	s	t		neither$^\frown$s$^\frown$nor$^\frown$t
LC	IC	A	A	$\longmapsto$	A

But now the cooccurrence restrictions reemerge: If we replace (and, IC) with (or, IC) in Domain(Coord) we would have to simultaneously replace (both, LC) with (either, LC).

However, in all the instances where these sorts of cooccurrence restrictrions have arisen at least one of the terms is drawn from a small closed class, {and, or, nor} in the case of coordination, {than, as} in the case of comparatives, as in *(many) more boys than girls, (twice) as many boys as girls*, etc. So it seems natural to introduce one item syncategorematically rather than positing a cooccurrence restriction between independent categories.

But there is a second, more significant, problem with (1). Recall that in Eng$_{RC}$ we placed a variety of conditions on elements such as (t, NP[NP]) and (who, NP[wh]). The latter blocks "relativizers" such as **with who*, in favor of *with whom*. The former allows 14 but blocks 15:

(14)   the senator who John interviewed every friend of t and some colleague of t

(15) *the senator who John interviewed t and some colleague of t.

But so far, the significant cases of this sort are ones in which the items with restricted distribution are lexical. So we posit (cautiously):

Axiom 2 For some n, for all $s, t \in L_G - Lex_n$,

$$Cat(s) = Cat(t) \Rightarrow \text{ for all } F \in Rule_G, Domain(F) = Domain(F)^{[s \leftrightarrow t]}.$$

Axiom 2 says that beyond a certain complexity level syntactic behavior is regular, at least to the extent that we cannot block tuples from Domain(F) based solely on their string coordinates. (See the Bounded Structure Theorem below for a candidate for this level). Note that Axiom 2 allows that the value of an F vary with the string: F might place a short NP string preverbally, and long one postverbally for example. Even so Axiom 2 is less secure than Axiom 1, its full converse, and it will force us to distinguish categories of expressions that some syntacticians identify, for example the bracketed constituents in (16a,b):

(16) a. Mary thinks [that Sue took the exam]

  b. the exam [which Sue took t]

But the constituent in (16b) contains an NP gap and in our relative clause grammar Eng_{RC} expressions with NP gaps have a different category, C[NP] than otherwise similar ones, C, without a gap. This is reasonable as they have a different distribution. Moreover for every n we can find expressions in $L_G - Lex_n$ with NP gaps, so to satisfy Axiom 2 these categories must be different. This seems to say that whenever expressions differ just in that one has an unresolved unbounded dependency and the other doesn't they they should have different categories.

Note that the right side of Axiom 2 determines a natural equivalence relation:

Definition 23 For all $F \in Rule$, $s =_F t$ iff $Domain(F) = Domain(F)^{[s \leftrightarrow t]}$. Generalizing, $s =_{Rule} t$ iff for all $F \in Rule$, $s =_F t$ is also an equivalence relation (which may fall short of being a congruence).

Theorem 13 *For all* $F \in Rule$, $=_F$ *is invariant, as is* $=_{Rule}$

Restated, Axiom 1 says that if $s =_{Rule} t$ then $Cat(s) = Cat(t)$. Axiom 2 is a limited converse when s and t are drawn from beyond a certain complexity level.

4.2 A language with agreement

Are the PH(C) invariant? In the grammars we have so far presented to model aspects of natural languages the PH(C) have all been invariant. However Span (Little Spanish) below, designed to model plain vanilla gender agreement between Nouns and Adjectives and Nouns and Dets (Determiners), allows that some automorphisms do not fix all the PH(C). This leads us to distinguish among automorphisms according as they are stable or not. The h in Aut$_{Span}$ which fail to fix some PH(C) are all unstable. And we take as axiomatic that all PH(C) are stable, in the sense of being fixed by all stable automorphisms.

Span=$\langle$V, Cat, Lex, Rule$\rangle$, a grammar for Little Spanish:

V:	man, woman, obstetrician, doctor, -a, -o, gentle, intelligent, every, some, very, moderately
Cat:	Nm, Nf, A, Am, Af, Amod, NPm, NPf, Agrm, Agrf D, Dm, Df
Lex:	Nm man, doctor
	Nf woman, obstetrician
	A gentle, intelligent
	D every, some
	Agrm -o
	Agrf -a
	Amod very, moderately
Rule:	GM (gender marking), Merge.

The functions in Rule are defined as follows:

Domain	GM	Value	Conditions
s t		s$^\frown$t	
C Agrm	$\longmapsto$	Cm	C $\in$ {D, A}
s t		s$^\frown$t	
C Agrf	$\longmapsto$	Cf	C $\in$ {D, A}

Domain	Merge	Value	Conditions
s t		s$^\frown$t	
Ax Nx	$\longmapsto$	Nx	x $\in$ {m, f}
s t		s$^\frown$t	
Dx Nx	$\longmapsto$	NPx	x $\in$ {m, f}
s t		s$^\frown$t	
Amod Ax	$\longmapsto$	Ax	x $\in$ {m, f}

With this grammar, we have derivations like this:

Merge:(every -a very intelligent -a obstetrician, NPf)

GM:(every -a, Df)   Merge:(very intelligent -a obstetrician, Nf)

(every, D)   (-a, Agrf)   Merge:(very intelligent -a, Af)   (obstetrician, Nf)

(very, Amod)   GM:(intelligent -a, Af)

(intelligent, A)   (-a, Agrf)

Merge:(some -o very gentle -o doctor, NPm)

GM:(some -o, Dm)   Merge:(very gentle -o doctor, Nm)

(some, D)   (-o, Agrm)   Merge:(very gentle -o, Am)   (doctor, Nm)

(very, Amod)   GM:(gentle -o, Am)

(gentle, A)   (-o, Agrm)

4.2.1 Some invariants of Span

Fact 17 Lex *is invariant (since* Range(GM) *and* Domain(Merge) *do not intersect* Lex*).*

Fact 18 PH(C) *is invariant for* C $\in$ {A, D, Agrm, Agrf, Amod}. *Note that each of these* PH(C) *coincides with* Lex(C), *since no expressions in these* PH(C) *are derived by GM or Merge.*

Fact 19 *Span is category functional (see U5 on page 28): the category of any derived expression is a function of the categories of the arguments of the function that derived it.*

Fact 20 *The generating functions (GM, Merge) are one to one and have disjoint ranges.*

So given Fact 17 and Fact 20, Span is unambiguous (in the sense defined on page 18).

Fact 21 *(Category Integrity) The sameness of category relation is invariant:*

Cat(s) = Cat(t) $\Rightarrow$ for all automorphisms h, Cat(h(s)) = Cat(h(t)).

Fact 22 *There is an automorphism g of Span which interchanges* (-a, Agrf) *and* (-o, Agrm). *g also interchanges* PH(Nm) *with* PH(Nf), PH(Am) *with* PH(Af), PH(Dm) *with* PH(Df) *and* PH(NPm) *with* PH(NPf). *So g interchanges masculine and feminine expressions.*

Proof. Let g_0 be that permutation of Lex_0 which interchanges (-a, Agrf) and (-o, Agrm), (man, Nm) and (woman, Nf), (doctor, Nm) and (obstetrician, Nf), and fixes all other elements of Lex. Then let g be that automorphism of L_{Span} which extends g_0 so that $g(\text{GM}(s,t)) = \text{GM}(g(s), g(t))$ and $g(\text{Merge}(s,t)) = \text{Merge}(g(s), g(t))$. (See note 1 on page 133.) □

Fact 23 *An automorphism h which fixes* $(-a, \text{Agrf})$ *and* $(-o, \text{Agrm})$, *fixes all* $\text{Lex}(C)$ *and so by U5, all* $\text{PH}(C)$.

4.2.2 Categorial symmetry and stable automorphisms

The possibility of category changing automorphisms in Span reveals a categorial symmetry present, in principle, in natural language. Noun classes partition a subset of the expressions in such a way that the blocks of the partition could be structurally interchanged. This possibility is "unstable" in the sense that many "minor" changes in the language – ones we agree are insignificant – result in languages in which these blocks cannot be interchanged. For example, in Span the existence of a category changing automorphism requires that the number of lexical Nm's and Nf's be the same. Add one more feminine N, (poet, Nf), with no compensating addition to the Nm's and we lose the possibility of interchanging expressions of different categories.

Ignoring this accidental possibility would be a mistake. A grammar with unequal numbers of lexical Nm's and Nf's could always be extended by adding new lexical items to one in which the numbers evened out again, permitting category changing automorphisms. And the ability to add new content words freely is a basic property of a natural language. More generally various types of allomorphy present a similar phenomenon. We might distinguish subcategories of NP in Korean according as their accusative marker was *-ul* or *-lul*. Then with matching cardinalities these two classes and the two accusative case markers could be interchanged by a structure map. In English we might distinguish classes of Nouns according to how their plural is formed: with /z/ as in *dog/dogs*, with /s/ as in *cat/cats*, with /əz/ in *judge/judges*, /f/ ⇒ /vz/ as in *leaf/leaves*, *-on* ⇒ *-a*, as in *phenomenon/phenomena*, no change as in *sheep* ⇒ *sheep*, etc.

We will treat agreement and allomorphy by distinguishing among automorphisms according as they remain stable under such changes. Informally, an automorphism is stable if it remains an automorphism after the addition of new expressions isomorphic to old ones. "New" means not inducing new derivations of expressions in the original language. (Thanks to Greg Kobele for this formulation, and thanks to Philippe Schlenker for the suggestion that we should treat allomorphy.)

Definition 24 For $G = \langle V, \text{Cat}, \text{Lex}, \text{Rule} \rangle$

a. For any finite $S \subseteq V \times \text{Cat}$, $G[S] =_{\text{df}} \langle V, \text{Cat}, \text{Lex} \cup S, \text{Rule} \rangle$.

And when no confusion will result, for any $s \in V \times \text{Cat}$, we write $G[s] =_{df} G[\{s\}]$.

b. G is *free for* expression $s \in V \times \text{Cat}$ iff

    i. for all $t \in L_{G[s]}$, if $t \in L_G$ then $\neg(s\text{CONt})$, and

    ii. for some $h \in \text{Aut}_{G[s]}$ and some $t \in \text{Lex}_G$, h interchanges s and t and fixes all other elements of $\text{Lex}_{G[s]}$.

c. G is *free for set* S iff for all $s \in S$, G is free for s and G[s] is free for $S - \{s\}$. (Note that all G are free for $\emptyset$.).

Condition (c) above entails that Span is not free for (gentle -o doctor, Nm) since that possible expression is a constituent of (in fact, it is identical to) an expression in L_{Span}. So (c) blocks adding as new lexical items expressions that are already in L_G.

Fact 24 *Span is free for* (poet, Nf).

Proof. (poet, Nf) is not a constituent of any $t \in L_{\text{Span}}$ since (i) it is not a constituent of any $t \in \text{Lex}_{\text{Span}}$ since it is not in Lex_{Span}, and (ii) it is not a constituent of any $v = \text{GM}(t, u)$ or $v = \text{Merge}(t, u)$ since if it were, *poet* would be a substring of string(v) since GM and Merge are concatenative, and a recursion proof on L_G shows that for all $v \in L_G$, *poet* is a not a coordinate of string(v).

    Define $h : L_{\text{Span}[(\text{poet},\text{Nf})]} \to L_{\text{Span}[(\text{poet},\text{Nf})]}$ as follows:

$$h(s, C) = (h'(s), C),$$

where h′ interchanges *poet* and *woman*, fixes all other lexical strings and extends to V^* coordinatewise. Prove that $h \in \text{Aut}_{G[(\text{poet},\text{Nf})]}$. □

And we now define:

Definition 25 1. $h \in \text{Aut}_G$ is *stable* iff h extends to an $h' \in \text{Aut}_{G[S]}$, for all finite S for which G is free. We write SAut_G for the stable automorphisms of G.

As before, we use "linguistic object" as a cover term for expressions, properties of expressions, relations between expressions and functions on expressions. A linguistic object over G is *stable* iff it is fixed by all stable automorphisms.

    Sometimes a stable object is referred to as a stable invariant, though this terminology suggests wrongly that the stable invariants are a subset of the invariants, whereas the inclusion goes just the other way. Since the stable automorphisms are a subset of Aut_G the objects fixed by all automorphisms are a subset of those fixed by all stable automorphisms.

Exercise 23 The FIX operator maps each $K \subseteq \text{Aut}_G$ to the set of objects fixed by all the $k \in K$. Show that when $K \subseteq K' \subseteq \text{Aut}_G$ then $\text{FIX}(K') \subseteq \text{FIX}(K)$.

Exercise 24 Exhibit a grammar Ger (Little German), like Span, but with three lexical noun classes Nm, Nf, Nn (masculine, feminine and neuter) and three agreement morphemes of categories Agrm, Agrf, and Agrn. Let Lex(Nm), Lex(Nf) and Lex(Nn) all have cardinality 3. Exhibit the five non-trivial permutations of the set of agreement markers and for each such permutation say for each noun class Nx which noun class Ny it gets mapped to. What is the minimum number of new nouns you can add so that each Lex(Nx) is fixed by all automorphisms of Ger?

(Recall that an n element set has n! permutations. So a three element set has $3! = 3 \cdot 2 \cdot 1 = 6$ permutations, of which the identity map is a trivial member.)

Fact 25 *If* $h \in \text{Aut}_{\text{Span}}$ *interchanges* $(\text{-}a, \text{Agrf})$ *and* $(\text{-}o, \text{Agrm})$ *then* h *is not stable.*

Proof. h as above must interchange Lex(Nm) and Lex(Nf) to preserve Domain(Merge). But adding s = (poet, Nf), for which Span is free, to Lex blocks this, since Lex(Nm) and Lex(Nf) have different numbers of members. So h can't extend to an automorphism of Span[(poet,Nf)], so h is not stable, as was to be shown. □

Corollary 14 *If* $h \in \text{Aut}_{\text{Span}}$ *is stable then* h *fixes* $(\text{-}a, \text{Agrf})$ *and* $(\text{-}o, \text{Agrm})$, *so it fixes all Lex(C), whence by U5 and category functionality, it fixes all PH(C).*

Conjecture 15 $h \in \text{Aut}_{\text{Span}}$ *is stable iff* h *fixes* $(\text{-}a, \text{Agrf})$ *and* $(\text{-}o, \text{Agrm})$.

Conjecture 16 *The category preserving automorphisms of Span are just the stable ones.*

Exercise 25 Exhibit a grammar in which some stable automorphisms fail to preserve category. (A trivial example suffices). This shows that Conjecture 16 does not hold for all G.

And we now adopt:

Axiom 3 (Category Stability) For all $C \in \text{Cat}_G$, PH(C) is stable, that is, fixed by all stable automorphisms.

For many purposes, of which Axiom 3 is an illustration, we modify our earlier linguistic generalizations replacing "automorphism" by "stable automorphism."

Definition 26 (revised from Lecture 1) The *grammatical constants* (formatives) of G are the lexical items fixed by all stable automorphisms. The *linguistic invariants* of G are those linguistic objects fixed by all stable automorphisms.

So the agreement markers in Span, (-a, Agrf), etc. are grammatical constants ("function words") even though they may fail to be fixed by all automorphisms. By Corollary 14 they are fixed by all stable automorphisms. Similarly for allomorphy (e.g. the two accusative markers *-ul, -lul* in Korean; or the two nominative markers *-i, -ka*, or the two topic markers *-un, -nun*). The important insight here is that what is to count as a grammatical property of a language does not vary with accidental properties, such as how many masculine nouns are in the lexicon.

In consequence we should study stable automorphisms carefully. The various generalizations in Lecture 1, U1-U10 remain valid replacing "automorphism" by "stable automorphism" since they all concerned objects fixed by all automorphisms, so in particular all stable automorphisms. And fundamental (though easily shown) in this regard is Theorem 18, as in proving objects to be invariant we have often relied on the group properties of automorphisms, especially closure under inverses. The proof is straightforward, but it may be helpful to see how it works. Even easier is Lemma 17:

Lemma 17 *Let G and G′ be grammars with the same V, Cat, and Rule, but* $\text{Lex}_G \subseteq \text{Lex}_{G'}$. *Then* $L_G \subseteq L_{G'}$.

Proof. Let $s \in L_G$. Then s is in the intersection of all the subsets of $V^* \times Cat$ which are closed with respect to all the $F \in \text{Rule}$ and which include Lex_G. This set contains all those that include $\text{Lex}_{G'}$ since $\text{Lex}_G \subseteq \text{Lex}_{G'}$. Hence s is in their intersection, that is, $s \in L_{G'}$. □

Theorem 18 *(Stable Subgroup Theorem) For any G,* SAut_G *forms a subgroup of* Aut_G.

Proof.

i. Clearly $\text{id}_G \in \text{SAut}_G$, since it extends to $\text{id}_{G[S]}$, any $S \subseteq V \times \text{Cat}$.

ii. We show that SAut_G is closed under function composition, ∘. Let $g, h \in \text{SAut}_G$, let S be arbitrary with G free for S. Let g′ and h′ be extensions of g and h respectively to G[S]. Then $g' \circ h' \in \text{Aut}_{G[S]}$ and for all $u \in L_G \subseteq L_{G[S]}$ we have:

$$
\begin{aligned}
(g' \circ h')(u) &= g'(h'(u)) \\
&= g'(h(u)) && \text{since } h' \text{ extends } h \\
&= g(h(u)) && \text{since } g' \text{ extends } g \\
&= (g \circ h)(u)
\end{aligned}
$$

whence $g' \circ h'$ extends $g \circ h$, so this latter is in SAut_G.

iii. $\mathrm{SAut_G}$ is closed under inverses. Letting $h \in \mathrm{SAut_G}$, we show $h^{-1} \in \mathrm{SAut_G}$. Let S arbitrary with G free for S. Let h extend to $h' \in \mathrm{Aut_{G[S]}}$. Then for $w \in \mathrm{L_G}$,

$$\begin{aligned}
h^{-1}(w) = u \quad &\text{iff } w = h(u) &&\text{def inverse} \\
&\text{iff } w = h'(u) &&h' \text{ extends } h \\
&\text{iff } h'^{-1}(w) = u &&\text{def inverse}
\end{aligned}$$

Thus h'^{-1} extends h^{-1}, whence $\mathrm{SAut_G}$ is a subgroup of $\mathrm{Aut_G}$.

$\square$

Corollary 19 *From the proof above we see that the map ' sending each stable automorphism h to an extension h' in* $\mathrm{Aut_{G[S]}}$ *is a homomorphism.from* $\mathrm{Aut_G}$ *to* $\mathrm{Aut_{G[S]}}$.

Corollary 20 *Given Axiom 3, stable automorphisms preserve sameness of category:*

$$\mathrm{Cat}(s) = \mathrm{Cat}(t) \Rightarrow \mathrm{Cat}(h(s)) = \mathrm{Cat}(h(t)) \text{ for h stable,}$$

but automorphisms in general may fail to do so.

No Splitting? In Span all automorphisms preserve sameness of category, even those that change category. And this might seem a reasonable requirement on categories in general. It would guarantee that expressions of the same category cannot be divided among two or more different categories preserving structure. But there are reasons to be cautious about this.

Default Coordination. Conjoining expressions in different gender classes is problematic. See Corbett (1991, Ch.9) for extensive discussion. Some languages like Chichewa (Mchombo 2000, p.185) disallow it. In others like Shona (Hawkinson and Hyman 1974) the verb agrees with the class of the higher conjunct on some Chain of Being hierarchy (e.g. human > animate non-human > inanimate).[1] A language may show agreement with the closest conjunct, as in Tamazight, Berber (Penchoen 1973, p.83). And still others have recourse to a default value, as in Hebrew and French when all conjuncts are third person. A coordination of two feminine NPs, such as *Marie et Isabelle*, is feminine plural, as shown by the agreements it triggers: *Marie et Isabelle sont heureuses* (fem.pl) 'Mary and Isabelle are happy'. But if the conjuncts differ in gender then the entire conjunction takes a default value, masculine (plural): *Marie et Philippe sont heureux* (m.pl). Below we add default agreement to Span; the resulting grammar Span' violates No Splitting. But when the grammar is further enriched with agreement between subjects and verbs all PH(C) are again invariant.

Define Span' as the grammar formed from Span by:

i. Adding *and* to V and (and, CONJ) to Lex.

ii. Adding Coord to Rule as follows,

Domain			Coord	Value	Conditions
and	s	t	$\longmapsto$	s $\frown$and$\frown$t	$x \neq y \in \{m, f\}$
CONJ	NPx	NPy		NPm	
and	s	t	$\longmapsto$	s $\frown$and$\frown$t	$x \in \{m, f\}$
CONJ	NPx	NPx		NPx	

Fact 26 *Span' fails No Splitting for all category changing automorphisms h.*

Both *every-o man* and *some-a woman and every-o man* are masculine NPs, the second by default, being the conjunction of a feminine NP with a masculine one. A category changing automorphism maps *every-o man* to a feminine NP but the complex one to a conjunction of a feminine NP and a masculine one, so the whole thing remains masculine. So a category changing automorphism in Span does not even preserve sameness of category.

But adding Subject-Verb Agreement forces fixity of all PH(C) (Benjamin George, p.c.). Add to Lex (laugha, VPf) and (crya, VPf), and (laugho, VPm) and (cryo, VPm). Extend Merge to map pairs $\langle (s, NPx), (t, VPx) \rangle$ to (s$\frown$t, S) when $x \in \{m, f\}$. The resulting grammar has no automorphisms which change category. For every $s = (u, VPm) \in L_G$,

$\langle (\text{every man -o}, NPm), s \rangle \in$ Domain(Merge), and
$\langle (\text{some woman -a and every man -o}, NPm), s \rangle \in$ Domain(Merge),

but the images of these two NPs have different categories under a category changing Automorphism h, so one of the resulting pairs will fail to be in Domain(Merge).

The fact that Subject-Verb agreement in Span' "filters out" the effects of default agreement forcing the automorphisms to fix gender class is, we feel, not accidental. The rich documentation in Corbett (1991) supports that the primary role of gender classes in a grammar is to license agreement. Corbett presents an extensive range of types of gender classes (noun classes) in natural languages, and we find no clear cases of a gender system with no form of agreement (Det or Adj agreement with the nouns, Predicate phrase agreement or pronoun/demonstrative agreement with the NPs built from the nouns,...). "...the determining criterion of gender is agreement...Saying that a language has three genders implies that there are three classes of nouns which can be distinguished syntactically by the agreements they take" (Corbett 1991, p.4). We propose as universal:

(**Agreement Invariance**)   Agreement classes are stable invariants.

Note that before this could be taken as an axiom or shown to follow from other axioms we would need a formal, language independent, definition of agreement. The form such a definition should take is not obvious, surprisingly, as agreement is a well recognized phenomenon in traditional grammar as well as generative grammar. Such a definition would have to build on a notion of semantic equivalence, to show, for example, that the bracketed constituents in (17a,b) are formally different ways of expressing the same property; and it would have to invoke a notion of substitution, to say that replacing the subject of (17a) by that of (17b) forces a change in agreement:

(17)   a.   Le   garçon est heureux
            The boy   is   happy   (m.sg.)

       b.   La   jeune fille est heureuse
            The young girl is   happy   (f.sg)

Moreover, internal to agreement, Corbett forces us to consider controller vs. target genders, subgenders, inquorate genders, defective nouns, and more. And externally, even the range of the phenomena to be covered is not pretheoretically clear: Should NPs like *no student, at most two students*, that license negative polarity items, as in *No one saw anything at all* vs. **Someone saw anything at all* constitute an agreement class separate from that of NPs that do not license such items? How should we distinguish agreement from more general "cooccurrence restrictions"?, etc. The working definition "systematic covariance" used by Corbett is correct but insufficiently formal to be taken as axiomatic. Still, we are clear about many cases of agreement and our proposed (Agreement Invariance) universal is helpful in identifying the agreement classes in some non-obvious cases. We consider in this regard a problem from Romanian, taken from Corbett (1991, Ch.6) who references the extensive discussion by other grammarians as well.

Traditional grammars of Romanian (Nandris 1969, Seiver 1953) distinguish two "pure" genders: masculine, such as *bărbat* 'man', and feminine *fată* 'girl'. They differ in agreements in two ways: they take different forms of the definite article in the singular and in the plural, and they trigger different forms of predicate adjectives, also in the singular and the plural:

(18)   a. bărbatul e bun
            man-the is good (m.sg.)

        b. fata   e bună
            girl-the is good (f.sg.)

(19)   a. bărbaţii sînt buni
            men-the are good (m.pl)

        b. fetele   sînt bune
            girls-the are good (f.pl)

However there are nouns of "mixed" gender, such as *scaun* 'chair', which trigger masculine forms of the definite article and predicate adjective in the singular and feminine ones in the plural:

(20)   a. scaunul e bun
            chair-the is good (m.sg)

        b. scaunele sînt bune
            chairs-the are good (f.pl)

The problem: how many gender classes does Romanian have? Corbett opts for three on the grounds that there are three distinct agreement patterns. But others have opted for two, claiming that the mixed cases are nouns whose gender agreement is always one of the two, the choice conditioned by context, as there is no form of article or predicate adjective that is peculiar to the mixed nouns. Absent a rigorous definition of agreement and gender class we cannot decide this issue. But support for Corbett's three class approach can be given in terms of (Agreement Invariance).

    It would be easy of course to present a model with three noun classes, Nmasc, Nfem, Nmixed, which cooccur with different articles and adjectives conditioned by number. But we would like to be able to say more than that the three class analysis is consistent (which was never in doubt, in any event). So let us try to make up a model with just two genders, Nm and Nf, and put the mixed nouns in both genders, designing the Merge rule so that we obtain the right cooccurrence relations.

    Rom=$\langle V, \text{Cat}, \text{Lex}, \text{Rule} \rangle$, a grammar for Little Romanian:

V: man, chair, girl, the.m, the.f, the.pl.m, the.pl.f

Cat: Nm, Nf, Det[sg.m], Det[sg.f], Det[pl.m], Det[pl.f],
Pred[sg.m], Pred[sg.f], Pred[pl.m], Pred[pl.f]

Lex:

Nm	chair,boy,...
Nf	chair,woman,...
Pred[sg.m]	is.good-ø
Pred[sg.f]	is.good-ă
Pred[pl.m]	is.good-i
Pred[pl.f]	is.good-e

Rule: Merge, defined as follows.

Domain		Merge	Value	Conditions
the.m	s		s⌢the.m	
Det[sg.m]	Nm	⟼	NP[sg.m]	none
the.f	s		s⌢the.f	
Det[sg.f]	Nf	⟼	NP[sg.f]	$s \notin$ string(PH(Nm))
the.pl.m	s		s⌢the.pl.m	
Det[pl.m]	Nm	⟼	NP[pl.m]	$s \notin$ string(PH(Nf))
the.pl.f	s		s⌢the.pl.f	
Det[pl.f]	Nf	⟼	NP[pl.f]	none
s	t		s⌢t	
NP[sg.m]	Pred[sg.m]	⟼	S	none
s	t		s⌢t	
NP[sg.f]	Pred[sg.f]	⟼	S	none
s	t		s⌢t	
NP[pl.m]	Pred[pl.m]	⟼	S	none
s	t		s⌢t	
NP[pl.f]	Pred[pl.f]	⟼	S	none

Definition 27 For all $(s, \text{Nm}) \in Lex$, (s, Nm) is a *pure* Nm iff $(s, \text{Nf}) \notin Lex$; otherwise (s, Nm) is *mixed*.

And for all $(s, \text{Nf}) \in Lex$, (s, Nf) is a *pure* Nf iff $(s, \text{Nm}) \notin Lex$; otherwise (s, Nf) is *mixed*.

Now, even though Rom only distinguishes two genders (and two numbers) in its category system, we claim that:

Fact 27 *In* Lex_{Rom}, *the set of pure Nms, the set of pure Nfs, and the mixed Ns are three pairwise disjoint stable invariants.*

Thus no stable automorphism can map (chair, Nm) or (chair, Nf) to a pure Nm or a pure Nf, and pure Nm's and pure Nf's cannot be interchanged by a stable automorphism. Thus even though the grammar was designed to have just two gender categories it still has three stable automorphism classes of lexical nouns. The reasoning which supports this is as follows:

Proof. First, Lex is invariant since it does not intersect Range(Merge). Second, the pure Nms and the pure Nfs in Lex cannot be interchanged by a stable automorphism here for the same reason as in Span: the grammar is free for new lexical Nm's and Nf's, so just add enough of one so that the two lexical classes have different cardinalities thereby blocking a bijection between them.

Now, suppose, leading to a contradiction, that some automorphism h maps some mixed (s, Nm) to a pure Nf. Then from the first and fourth clauses of definition of Merge, h maps $(the.m, Det[sg, m])$ either to $(the.f, Det[sg, f])$ or to $(the.pl.f, Det[pl.f])$. In the first case, since $\langle(the.m, Det[sg.m]), (man, Nm)\rangle \in Domain(Merge)$ it must map (man, Nm) to some (t, Nf), which it cannot do as we saw above. Similarly in the second case. The analogous arguments hold if an automorphism were to map a mixed (s, Nf) to a pure Nm, completing the proof. $\square$

Note that we established our result just by looking at the choice of article, but a similar conclusion would follow from consideration of predicate agreement. We consider then that (Agreement Invariance) gives an objective reason for supporting Corbett's analysis in which Romanian has three gender classes, since even when we attempt to code a system with just two genders we must still distinguish three stable automorphism classes.

There is one other constraint on the role of categories that has already been mentioned above:

Axiom 4 (Category Functionality) Grammars of natural languages are category functional.

Axiom 4, satisfied by all the model grammars considered so far, disallows that the category of a derived expression could vary with the string coordinates of its arguments holding their categories fixed. So far the closest thing to a counterexample we have found concerns grammatical formatives such as the case markers in Korean. In our grammar we assigned them different categories, Kn and Ka. They combine with NPs to form expressions in different categories, KPn and KPa, so assigning them the same category would have violated Axiom 4.

This concludes our discussion of axioms which specifically concern categories. We turn now to ones that concern more directly the kinds of recursion in natural languages.

4.3 Constraints on recursion

Axiom 5 (Finite Generators) Lex is finite

The motivation for this common assumption is familiar. Lex_G is a set of expressions in general not derived by rule. We can memorize the form and meaning of finitely many unrelated items, but not infinitely many. In the cases where a linguist has proposed a "lexical" rule that would iterate yielding infinitely many expressions we would just include that rule in Rule and items generated by n iterations would be in Lex_n, not $Lex_0 = Lex.$[2] This intuition is not disturbed by approaches that invoke infinitely many "variables" or indexed gaps. Such have their interpretations determined "on line" as part of the recursive interpretative mechanism. (And even here it is unclear that we need more than a few distinct variables).

It is less motivated to require that Cat and Rule be finite. It is often at least easier to define the set of categories and rules in such way that there are infinitely many. For example in Categorial Grammar Cat is normally infinite. Still, plausible is

Axiom 6 (Useful Categories) $\{C \in Cat_G | PH(C) \neq \emptyset\}$ is finite.

Thus for some n, there are no expressions of new categories in Lex_m, any $m > n$. So given L_G infinite, some $PH(C)$ must be infinite. Note that Axiom 6 blocks unbounded Lifting in Categorial Grammar.

Axiom 5 has one non-obvious consequence, suggested to us by Marcus Kracht: For a large natural class of grammars it tells us that the structure of expressions in general is determinable on the basis of the structure of expressions of limited derivational depth. The theorem is technical in appearance, so let us focus first on the phenomenon it describes. The underlying question we are asking is "How much can you tell about the structure of expressions in general just by looking at Lex_0? Lex_1?... Lex_n? How far up the complexity hierarchy must we go to find a representative sample of the expressions in L_G? Let us take Span' as an example:

$Lex_0 = Lex$

$Lex_1 = Lex_0 +$ the gender marked adjectives and determiners:
   $(\text{gentle -o}, Am), (\text{every -a}, Df),$ etc.

$Lex_2 = Lex_1 +$ modified Ns and As, and basic NPs:
   $(\text{gentle -o doctor}, Nm), (\text{very gentle -o}, Am), \ldots$

$Lex_3 = Lex_2+$
   $(\text{every -o man and some -a woman}, NPm), \ldots$

$Lex_4 = Lex_3+$
   $(\text{every -o very gentle -o doctor}, NPm), \ldots$

So notice that no expressions in Lex_1 (and hence Lex_0) are created by Merge, which doesn't become active until Lex_2. And at this level Coord has still not created anything. It only becomes active in Lex_3, with conjunctions of NPs. In fact every lexical item that occurs in a derived expression in $L_{Span'}$ occurs in one in Lex_3, and every generating function (CM, Merge, Coord) can apply to some tuples in Lex_3. However we only get full NPs with adverbially modified adjectives in Lex_4. So we might feel that Lex_4 gives us a representative sample of the structure types in $L_{Span'}$. But how to say this precisely?

Here is one way. Given a grammar G, pick a level Lex_n and think of it as a language. The structure of its expressions is determined by its automorphisms - the bijections from Lex_n to Lex_n which fix the domains of the generating functions restricted to Lex_n, and which commute with them. Call such functions (defined below) *partial automorphisms*. They include all the real automorphisms restricted to Lex_n, but typically include much else besides. If n is chosen small enough not all the generating functions are active on Lex_n and so there will be sets of tuples that need not be fixed by the partial automorphisms.

For example, consider Lex_0 in Span'. The only generating function that applies to tuples in Lex_0 is GM, Gender Marking. So a partial automorphism h_0 of Lex_0 is just a bijection of Lex_0 which fixes the domain of GM, which just consists of pairs $\langle s, t \rangle$ where t is an Agrx and s is an A (Adjective) or a D (Determiner). So aside from being a bijection we know that h_0 can't map As or Ds to Nm's for example, though it could interchange As and Ds preserving Domain(GM). The map k_0 which interchanges (man, Nm) and (woman, Nf) and fixes everything else in Lex_0 is a partial automorphism of Lex_0. So also of course are the real automorphisms of Span' restricted to Lex_0. In this sense the partial automorphisms of Lex_0 include all the real automorphisms and much else - pseudo-automorphisms - besides.

Now as we move to Lex_1 two new aspects of structure come into play. First, Merge applies to some tuples $\langle s, t \rangle$, such as

$$\langle (\text{gentle -o, Am}), (\text{doctor, Nm}) \rangle,$$

so the set of such pairs must be fixed by any automorphism h_1 of Lex_1. This tells us that Nm's can't be mapped to Amod's preserving Domain(Merge) on Lex_1, but it tells us something of much greater interest: the pseudo-automorphism k_0 above does not extend to an automorphism of Lex_1. The reason is that it maps (doctor, Nm) to itself and therefore must map Am's to Am's to preserve Domain(Merge). But k_0 also maps (man, Nm) to (woman, Nf), whence to preserve Domain(Merge) it would have to map Am's, such as (gentle -o, Am) to

Af's, which we've just seen it can't do. So any partial automorphism h_1 of Lex_1 must treat lexical Nm's (and lexical Nf's) uniformly, mapping them all to Nm's or all to Nf's, but not splitting them.

A second new structural fact about Lex_1 is that the values GM assigns to pairs from Lex_0 lie in Lex_1. So the set of triples $\langle s, t, u \rangle$ where s is an A or a D, t an Agrf or Agrm, and u an Am, Af, Dm, or Df must be fixed by any partial automorphism h_1 of Lex_1.

In this way then, starting with the automorphisms of Lex_0 and moving up the complexity hierarchy we increasingly eliminate pseudo-automorphisms until we reach a level n at which the only automorphisms of Lex_n are the automorphisms of G restricted to Lex_n. All pseudo-automorphisms are eliminated. In this sense the structures (invariants) of G are determined by the structures on Lex_n. This number n will be called the "structure point" of G. Theorem 21 below guarantees that grammars meeting certain very general conditions have a structure point.

To state the theorem precisely we first define the set Aut_n of partial automorphisms of depth n. For $F \in Rule$, write F_n for $F \upharpoonright Lex_n$.

Definition 28 $h \in Aut_n$ iff

  i. h is a bijection: $Lex_n \rightarrow Lex_n$, and

  ii. h fixes $Domain(F_n)$, all $F \in Rule$, and

  iii. if $n > 0$, $h(F_n(t)) = F_n(h(t))$, all $t \in Lex_{n-1}^* \cap Domain(F)$

Note that for each $h \in Aut_G$, $h \upharpoonright Lex_n$ is in Aut_n. But Aut_n may contain other functions, namely the pseudo-automorphisms, mentioned above.

Theorem 21 *(Bounded Structure) If* Lex *is finite and for all* F, $Lex \cap Range(F) = \emptyset$, *then for some n, the set of partial automorphisms on* Lex_n *is exactly the set of automorphisms of G restricted to* Lex_n.

Proof provided in Appendix A.

Definition 29 If n is the least such that $Aut_n = Aut_G \upharpoonright Lex_n$ then n is called the *structure point* of G and noted nG. If no such n exists set $nG = \infty$.

For each $F \in Rule$, if n is least such that tuples of elements of Lex_n lie in $Domain(F)$ then n is the *start point* of F, noted nF. If no such n exists we set $nF = \infty$.

Theorem 21 tells us that there is a finite bound on the derivational depth of expressions you need consider to determine the automorphisms, and in this sense, the structure, of G. If Rule itself is finite then Aut_G is determinable on the basis of a finite sample of expressions. A grammar G which lacked a structure point, $nG = \infty$, would be "intractable." It would mean that no matter what complexity level of expressions you considered, say $n = 10^{10}$, you could always find yet more complex ones with structural properties not derivable from those you had already had. This seems implausible, so we might consider taking as axiomatic that natural language grammars have a structure point. But given Axiom 5 "Lex is finite," the existence of a structure point follows for all G in which no derived expressions are in Lex. And Axiom 9, Foundation, introduced below, guarantees that we can drop finitely many derived elements of Lex without changing L_G or Aut_G (Theorem 25). Thus our other axioms essentially guarantee the antecedent of Theorem 21.

Exercise 26 What is the structure point of Span'? Can you prove it?

Sleeper functions? How far up the complexity hierarchy can the structure point be? Note that it is possible that some $nF = \infty$. F is defined on $V^* \times Cat$. F might be a very non-trivial function with no expressions in any Lex_n in its domain, so a user of L_G would have no reason to suspect its existence. Call such an F a *deep sleeper*. One might want to rule out deep sleepers axiomatically, but it is hard to find empirical evidence that they don't exist. In fact we can start to imagine cases where we might want them. Perhaps the grammar of some natural language has some very specific conditions on its generating functions which make the domains of another function H empty, even though H is productive in other natural languages. So we might want to say that all G for natural languages have an H type function, but in some G its application is vacuous due to preemption by other more specific functions.

A case we are more inclined to rule out, but do not know how to formulate insightfully, are *shallow sleepers*. Imagine a G with $nF \leq 10$ for all $F \in Rule$ except one, F', with $nF' = 100$. So most functions apply gleefully at Lex_{10}, iterating and feeding each other, creating derived expressions in $Lex_{11}, Lex_{12}, \ldots$ and then at Lex_{100} F' suddenly applies creating a new type of structure. Users of L_G could say a lot with no reason to suspect the existence of F' until a certain quite high complexity level. So it would be possible to be an apparently competent speaker without ever knowing F' as long as you didn't exceed complexity level 99. This seems implausible for a grammar of a natural language, but just how shallow can a sleeper be before the grammar becomes plausible? Rather than pontificate here we should study the competence of speakers on complex expressions. Generative grammarians tend to accept that children become competent in their native language very quickly, but perhaps there are aspects of competence that only show up in more complex expressions that young children haven't yet mastered. Huttenlocher et al. (2002) is suggestive in this regard.

We turn now to our first attempt to characterize the type of recursion mechanisms natural languages present.

Definition 30 For $c = \langle C_1, \ldots, C_n \rangle \in \mathrm{Cat_G}^n$, and for every positive integer k, we define $k \cdot c$ by:

$$1 \cdot c = c$$
$$(k+1) \cdot c = \langle C_1, \ldots, C_{n-1} \rangle^\frown (k \cdot c)$$

Definition 31 A sequence $s = \langle s_1, \ldots, s_n \rangle$ of expressions is an *embedding sequence for* $c = \langle C_1, \ldots, C_n \rangle \in \mathrm{Cat_G}^n$ iff

  i. each s_i is of category C_i, $1 \le i \le n$, and

  ii. each $s_i \mathrm{ICONs}_{i+1}$, $1 \le i < n$,

An expression t *embeds* c iff for some embedding sequence $\langle s_1, \ldots, s_n \rangle$ for c, we have $s_n \mathrm{CONt}$.

Call $c = \langle C_1, \ldots, C_n \rangle$ a *cycle* iff $n > 1$, $C_n = C_1$ and for every positive integer k, there is a t which embeds $k \cdot c$. c is a *minimal cycle* iff $C_1, \ldots, C_{n-1}$ are all distinct. (Note that if a cycle c has length n then $k \cdot c$ has length $n + (n-1)(k-1)$.)

A *proper cycle* c is a minimal cycle such that for every embedding sequence $\langle s_1, \ldots, s_n \rangle$ for c, $|\mathrm{string}(s_n)| > |\mathrm{string}(s_1)|$.

Expression t is a *cyclic extension* of u iff there is a proper cycle $c = \langle C_1, \ldots, C_n \rangle$ such that for some positive integer k, $k \cdot c$ has an embedding sequence s with $s_1 = u$ and $s_{|s|} = t$. (Recall: the length of a sequence s is noted $|s|$ and its i'th coordinate s_i. So $s_{|s|}$ is its last coordinate.)

Category C is a *cyclic category* if there is a minimal cycle c with first coordinate C. Expression u is a *cyclic expression* iff it is the first coordinate of an embedding sequence for a minimal cycle.

Axiom 7 (Cyclicity) Every G has a proper cycle.

Fact 28 *Cyclicity entails that for some C, PH(C) is infinite, whence* L_G *is infinite.*

Examples from the syntax of $\mathrm{Eng_{RC}}$ (recalled from page 88):

Fact 29 $c = \langle \mathrm{NP}, \mathrm{NP/N}, \mathrm{NP} \rangle$ *is a proper cycle, embedded by*

$$(\text{John's teacher's doctor}, \mathrm{NP}).$$

One embedding sequence is

$$\langle (\text{John}, \mathrm{NP}), (\text{John's}, \mathrm{NP/N}), (\text{John's teacher}, \mathrm{NP}) \rangle.$$

So (John's teacher, NP) *is a cyclic extension of* (John, NP). *Another embedding sequence for c is*

$$\langle (\text{John's teacher}, \text{NP}), \\ (\text{John's teacher's}, \text{NP/N}), \\ (\text{John's teacher's doctor}, \text{NP}) \rangle.$$

$2 \cdot c = \langle \text{NP}, \text{NP/N}, \text{NP}, \text{NP/N}, \text{NP} \rangle.$ *It is embedded by*

$$\langle (\text{John}, \text{NP}), \\ (\text{John's}, \text{NP/N}), \\ (\text{John's teacher}, \text{NP}), \\ (\text{John's teacher's}, \text{NP/N}), \\ (\text{John's teacher's doctor}, \text{NP}) \rangle.$$

So (John's teacher's doctor, NP) *is a cyclic extension of* (John, NP).

Fact 30 *If t is an embedding sequence for* $k \cdot \langle \text{NP}, \text{NP/N}, \text{NP} \rangle$ *then*

$$\langle t, (t^\frown \text{'s}, \text{NP/N}), (t^\frown \text{'s doctor}, \text{NP}) \rangle$$

is an embedding sequence for $(k + 1) \cdot \langle \text{NP}, \text{NP/N}, \text{NP} \rangle.$

Fact 31 $\langle \text{NP/N}, \text{NP}, \text{NP/N} \rangle$ *is embedded by* (John's teacher's doctor, NP) *with embedding sequence*

$$\langle (\text{John's}, \text{NP/N}), \\ (\text{John's father}, \text{NP}), \\ (\text{John's father's}, \text{NP/N}) \rangle$$

Definition 32 A category C of G is *unbounded* iff for all n there is an $m > n$ such that $\text{PH}(C) \cap (\text{Lex}_m - \text{Lex}_n) \neq \emptyset.$

So if C is unbounded we know that whenever some (s, C) is in some Lex_n we can always find a new expression of category C in some Lex_m, $m > n$.

Fact 32 *All cyclic categories are unbounded, so all bounded categories are non-cyclic*

Axiom 8 All unbounded categories are cyclic.

Axioms 7 and 8 jointly yield something like the "constant growth property" (Joshi et al. 1991, Stabler 2003a) applied to structures, not strings: beyond some Lex_n, new expressions are cyclic extensions of old ones. And since each cycle has a fixed length new expressions beyond Lex_n differ in a fixed structural way from the expression in Lex_n they are cyclic extensions of. This should guarantee:

Conjecture 22 *There is an n such that for all* $m > n$, *all* $s \in \text{Lex}_m - \text{Lex}_{m-1}$, *s is a cyclic extension of an* $s' \in \text{Lex}_n$ *or s properly embeds such an extension but has itself no cyclic extensions.*

The idea here is that in moving up the complexity hierarchy we reach a level Lex_n beyond which we only get new expressions by cyclic extensions simpliciter or by cyclic extensions followed by some operations, e.g. Yes-No question Formation, which block further cyclic embedding of the expression. (Thanks to Philippe Schlenker for discussion of this idea).

Axiom 9 (Foundation) For $s, t \in L_G$, if $sPCONt$ then $s \neq t$.

Foundation fails for some G due to a failure of antisymmetry in constituency. Consider functions f,g such that, inter alia,

$$g(t, C) = (a^\frown t, C') \text{ and } f(a^\frown t, C') = (t, C).$$

Then $(t, C)PCON(t, C)$ contradicting Foundation. This happens in many familiar, non-linguistic settings. For example in integer arithmetic let *suc* be addition of 1, *pred* subtraction of 1. Observe that the integers are the closure of $\{0\}$ under $\{$suc,pred$\}$. (We could bring this fully into the grammatical setting by giving all numbers the same category Z.) Then $0ICONsuc(0), suc(0)ICONpred(suc(0))$, so $0PCONpred(suc(0))$, contradicting Foundation since $0 = \text{pred}(1) = \text{pred}(\text{suc}(0))$. Thus by the Foundation Axiom, the integers, so constructed, are not a possible natural language. The axiom also rules out "symmetric" grammars like the Lambek calculus, Pregroup Grammars, and Multimodal Type-Logical Grammars, as discussed in §3.2.3 above. But it would have three possibly desirable consequences:

Theorem 23 *Foundation* $\Rightarrow$ *CON is antisymmetric (and thus a reflexive partial order).*

Proof. Let sCONt and tCONs. Show s = t. Let u,v be IC sequences (sequences of expressions in which each non-last one is an immediate constituent of the next one) with $|u| = n \geq 1$ and $|v| = m \geq 1$ such that $s = u_1$ and $t = u_n$ and $t = v_1$ and $s = v_m$. If n = 1 then $u = \langle b \rangle$ for some b, and s = b = t, so s = t as was to be shown. Similarly if m = 1 then s = t. And these are the only possibilities, for suppose that $n, m > 1$. Then $\langle u_1, \ldots, u_n, v_2, \ldots, v_m \rangle$ is an IC sequence of length $n + (m - 1) > 1$. Thus u_1PCONv_m so by Foundation $u_1 \neq v_m$. But $u_1 = s$ and $v_m = s$, a contradiction, completing the proof. $\square$

Definition 33 The *ith projection function* of arity n, $p[i, n]$ is that map from $L_G{}^n$ into L_G sending each n-ary sequence of expressions to its ith coordinate. So then $\text{id}_G = p[1, 1]$.

Theorem 24 *No projection function on L_G is in Rule$_G$.*

Exercise 27 Prove Theorem 24.

Theorem 25 *(Elimination of Derived Lexical Items) Write G/s for that grammar like G except that* $\mathrm{Lex}_{G/s} = \mathrm{Lex}_G - \{s\}$. *Then, given Foundation, if* s $\in$ Lex_G *is derived then* $L_G = L_{G/s}$ *and* $\mathrm{Aut}_G = \mathrm{Aut}_{G/s}$.

Proof in Appendix B.

Exercise 28 Why do we need the assumption of Foundation in Theorem 25?

Economy? Foundation blocks some cases that linguists might rule out on "economy" grounds: Consider the context free grammar:

> **V:** John
> **Cat:** NP

And where ⇢ is given by the following:

> NP⇢John   NP⇢NP

This grammar allows derivations of arbitrary length of the string *John* from NP. Obviously, the second rule can be removed from G without changing the language generated. Translating the grammar into a bare grammar bg(G) in the way described on page 101, the second rule becomes

$$\begin{array}{c} S \\ NP \end{array} \xrightarrow{F_{NP\rightarrow NP}} \begin{array}{c} S \\ NP \end{array}$$

This function $F_{NP\rightarrow NP}$ is exactly the identity map $\mathrm{id}_{bg(G)}$ on the language, and so the grammar violates Foundation.

Duke of York Derivations (DYDs). An apparent empirical challenge to Foundation are DYDs, first discussed by Pullum (1976) and recently elaborated by McCarthy (2003). Simplifying their phonetic notation slightly, a DYD in Nootka phonology is given as follows:

$$\mathrm{mo:q} \xrightarrow{\mathrm{Lab}} \mathrm{mo:q^w} \xrightarrow{\mathrm{DeLab}} \mathrm{mo:q}$$

Labialization applies to a dorsal consonant (e.g. q) when it follows a rounded vowel (e.g. o:). Delabialization applies to dorsal consonants when syllable final. This yields an ICON sequence of length 3, as above, with identical first and last elements, *mo:q*, contrary to Foundation.

We are not sure that DYDs are counterexamples to Foundation. The direct formulation of (De)Lab as functions is unsound, generating expressions like *mo:qw* which are not grammatical. We find it hard to see why the rules were formulated in this unnatural way. Here for example is a direct formulation of the phenomenon compatible with Foundation: k ranges over dorsal consonants, L is the function we're defining.

Domain	L	Value	Conditions
$\langle \ldots, s, k, t, \ldots \rangle$	$\mapsto$	$\langle \ldots, s, k^w, t, \ldots \rangle$	s a round vowel t a vowel

In other words you just labialize a dorsal consonant when it follows a round vowel and begins a syllable. Obviously more Nootka data than the little McCarthy gives to illustrate the DYD are needed to justify or refute the adequacy of a function like L in (18). But McCarthy does note that there is no reason in Nootka to have the intermediate state in (17), as it is not well formed and no other functions apply to it to "save" it from oblivion.

But if further empirical work supports the insightfulness of DYDs or the Lambek grammars, we should consider weakening Foundation. Weak Foundation below is one such. Another candidate is Axiom 11.

Axiom 10 (Weak Foundation) For all $s, t \in L_G$, sICONt $\Rightarrow s \neq t$.

Weak Foundation still implies Theorem 24 above, and so blocks a function that would map an expression to itself. But it does not entail Foundation or Theorem 23 or 25, and it allows IC sequences of length $n > 2$ in which the first and last coordinates are identical. That is, the effect of a rule applied early can be nullified later.

Axiom 11 Every minimal cycle is proper.

This implies that the first and last expressions in a minimal cycle are not identical and thus guarantees Foundation for cyclic expressions.

4.4 Constraints relating form and meaning

We assume some familiarity with the basics of a model theoretic interpretation for languages. We take an extensional model for a natural language to be a triple $\langle E, 2, m \rangle$ where E is a non-empty set (of entities), 2 is the minimal boolean lattice $\{1, 0\}$ of truth values, and m is a function mapping lexical expressions to elements in the sets in the type hierarchy generated by E and 2, TH(E, 2). TH(E, 2) is the least collection of sets containing E and 2 and closed under finite products and the formation of function spaces (meaning the set $[A \rightarrow B]$ of functions from A into B is in TH(E,2) whenever A and B are). Here we replace (E, 2) with an arbitrary ontology O, a collection of sets usually with designated relations (functions, elements). E.g. for natural language models we may want our ontology to include a set T of times, or intervals, with an order (or overlap) relation, a set of possible worlds with an accessibility relation, etc. So a model is now simply a pair (O,m). Different languages might have different ontologies O.

Given a set A on which are defined a family of relations R_i, an automorphism is a bijection on A which fixes each relation R_i. An invariant of this structure is any object over A (element of A, subset of A,...) fixed by all the automorphisms. For example suppose that our structure is the three element set $\{x, y, z\}$ on which is defined a single partial order relation $\leq$ represented by the Hasse diagram below:

All automorphisms of this structure fix x (map it to itself), but an automorphism may interchange y and z. So x is a fixed object, the set $\{y, z\}$ is fixed, etc. We refer to these objects as semantic invariants when $(A, \leq)$ is used as a denotation set for expressions in a language. We turn now to some general properties relating form and meaning in natural language.

Axiom 12 (Global Compositionality) (Fulop and Keenan 1998, Keenan and Stabler 2002) For each G, $M_G = \{m|\ \exists O,\ (O, m)$ is a model of $L_G\}$ satisfies, for each $F \in F_G$,

$$\{\langle m(d), m(F(d))\rangle|\ d \in \text{Domain}(F)\ \&\ m \in M_G\}\text{ is a function.}$$

Theorem 26 *Global Compositionality* $\Rightarrow$ *Globality. That is, for all* $d, d' \in \text{Domain}(F)$, *all* $m, m' \in M_G$,

$$\text{if } m(d) = m'(d'),\text{ then } m(F(d)) = m'(F(d'))$$

Furthermore, Global Compositionality $\Rightarrow$ *Compositionality. That is, for all* $F \in F_G$, *all models* (O, m) *of* L_G,

$$\{\langle m(d), m(F(d))\rangle|\ d \in \text{Domain}(F)\}\text{ is a function.}$$

Axiom 13 (Model Closure under isomorphism, MC) For each model (O, m) of L_G and isomorphism π of O, $(\pi(O), \pi \circ m)$ is a model of L_G.

Theorem 27 *If d is semantically constant in the sense of having the same denotation in all models with the same ontology then for all models (O,m), m(d) is a semantic invariant. (Keenan and Stavi 1986, Keenan 2001)*

Proof. Let d be semantically constant. Show for all $M = (O, m)$, all automorphisms μ of O, that $\mu(m(d)) = m(d)$. Observe that $\mu(M) = (O, \mu \circ m)$ is a model, by MC. Whence

$$
\begin{aligned}
\mu(m(d)) &= (\mu \circ m)(d) &&\text{Model closure}\\
&= m(d) &&\text{d is a semantic constant}
\end{aligned}
$$

$\square$

Note that, *contra* Etchemendy (1990, esp. Ch.12) (i) denoting invariant objects does seem to be a property common to the denotations of "logical constants," and (ii) holding interpretations of an expression constant cannot be done freely, i.e. if we hold constant *is a senator* then in any model M it denotes the empty set or all of E, as they are the only invariant subsets of E.

Axiom 14 (Meaning Recoverability, MR) For $F \in \text{Rule}_G$ and $d, d' \in \text{Domain}(F) \cap \text{Lex}_G{}^*$, if $d \simeq d'$ and $d \neq d'$ then $F(d) \neq F(d')$

Notice that $d \simeq d'$ entails $F(d) \simeq F(d')$. The intuition here is easy: simple expressions which are distinct but isomorphic may almost always be interpreted differently.[3] *Mary* vs. *Sue*; *laughed* vs. *cried*; *Bill laughed* vs. *John cried*. So e.g. if *laugh* and *cry* are isomorphic but distinct we expect (correctly) their infinitival forms *to laugh* and *to cry* to be distinct (and isomorphic) as well as their gerund forms *laughing* and *crying*. If the gerund forms of *laugh* and *cry* were both *blicking*, and so MR failed, the meaning of each would be unrecoverable from the derived form. Similarly the gerundive nominal *Bill's laughing* is distinct but isomorphic to *John's crying*; if they were both *Sam's talking* an inherent loss of meaning would be associated with the nominalization process. There may be occasional counterexamples to MR, but the claim is that there are no "systematic" ones.

Axiom 14 tells us that syntactically invariant expressions are either lexical items or built by rule from grammatically invariant lexical items, Theorem 28 below. We write K_{GC} for the set of invariant expressions (grammatical constants) in $K \subseteq L_G$,

Theorem 28 MR $\Rightarrow L_{GC} = \text{closure}(\text{Lex}_{GC}, \text{Rule}_G)$

<u>Proof.</u> ($\supseteq$) We first show $\text{Lex}_{GC} \subseteq L_{GC}$ and L_{GC} is closed with respect to arbtrary $F \in \text{Rule}_G$.

i. Let $d \in \text{Lex}_{GC} \subseteq \text{Lex}_G$. Then $d \in L_G$ and d is grammatically constant so $d \in L_{GC}$.

ii. Let $d_1, \ldots, d_n \in L_{GC}$ with $d = \langle d_1, ..., d_n \rangle \in \text{Domain}(F)$. Show $F(d) \in L_{GC}$.

Letting π be any syntactic automorphism,

$$\pi(F(d_1, \ldots, d_n)) = F(\pi(d_1), \ldots, \pi(d_n)) = F(d_1, \ldots, d_n),$$

since $d_1, \ldots, d_n \in L_{GC}$, so $\pi(F(d)) = F(d)$ and so $F(d) \in L_{GC}$.

($\subseteq$) Set $K = \{d \in L_G | \text{ if } d \in L_{GC} \text{ then } d \in \text{closure}(\text{Lex}_{GC}, \text{Rule}_G)\}$.

i. ($\text{Lex} \subseteq K$) Let $d \in \text{Lex}$ and suppose $d \in L_{GC}$. Then $d \in \text{Lex}_{GC} \subseteq \text{closure}(\text{Lex}_{GC}, \text{Rule}_G)$.

ii. Let d be a tuple of elements of K with $d \in Domain(F)$. Show $F(d) \in K$. Suppose $F(d) \in L_{GC}$. Show $F(d) \in closure(Lex_{GC}, Rule_G)$. Suppose, leading to a contradiction, that some $d_i \notin L_{GC}$. Let π be an automorphism such that $\pi(d_i) \neq d_i$. Thus $\pi(d) \neq d$. Since trivially $d \simeq \pi(d)$ we have that $F(d) \simeq F(\pi(d))$. But $F(\pi(d)) = \pi(F(d))$ since π commutes with generating functions, and $\pi(F(d)) = F(d)$ since $F(d) \in L_{GC}$. So $F(d) = F(\pi(d))$, a contradiction. Thus all $d_i \in L_{GC}$, so each $d_i \in closure(Lex_{GC}, Rule_G)$, and so $F(d) \in closure(Lex_{GC}, Rule_G)$, since this set is closed with respect to F, completing the proof.

$\square$

Notice that Theorem 28 has no semantic analogue: Semantic constants may be syntactically complex without being built from (simpler) semantic constants. E.g. *Either there exist pink swans or there don't* is semantically constant even though *pink* and *swans* are not.

Finally, we provide a slightly more refined version of Thesis 2 from Lecture 1:

Axiom 15 Syntactic invariants denote semantic invariants in the following sense:

i. If an expression d is invariant then in any model (O,m), m(d) is invariant.

ii. Invariant expressions have the same denotation in all models with the same ontology (And these denotations are invariant; Theorem 27)

iii. Syntactically invariant expressions are isomorphism invariant: For all models $\mathcal{M} = (O, m)$ and $\mathcal{M}' = (O', m')$ and all isomorphisms $\pi : \mathcal{M} \to \mathcal{M}'$, $m'(d) = \pi(m(d))$.

iv. If PH(C) is a closed class (that is, it does not add new members freely), then Den(C) is absolutely upper bounded; that is, $\exists n \forall O \, |Den_O C| \leq n$.

We first give a few unsystematic examples, assuming the relevant expressions to be syntactically invariant, and then one more systematically modeled one, Case Marking. We assume a standard extensional ontology.

1. The reflexive *himself* interpreted as SELF, as in,

    Each worker criticized himself in front of his buddies.

    SELF maps binary relations to properties by: $\text{SELF}(R) = \{a|\ aRa\}$

2. The passive operator interpreted as PASS, as in,

    The door was opened $\ = (\text{The door})(\text{Pass}(\text{open}))$,

    where PASS maps binary relations to properties by: $\text{PASS}(R) = \{b|\ \exists a, aRb\}$.

3. The agentive *by* interpreted as BY, as in,

    The door was opened by Fred $\ = (\text{The door})(\text{Pass}(\text{open by Fred}))$.

    BY maps individuals to maps from binary (n-ary) relations to binary (n-ary) relations:

    $$\text{BY}(x)(R) = \{\langle a, b\rangle|\ a = x \wedge \langle a, b\rangle \in R\}$$

4. Case Marking. In Kor for all models (O,m), m(-acc, Ka) = ACC is semantically invariant.

Exercise 29 Using the definitions just above, compute that (a) and (b) are logically equivalent:

a. John hugged Bill

b. Bill was hugged by John (= Bill Pass(hug (by John)))

Notice that there are semantic constants which are not grammatical constants. For example, *sixty-seven* and *fifty-seven* are semantic constants but can be interchanged by a syntactic automorphism of English.

It is easy to see that Axiom 15 constrains the form of allowable grammars. We could not enrich an adequate grammar of English with the apparently redundant rule F whose domain was {(John, NP)} and whose value at its only argument is (John, NP) (or for that matter, anything at all). The reason is simply that syntactic automorphisms fix the domains of generating functions, so English+F requires that all syntactic automorphisms map (John, NP) to itself, so it is a grammatical constant, whence by Axiom 15.1 it is a semantic constant. But in fact it is not a semantic constant; in different models (with the same ontology) *John* may denote different individuals.

It is also easy to see that Axiom 15 constrains the content of models. In simple Ss the present/past/future tense marking in Malagasy seems interchangeable:

(21)   m-/n-/h-ianatra   teny   angilisy Rabe
       pres-/past-/fut-study language English Rabe

'Rabe is studying/studied/will-study English'

Nor does it seem unreasonable that tense marking might be semantically symmetric: we could systematically permute past and future, holding present constant for example. But more detailed study reveals that they cannot be interchanged. For example, many verbs select complements in the future tense:

(22)   n-ibaiko   an-dRabe *m-/*n-/h-anolo   ny kodiarana
       past-order acc-Rabe pres/past/fut-replace the tire
       Rasoa
       Rasoa

'Rasoa ordered Rabe to change the tire'

Also many root adjectives, and the very few root verbs, mark future but do not distinguish past and present:

(23)   a. Tonga Rabe
            Arrive Rabe

            'Rabe arrived/is-arriving'

        b. Ho tonga Rabe
            Fut arrive Rabe

            'Rabe will arrive'

So future tense marking appears to be a fixed point of syntactic automorphisms, whence by Axiom 15 it must denote an invariant object. So Future and Past must not be symmetrically related in interpretations of Malagasy. This will be so for example in a model in which in addition to E and 2 we have a set T of "times" (or intervals) equipped with a temporal ordering relation $>$, a distinguished point NOW with FUTURE defined as $>$ NOW. (Semantic automorphisms fix the temporal order and fix the NOW point).

These fleeting remarks relating form and interpretation are all too fleeting. They serve nonetheless to illustrate natural hypotheses specific to our invariance perspective, ones which, while in need of refinement, help clarify the distinction between syntactic and semantic properties of grammatical formatives.

Appendix A. The bounded structure theorem

We prove Theorem 21, stated on page 156:

(Bounded Structure) If Lex is finite and for all F, Lex∩Range(F) = ∅, then for some n, the set of partial automorphisms on Lex_n is exactly the set of automorphisms of G restricted to Lex_n.

Lemma 29 $\{h \upharpoonright Lex_n | \ h \in Aut_G\} \subseteq Aut_n$

Proof. Write h_n for $h \upharpoonright Lex_n$. By U4 on page 28, Lex_n is invariant, so

$$Lex_n = h(Lex_n) = \{h(s)| \ s \in Lex_n\} = \{h_n(s)| \ s \in Lex_n\} = h_n(Lex_n).$$

So h_n is a bijection on Lex_n. h in Aut_G fixes each Domain(F), so for $t \in Domain(Fn) \subseteq Lex_{n-1}^*$, $h(t) \in Domain(F_n)$, so $h(Domain(F_n)) \subseteq Domain(F_n)$, whence equality holds since h was arbitrary. Thus $h_n(Domain(F_n)) = Domain(F_n)$. And $h_n(F_n(t)) = h(F(t)) = F(h(t)) = F_n(h_n(t))$, so h_n commutes with F_n. □

Lemma 30 *For all n, all* $h', h'' \in Aut_n$, *if* h' *and* h'' *extend* $h_0 \in Aut_0$ *then* $h' = h''$.

Proof. By induction on n. Fix h_0, set $K = \{n|$ the lemma holds$\}$

i. $(0 \in K)$. Let s be arbitrary in Lex_0. Then $h'(s) = h_0(s) = h''(s)$ since h', h'' extend h_0.

ii. Assume $n \in K$. Show $n + 1 \in K$. Let $s \in Lex_{n+1}$. If $s \in Lex_n$ the lemma holds by the IH. So we assume $s \in Lex_{n+1} - Lex_n$. So $s = F(t)$, some $t \in Lex_n^* \cap Domain(F)$. So each $t_i \in Lex_n$, so by the IH, $h'(t_i) = h''(t_i)$. Whence $h'(s) = h'(F(t)) = F(h'(t)) = F(h''(t)) = h''(F(t)) = h''(s)$.
□

Thus if an h_0 in Aut_0 extends to an Aut_n it extends uniquely.

Lemma 31 $h \in Aut_n \Rightarrow h^{-1} \in Aut_n$

Proof. Assume the antecedent. Then h^{-1} is a bijection on Lex_n. And since $Domain(F_n) = h(Domain(F_n))$ then

$$h^{-1}(Domain(F_n)) = h^{-1}(h(Domain(Fn))) = Domain(Fn).$$

And for any $t \in Domain(F_n)$, $h^{-1}(t) \in Domain(Fn)$, and $F_n(h^{-1}(t)) = h^{-1}(h(F_n(h^{-1}(t)))) = h^{-1}(F_n(h(h(h^{-1}(t))))) = h^{-1}(F_n(t))$ so h commutes with each F_n proving that $h^{-1} \in Aut_n$. □

Lemma 32 *For every n, each* $h \in Aut_n$ *extends some* $h' \in Aut_0$.

Proof. Let n arbitrary, $h \in Aut_n$ arbitrary. Write h_0 for $h \upharpoonright Lex_0$. We show that $h_0 \in Aut_0$. h_0 is one to one since h is. For onto, let

$s \in \text{Lex}_0$. Then $h(s) = h_0(s) \in \text{Lex}_0$, otherwise $h(s) = F(t)$, some F, t. But then $s = h^{-1}(h(s)) = h^{-1}(F(t)) = F(h^{-1}(t))$, contradicting U4 (using Lemma 31). Thus $h_0(\text{Lex}_0) \subseteq \text{Lex}_0$. For equality, let $t \in \text{Lex}_0$, let t' such that $h(t') = t$, since h is onto Lex_n. Again if $t' \notin \text{Lex}_0$ then t' is some $F(u)$ and $t = h(F(u)) = F(h(u))$, contradicting U4. Thus $t' \in \text{Lex}_0$, so $h_0(t') = t$, so h_0 is onto Lex_0 and thus a bijection. Similarly let $u \in \text{Domain}(F_0)$. Then since h fixes $\text{Domain}(F)$, $h(u) = h_0(u) \in \text{Domain}(F) \upharpoonright \text{Lex}_0^* = \text{Domain}(F_0)$ since $h_0(u_i) \in \text{Lex}_0$. Thus $h_0(\text{Domain}(F_0)) \subseteq \text{Domain}(F_0)$. For equality, again let $u \in \text{Domain}(F_0)$, let $h(u') = u$. If $u' \in \text{Lex}_0^*$ then some u_i' is some $F(v)$, whence $h(u_i') = h(F(v)) = F(h(v)) \in \text{Lex}_0$, contradicting A2. Thus $u' \in \text{Lex}_0^*$ and so $h_0(u') = u$, whence h_0 is onto. Thus h_0 is bijective on Lex_0 and fixes each $\text{Domain}(F_0)$. h_0 commutes with each F_0 vacuously, since for all $u \in \text{Domain}(F_0)$, $F(u) \in \text{Lex}_0$ by A2. Thus $h_0 \in \text{Aut}_0$ and h is, trivially, an extension of h_0. $\qquad\square$

Lemma 33 *If for all n, $h_0 \in \text{Aut}_0$ extends to some $h_n \in \text{Aut}_n$, then for all k,m with $k < m$, h_m extends h_k.*

Proof. Let h_0 extend as per the lemma. By Lemma 30 each h_n is unique. Set $K = \{n \in N|$ for all $m > n$, h_m extends $h_n\}$

i. $0 \in K$ since each h_m is given as an extension of h_0.

ii. Suppose $n \in K$, show $n + 1 \in K$. Let $m > n + 1$, let $s \in \text{Lex}_{n+1}$. Show $h_m(s) = h_n(s)$.

Case 1. $s \in \text{Lex}_n$. Then by the IH since $m, n + 1 > n$, $h_m(s) = h_n(s) = h_{n+1}(s)$.

Case 2. $s \in \text{Lex}_{n+1} - \text{Lex}_n$. So $s = F(u)$, some $u \in \text{Lex}_n^*$, so h_m and h_{n+1} agree on the u_i, by reasoning analogous to case 1. Whence $h_m(s) = h_m(F(u)) = F(h_m(u)) = F(h_n(u)) = h_n(F(u)) = h_n(s)$. $\qquad\square$

Lemma 34 *If for all n, $h_0 \in \text{Aut}_0$ extends to some $h_n \in \text{Aut}_n$, then $h^* : L_G \to L_G$ defined by $h^*(s) = h_m(s)$, m least such that $s \in \text{Lex}_m$ is in Aut_G and h^* extends h_0.*

Proof.

i. h^* is a function: if $\langle s, t \rangle \in h^*$ and $\langle s, t' \rangle \in h^*$ then for some m, m', $\langle s, t \rangle \in h_m$ and $\langle s, t' \rangle \in h_{m'}'$. So $t = t'$ since one of h_n, h_m extends the other by Lemma 33.

ii. h^* extends h_0 directly from def h^*

iii. $\text{Domain}(h^*) = \bigcup_n(\text{Domain}(h_n)) = L_G$. Similarly $\text{Range}(h^*) = \bigcup_n(\text{Range}(h_n)) = L_G$ since each h_n is onto Lex_n and any $s \in L_G$ lies in some Lex_n. So h^* is onto.

iv. h^* is one to one. Let $s \neq s' \in L_G$. Let n least such that both $s, s' \in \text{Lex}_n$. Then $h^*(s) = h_n(s) \neq h_n(s')$, since h_n is one to one, $= h^*(s')$.

v. h^* commutes with each F in Rule. Let $F(t) \in L_G$ with n least such that $F(t) \in \text{Lex}_n$. Then $h^*(F(t)) = h_n(F(t)) = F(h_n(t)) = F(h^*(t))$.

□

Finally, the Bounded Structure Theorem can be stated as follows:

Theorem 25 For some n, $\text{Aut}_n = \{h \restriction \text{Lex}_n \mid h \in \text{Aut}_G\}$.

Proof. The right to left direction is just Lemma 29. For the left to right direction observe that for each $h \in \text{Aut}_0$ that does not extend to an $h' \in \text{Aut}_G$ there is an n such that h does not extend to any $h'' \in \text{Aut}_n$. Otherwise for every n, h would extend to an element of Aut_n and thus by Lemma 34 to an $h' \in \text{Aut}_G$, a contradiction. Since Aut_0 is finite (it is a subset of $\text{PERM}(\text{Lex}_0)$ and Lex_0 is finite), there is a least n such that all $h \in \text{Aut}_0$ which do not extend to an $h' \in \text{Aut}_G$ do not extend to Aut_n. So for that n all $h \in \text{Aut}_n$ extend to an h' in Aut_G, that is, $\{h \restriction \text{Lex}_n \mid h \in \text{Aut}_G\} \subseteq \text{Aut}_n$, completing the proof. □

Appendix B. Elimination of Derived Lexical Items

We prove Theorem 25, stated on page 161:

(Elimination of Derived Lexical Items)   Write G/s for that grammar
like G except that $\mathrm{Lex}_{G/s} = \mathrm{Lex}_G - \{s\}$. Then, given Foundation, if $s \in \mathrm{Lex}_G$ is derived then $L_G = L_{G/s}$ and $\mathrm{Aut}_G = \mathrm{Aut}_{G/s}$.

Lemma 35 *If sCONt and tICONu then sPCONu.*

Proof. If $s = t$ then sICONu so (s, u) is an IC sequence showing that
sPCONu. If $s \neq t$ then let v be an IC sequence which shows that
sPCONt. $\langle v_1, \ldots, v_n, u \rangle$ is an IC sequence of length $n + 1 > 1$, which
shows that sPCONu.   □

Lemma 36 *If sICONt and tCONu then sPCONu.*

An easy variant of the proof above works here as well.

Theorem 37 *Let* $h \in \mathrm{Aut}_G$, $s \in \mathrm{Lex}$. *Suppose that* $h(s) \notin \mathrm{Lex}$. *Then*
s itself is derived. That is, $s = F(d)$ *for some* $F \in \mathrm{Rule}_G$ *and some*
tuple $d \in L_G{}^* \in \mathrm{Domain}(F)$.

Proof. Since $h(s) \notin \mathrm{Lex}$ and $h(s) \in L_G$ we have that for some F
and some tuple u in $\mathrm{Domain}(F)$, $h(s) = F(u)$. So $s = h^{-1}(h(s)) =$
$h^{-1}(F(u)) = F(h^{-1}(u))$, so s is derived.   □

Moral. The value of an automorphism h at a derived expression,
whether it is in Lex or not, is determined by its values at what it
is derived from. So in defining automorphisms we need only consider
their values at lexical items, and we can ignore lexical items that are
also derived.

Theorem 38 *Given* $G = \langle V, \mathrm{Cat}, \mathrm{Lex}, \mathrm{Rule}\rangle$, *let* $s \in \mathrm{Lex}$ *be derived.*
That is, $s = F(d)$, *for some tuple d. Set* $G/s = \langle V, \mathrm{Cat}, \mathrm{Lex} - \{s\}, \mathrm{Rule}\rangle$.
Recall that $\mathrm{Domain}(F) \subseteq (V^* \times Cat)^*$. *Then*

$$\text{if } L_{G/s} = L_G \text{ then } \mathrm{Aut}_{G/s} = \mathrm{Aut}_G.$$

Proof. Assume the antecedent. Then

$h \in \mathrm{Aut}_{G/s}$ iff h is a bijection on $L_{G/s}$ and h fixes all $F \in \mathrm{Rule}$
                                     iff h is a bijection on L_G and h fixes all $F \in \mathrm{Rule}$
                                     iff $h \in \mathrm{Aut}_G$

                                                                                               □

Remark. If s in Lex was crucially derived from itself in some way then
removing it from Lex might remove it from the language.

Example. $\mathrm{Lex}_G = \{s\}$, $\mathrm{Rule}_G = \{\mathrm{id}_{V^* \times \mathrm{Cat}}\}$. Then $L_G = \{s\}$ and
$L_{G/s} = \emptyset$. A less trivial example is the language of the integers given

earlier: $L_G = \mathrm{closure}(\{(0, Z)\}, \{\mathrm{suc}, \mathrm{pred}\}$. Then L_G is the set of integers (positive, negative and zero). But removing $(0, Z) = \mathrm{suc}(\mathrm{pred}(0, Z))$ from Lex results in the empty language.

Theorem 39 *If G satisfies Foundation and* $s \in$ *Lex is derived, then* $L_G = L_{G/s}$.

Lemma 40 *For any G (with Foundation or not) with some* $s = F(d) \in$ *Lex$_G$, for all* $t \in L_G$, *if* $\neg(sCONt)$ *then* $t \in L_{G/s}$.

Proof. Set $K = \{t \in L_G |$ if $\neg(sCONt)$ then $t \in L_{G/s}\}$

i. Show Lex$_G \subseteq K$. Let $t \in$ Lex$_G$ and assume $\neg(sCONt)$. Then $t \neq s$, so $t \in$ Lex$_G - \{s\} = $ Lex$_{G/s} \subseteq L_{G/s}$

ii. Show K closed under the generating functions F. Let $F \in$ Rule, d a tuple of expressions each of which is in K. Show $F(d) \in K$. Assume $\neg sCON(F(d))$. Then for each coordinate d_i of d, $\neg(sCONd_i)$, otherwise $sCONd_i$ and $d_iICON(F(d))$, whence $sCON(F(d))$, contradicting the assumption on s. Thus each $d_i \in L_{G/s}$, whence $F(d) \in L_{G/s}$ since $L_{G/s}$ is closed under F.

$\square$

Lemma 41 *For any G with* $g \in$ *Rule$_G$,* $u \in L_G{}^* \cap \mathrm{Domain}(g)$ *and s a derived expression* $F(d) \in$ *Lex$_G$,*

$$\text{if } \neg(sCONu_i), \text{ all } 1 \leq i \leq |u|, \text{ then } g(u) \in L_{G/s}.$$

Proof. Assume the antecedent. Then each $u_i \in L_{G/s}$ by Lemma 40. Whence $g(u) \in L_{G/s}$ since $L_{G/s}$ is closed under g. $\square$

Theorem 42 *Given G satisfying Foundation and* $s = F(d) \in$ *Lex as above,* $L_G = L_{G/s}$, *whence by Theorem 38,* Aut$_G = $ Aut$_{G/s}$.

Proof. Since $s = F(d)$ then $\neg(sCONd_i)$, any coordinate d_i of d, otherwise $sCONd_i$ and $d_iICONF(d)$ so $sPCONF(d)$, whence by Foundation $s \neq F(d)$, contradicting our assumption. Thus $\neg(sCONd_i)$, all coordinates d_i of d. Thus by Lemma 36, $F(d) \in L_{G/s}$. Now, set $K = \{w \in L_G | w \in L_{G/s}\}$.

i. Lex$_G \subseteq K$. Let $t \in$ Lex$_G$. If $t \neq s$ then $t \in$ Lex$_G - \{s\} = $ Lex$_G \subseteq L_{G/s}$. If $t = s = F(d)$ then $t \in L_{G/s}$ by the reasoning immediately above.

ii. K is closed under the g in Rule. Let u be a tuple of elements of K which lies in Domain(g). Show $g(u) \in L_{G/s}$. But each $u_i \in K$, so each $u_i \in L_{G/s}$, whence $g(u) \in L_{G/s}$, since $L_{G/s}$ is closed under g.

Thus $L_G \subseteq L_{G/s}$; and since $L_{G/s} \subseteq L_G$ because Lex$_{G/s} \subseteq$ Lex$_G$, equality holds proving the theorem. $\square$

Corollary 43 *Let* $G = \langle V, Cat, Lex, R \rangle$ *satisfy Foundation. If* $D = \{s \in Lex_G | \; s \text{ is derived}\}$ *is finite then* $L_G = L_{G'}$ *and* $Aut_G = Aut_{G'}$, *where* $G' = \langle V, Cat, Lex - D, R \rangle$.

Proof by induction on $card(D)$.

We conclude that when the number of derived expressions in Lex is finite - which of course is the case when Lex itself is finite - then we can treat Lex as though it had no derived expressions as far as deciding what the expressions in the language are and what their structure is.

Notes

[1]A person hierarchy, $1 > 2 > 3$ is used when conjuncts are in different persons. Thus the French *Isabelle et moi*, 'Isabelle and I', and *toi et moi* 'you and I', trigger 1st person plural verb agreement; while *toi et lui* 'you and he' triggers 2nd person plural agreement.

[2]Although many morphological rules have restricted domains that block iteration, lexical rules that can "iterate" do seem to occur. The Bambara reduplication mentioned earlier (page 137) is claimed to be productive in this way. In English, we have the prefixation of *anti-* and noun compounding, for example.

[3]See for example, Clark (1987), Di Sciullo and Williams (1987), and Carstairs-McCarthy (1999).

Acknowledgements

We owe thanks to the following scholars for discussions of this work:
Gerard Huet, Graham Katz, Greg Kobele, Marcus Kracht, Uwe Mönnich,
Yiannis Moschovakis, Ian Pratt, Geoffrey Pullum, and Philippe Schlenker.

References

Asher, R.E. 1985. *Tamil.* London: Croom Helm. Reprinted 1989, London: Routledge.

Avelino, Heriberto. 2004. *Topics in Yalálag Zapotec Grammar.* Doctoral dissertation, UC, Los Angeles. to appear.

Baker, Mark C. 1988. *Incorporation: a theory of grammatical function changing.* Cambridge, Massachusetts: MIT Press.

Baker, Mark C., Kyle Johnson, and Ian Roberts. 1989. Passive arguments raised. *Linguistic Inquiry* 20:219–251.

Bar-Hillel, Y., C. Gaifman, and E. Shamir. 1960. On categorial and phrase structure grammars. *Bulletin of the Research Council of Israel* F9:155–166. Reprinted in Y. Bar-Hillel, *Language and Information: Selected Essays on their Theory and Application.* NY: Addison-Wesley, 1964.

Barton, G. Edward, Robert C. Berwick, and Eric Sven Ristad. 1987. *Computational Complexity and Natural Language.* Cambridge, Massachusetts: MIT Press.

Berwick, Robert C., and Amy S. Weinberg. 1984. *The Grammatical Basis of Linguistic Performance: Language Use and Acquisition.* Cambridge, Massachusetts: MIT Press.

Bird, Steven. 1995. *Computational Phonology: A Constraint-Based Approach.* NY: Cambridge University Press.

Birkhoff, Garrett. 1940. *Lattice Theory.* Providence, Rhode Island: American Mathematical Society. Reprinted 1967.

Black, Cheryl. 1996. A backwards binding construction in Zapotec. *Working Papers of the Summer Institute of Linguistics* 40:75–87.

Bresnan, Joan. 2001. *Lexical-Functional Syntax.* Oxford: Blackwell.

Bresnan, Joan, Ronald M. Kaplan, Stanley Peters, and Annie Zaenen. 1982. Cross-serial dependencies in Dutch. *Linguistic Inquiry* 13(4):613–635.

Bromberger, Sylvain, and Morris Halle. 1989. Why phonology is different. *Linguistic Inquiry* 20:51–70.

Büchi, J. Richard. 1960. Weak second-order arithmetic and finite automata. *Zeitschrift für mathematische Logik und Grundlagen der Mathematik* 6:66–92.

Buszkowski, Wojciech. 1988. Gaifman's theorem on categorial grammars revisited. *Studia Logica* 47(1):21–33.

Buszkowski, Wojciech. 2001a. Lambek Grammars Based on Pregroups. In *Logical Aspects of Computational Linguistics*, ed. Philippe de Groote, Glyn Morrill, and Christian Retoré. Lecture Notes in Artificial Intelligence, No. 2099. NY: Springer.

Buszkowski, Wojciech. 2001b. Pregroups: models and grammars. Adam Mickiewicz University, Poznań, Poland.

Butler, Inez. 1976. Reflexive constructions of Yatzachi Zapotec. *International Journal of American Linguistics* 42:331–337.

Carstairs-McCarthy, Andrew. 1999. *The Origins of Complex Language*. Oxford: Cambridge University Press.

Casadio, Claudia. 2001. Non-commutative linear logic in linguistics. *Grammars* 4(3):167–185.

Casadio, Claudia, and Joachim Lambek. 2002. A tale of four grammars. *Studia Logica* 71(3):315–329.

Chomsky, Noam. 1956. Three models for the description of language. *IRE Transactions on Information Theory* IT-2:113–124.

Chomsky, Noam. 1965. *Aspects of the Theory of Syntax*. Cambridge, Massachusetts: MIT Press.

Chomsky, Noam. 1973. Conditions on transformations. In *A Festschrift for Morris Halle*, ed. Stephen R. Anderson and Paul Kiparsky. NY: Holt, Rinehard & Winston. Reprinted in Chomsky's (1977) *Essays on Form and Interpretation*. Amsterdam: North-Holland.

Chomsky, Noam. 1977. On wh-movement. In *Formal Syntax*, ed. P. Culicover, T. Wasow, and A. Akmajian. Academic.

Chomsky, Noam. 1986. *Knowledge of Language*. NY: Praeger.

Chomsky, Noam. 1995. *The Minimalist Program*. Cambridge, Massachusetts: MIT Press.

Clark, Eve V. 1987. The principle of contrast: a constraint on language acquisition. In *Mechanisms of Language Acquisition*, ed. Brian MacWhinney. 1–33. Hillsdale, New Jersey: Lawrence Erlbaum.

Cohn, P.M. 1965. *Universal Algebra*. NY: Harper and Row.

Corbett, Grenville. 1991. *Gender*. NY: Cambridge University Press.

Corver, Norbert, and Henk C. Van Riemsdijk (ed.). 2001. *Semi-Lexical Categories : The Function of Content Words and the Content of Function Words.* Studies in Generative Grammar, 41. Berlin: De Gruyter.

Culy, Christopher. 1985. The Complexity of the Vocabulary of Bambara. *Linguistics and Philosophy* 8(3):345–352.

Di Sciullo, Anna Maria, and Edwin Williams. 1987. *On the definition of word.* Cambridge, Massachusetts: MIT Press.

Elgot, Calvin C. 1961. Decision problems of finite automata design and related arithmetics. *Transactions of the American Mathematical Society* 98:21–52.

Emonds, Joseph E. 1985. *A Unified Theory of Syntactic Categories.* Dordrecht: Foris.

Enderton, Herbert B. 1972. *A Mathematical Introduction to Logic.* NY: Academic Press.

Etchemendy, John. 1990. *The Concept of Logical Consequence.* Cambridge, Massachusetts: Harvard University Press.

Fiengo, Robert, and Robert May. 1995. *Indices and Identity.* Cambridge, Massachusetts: MIT Press.

Fontana, Josep. 1996. Phonology and syntax in the interpretation of the Tobler-Mussafia law. In *Approaching Second*, ed. Aaron L. Halpern and Arnold M. Zwicky. Stanford, California: CSLI Publications.

Fulop, Sean, and Edward L. Keenan. 1998. Compositionality: A global perspective. *Sonderheft Semantik* 9.

Geach, P.T. 1962. *Reference and Generality.* Ithaca, New York: Cornell University Press.

Gildersleeve, B.L., and Gonzalez Lodge. 1913. *Latin Grammar Third Edition.* NY: MacMillan.

Grätzer, George. 1968. *Universal Algebra.* NY: van Nostrand.

Grimshaw, Jane. 1997. Projection, heads, and optimality. *Linguistic Inquiry* 28:373–422.

Haïk, Isabelle. 1987. Bound variables that need to be. *Linguistic Inquiry* 11:503–530.

Hale, Kenneth. 1983. Warlpiri and the grammar of non-configurational languages. *Natural Language and Linguistic Theory* 1:5–47.

Hale, Mark. 1996. Deriving Wackernagel's law: prosodic and syntactic factors determining clitic placement in the language of the Rigveda. In *Approaching Second*, ed. Aaron L. Halpern and Arnold M. Zwicky. Stanford, California: CSLI Publications.

Halpern, Aaron L., and Arnold M. Zwicky (ed.). 1996. *Approaching Second.* Stanford, California: CSLI Publications.

Harkema, Henk. 2000. A recognizer for minimalist grammars. In *Sixth International Workshop on Parsing Technologies, IWPT'2000.*

Harkema, Henk. 2001. A characterization of minimalist languages. In *Logical Aspects of Computational Linguistics,* ed. Philippe de Groote, Glyn Morrill, and Christian Retoré, 193–211. Lecture Notes in Artificial Intelligence, No. 2099. NY. Springer.

Hawkinson, Annie, and Larry Hyman. 1974. Hierarchies of natural topic in Shona. *Studies in African Linguistics* 5:147–170.

Heim, Irene, and Angelika Kratzer. 1988. *Semantics in Generative Grammar.* Oxford: Blackwell.

Higginbotham, James. 1985. On semantics. *Linguistic Inquiry* 16:547–593.

Hodges, Wilfrid. 1993. *A Shorter Model Theory.* Cambridge: Cambridge University Press.

Hopper, Paul J., and Elizabeth Closs Traugott. 1993. *Grammaticalization.* NY: Cambridge University Press.

Hornstein, Norbert. 1995. *Logical Form: From GB to Minimalism.* Oxford: Basil Blackwell.

Huang, Cheng-Teh James. 1991. Modularity and Chinese A-not-A questions. In *Interdisciplinary Approaches to Language: Essays in Honor of S.-Y. Kuroda,* ed. C. Georgopoulos and R. Ishihara. Dordrecht: Kluwer.

Huang, Cheng-Teh James. 1995. Logical form. In *Government and Binding Theory and the Minimalist Program,* ed. Gert Webelhuth. Cambridge, Massachusetts: MIT Press.

Huttenlocher, Janellen, Marina Vasilyeva, Elina Cymerman, and Susan Levine. 2002. Language input and child syntax. *Cognitive Psychoogy* 45:337–374.

Huybregts, M.A.C. 1976. Overlapping dependencies in Dutch. Technical report. University of Utrecht. Utrecht Working Papers in Linguistics.

Joshi, Aravind. 1985. How much context-sensitivity is necessary for characterizing structural descriptions. In *Natural Language Processing: Theoretical, Computational and Psychological Perspectives,* ed. D. Dowty, L. Karttunen, and A. Zwicky. 206–250. NY: Cambridge University Press.

Joshi, Aravind K., K. Vijay-Shanker, and David Weir. 1991. The convergence of mildly context sensitive grammar formalisms. In *Foundational Issues in Natural Language Processing,* ed. Peter Sells, Stuart

Shieber, and Thomas Wasow. 31–81. Cambridge, Massachusetts: MIT Press.

Keenan, Edward L. 1985. Passive in the world's languages. In *Language Typology and Syntactic Description, Volume 1: Clause Structure*, ed. T. Shopen. Cambridge: Cambridge University Press.

Keenan, Edward L. 1987. Unreducible n-ary quantifiers in natural language. In *Generalized Quantifiers*, ed. P. Gardenfors. Dordrecht: Reidel.

Keenan, Edward L. 1988. On semantics and the binding theory. In *Explaining Language Universals*, ed. J. Hawkins. 105–145. Oxford: Blackwell.

Keenan, Edward L. 1993. Anaphor-antecedent asymmetry: a conceptual necessity? In *Proceedings of SALT III*, ed. Utpal Lahiri and Zachary Wyner. Amsterdam.

Keenan, Edward L. 2001. Logical objects. In *Logic, Meaning and Computation: Essays in Memory of Alonzo Church*, ed. C.A. Anderson and M. Zeleny. 149–180. Boston: Kluwer.

Keenan, Edward L. 2003. Language invariants and the theta generalization. UCLA Syntax/Semantics Seminar.

Keenan, Edward L., and Avery Andrews. 2004. Relative Clauses. In *Language Typology and Syntactic Description (Revised Edition)*, ed. T. Shopen. Cambridge: Cambridge University Press. forthcoming.

Keenan, Edward L., and Leonard M. Faltz. 1985. *Boolean Semantics for Natural Language*. Dordrecht: Reidel.

Keenan, Edward L., and Edward P. Stabler. 1996. Abstract Syntax. In *Configurations: Essays on Structure and Interpretation*, ed. Anna-Maria Di Sciullo, 329–344. Somerville, Massachusetts. Cascadilla Press.

Keenan, Edward L., and Edward P. Stabler. 2002. Syntactic Invariants. In *Algebras, Diagrams and Decisions in Language,Logic and Information*, ed. Ann Copestake and Kees Vermeulen. Stanford, California. CSLI Publications.

Keenan, Edward L., and Jonathan Stavi. 1986. A semantic characterization of natural language determiners. *Linguistics and Philosophy* 9:253–326.

King, Paul J., Kiril Ivanov, and Bjorn Aldag. 1999. The complexity of modellability in finite and computable signatures of a constraint logic for head-driven phrase structure grammar. *Journal of Logic, Language and Information* 8:83–110.

Kracht, Marcus. 1998. Strict compositionality and literal movement grammars. In *Proceedings, Logical Aspects of Computational Linguistics, LACL'98*. 126–142. NY: Springer.

Ladusaw, William. 1983. Logical form and conditions on grammaticality. *Linguistics and Philosophy* 6:389–422.

Lambek, Joachim. 1958. The Mathematics of Sentence Structure. *American Mathematical Monthly* 65:154–170.

Lambek, Joachim. 1993. From categorial grammar to bilinear logic. In *Substructural Logics*, ed. Peter Schroeder-Heister and Kosta Došen. Oxford: Oxford University Press.

Lambek, Joachim. 1995. Bilinear logic in algebra and linguistics. In *Advances in Linear Logic*, ed. Jean-Yves Girard, Yves Lafont, and Laurent Regnier. Cambridge: Cambridge University Press.

Lambek, Joachim. 1999. Type grammars revisited. In *Logical Aspects of Computational Linguistics*, ed. A. Lecomte, F. Lamarche, and G. Perrier. 1–27. Lecture Notes in Artificial Intelligence, No. 1582. NY: Springer.

Lambek, Joachim. 2001. Type grammars as pregroups. *Grammars* 4:21–35.

Lehmann, Christian. 1979. Der Relativsatz. Report 36. Akup Arbeiten des Kölner Universalien-Projekts.

Lehmann, Christian. 1985. Grammaticalization: synchronic variation and diachronic change. *Lingua e Stile* 20(3):303–318.

Manaster-Ramer, Alexis. 1986. Copying in natural languages, context freeness, and queue grammars. In *Proceedings of the 1986 Meeting of the Association for Computational Linguistics*.

May, Robert. 1985. *Logical Form: Its Structure and Derivation*. Cambridge, Massachusetts: MIT Press.

McCarthy, John. 2003. Sympathy, cumulativity and the Duke-of-York gambit. In *The Syllable in Optimality Theory*, ed. Caroline Féry and Ruben van de Vijver. NY: Cambridge University Press. Manuscript version available from the Rutgers Optimality Archive.

Mchombo, Sam. 2000. Quantification and verb morphology: the case of reciprocals in African languages. *Linguistic Analysis* 29:182–213.

McKenzie, Ralph N., George F. McNulty, and Walter F. Taylor. 1987. *Algebras, Lattices and Varieties, Volume I*. Cambridge, Massachusetts: MIT Press.

McNaughton, Robert, and Seymour Papert. 1971. *Counter-Free Automata*. Cambridge, Massachusetts: MIT Press.

Michaelis, Jens. 1998. Derivational minimalism is mildly context-sensitive. In *Proceedings, Logical Aspects of Computational Linguistics, LACL '98.* NY. Springer.

Michaelis, Jens. 2001. Transforming linear context free rewriting systems into minimalist grammars. In *Logical Aspects of Computational Linguistics*, ed. Philippe de Groote, Glyn Morrill, and Christian Retoré, 228–244. Lecture Notes in Artificial Intelligence, No. 2099. NY. Springer.

Mohanan, K.P. 1982. Grammatical relations and clause structure in Malayalam. In *The Mental Representation of Grammatical Relations*, ed. Joan Bresnan. Chap. 8, 504–589. MIT Press.

Mönnich, Uwe. 2001. Regular description of HPSG. Manuscript, Seminar für Sprachwissenschaft, Universität Tübingen.

Montague, Richard. 1969. English as a formal language. In *Linguaggi nella Societá e nella Tecnica*, ed. B. Visentini et al. Milan: Edizioni di Communitá. Reprinted in R.H. Thomason, editor, *Formal Philosophy: Selected Papers of Richard Montague.* New Haven: Yale University Press, §6.

Moortgat, Michael. 1996. Categorial type logics. In *Handbook of Logic and Language*, ed. Johan van Benthem and Alice ter Meulen. Amsterdam: Elsevier.

Moshier, M. Andrew. 1997. Featureless HPSG. In *Specifying Syntactic Structures*, ed. Patrick Blackburn and Maarten de Rijke. 115–156. Stanford, California: CSLI Publications.

Mundy, Joseph L., and Andrew Zisserman. 1992. *Geometric Invariance in Computer Vision.* Cambridge, Massachusetts: MIT Press.

Nandris, Grigore. 1969. *Colloquial Rumanian.* London: Routledge and Kegan Paul.

O'Grady, William. 1987. The interpretation of Korean anaphora. *Language* 63:251–277.

Park, Sung-Hyuk. 1986. Parametrizing the Theory of Binding: the Implications of *caki* in Korean. *Language Research* 22:229–253.

Penchoen, Thomas. 1973. *Tamazight of the Ayt Ndhir.* Los Angeles: Undena Publications.

Pollard, Carl. 1999. Strong generative capacity in HPSG. In *Lexical and Constructional Aspects of Linguistic Explanation*, ed. Gert Webelhuth, Jean-Pierre Koenig, and Andreas Kathol. 281–297. Stanford, California: CSLI Publications.

Pullum, Geoffrey K. 1976. The Duke of York gambit. *Journal of Linguistics* 12:83–102.

Quine, Willard van Orman. 1974. *The Roots of Reference.* NY: Open Court.

Radford, Andrew. 1997. *Syntactic Theory and the Structure of English: A Minimalist Approach.* Cambridge Textbooks in Linguistics. Cambridge: Cambridge University Press.

Radzinski, Daniel. 1990. Unbounded syntactic copying in Mandarin Chinese. *Linguistics and Philosophy* 13:113–127.

Rajemisa-Raolison, Régis. 1971. *Grammaire Malagache, 7th Edition.* Madagascar: Fianarantsoa.

Richter, Frank. 2000. *A Mathematical Formalism for Linguistic Theories with an Application in Head-Driven Phrase Structure Grammar.* Doctoral dissertation, Eberhard-Karls-Universität, Tübingen. (April 28, 2000 version).

Ristad, Eric. 1993. *The Language Complexity Game.* Cambridge, Massachusetts: MIT Press.

Rogers, James. 1999. *A Descriptive Approach to Language-Theoretic Complexity.* NY: Cambridge University Press.

Ross, John R. 1967. *Constraints on Variables in Syntax.* Doctoral dissertation, Massachusetts Institute of Technology.

Schachter, Paul. 1984. Studies in the Structure of Toba Batak. Technical Report UCLA Occasional Papers in Linguistics, Number 5. Los Angeles: UCLA.

Seiver, George O. 1953. *Introduction to Romanian.* NY: Hafner.

Seki, Hiroyuki, Takashi Matsumura, Mamoru Fujii, and Tadao Kasami. 1991. On multiple context-free grammars. *Theoretical Computer Science* 88:191–229.

Shieber, Stuart M. 1985. Evidence Against the Context-Freeness of Natural Language. *Linguistics and Philosophy* 8(3):333–344.

Smith, Marcus. 2002. Partial Agreement in Pima. UCLA M.A. thesis.

Stabler, Edward P. 1997. Derivational minimalism. In *Logical Aspects of Computational Linguistics*, ed. Christian Retoré. 68–95. NY: Springer-Verlag (Lecture Notes in Computer Science 1328).

Stabler, Edward P. 2001. Minimalist grammars and recognition. In *Linguistic Form and its Computation*, ed. Christian Rohrer, Antje Rossdeutscher, and Hans Kamp. Stanford, California: CSLI Publications. (Presented at the SFB340 workshop at Bad Teinach, 1999).

Stabler, Edward P. 2003a. *Computational Minimalism: Acquiring and parsing languages with movement.* Oxford: Basil Blackwell. Forthcoming.

Stabler, Edward P. 2003b. *Language and Evolution*. Los Angeles: UCLA. Lecture notes, forthcoming.

Stabler, Edward P. 2004. Varieties of crossing dependencies: Structure dependence and mild context sensitivity. *Cognitive Science*. Forthcoming.

Steedman, Mark J. 2000. *The Syntactic Process*. Cambridge, Massachusetts: MIT Press.

Taylor, Ann. 1996. A prosodic account of clitic position in Ancient Greek. In *Approaching Second*, ed. Aaron L. Halpern and Arnold M. Zwicky. Stanford, California: CSLI Publications.

Thomas, Wolfgang. 1997. Languages, automata and logic. In *Handbook of Formal Languages, Volume 3: Beyond Words*, ed. G. Rozenberg and A. Salomaa. 389–455. NY: Springer.

Traugott, Elizabeth C., and Bernd Heine. 1991. *Approaches to Grammaticalization*. Amsterdam: John Benjamins.

van Benthem, Johan. 1989. Logical constants across varying types. *Notre Dame Journal of Formal Logic* 30(3):315–342.

Vijay-Shanker, K., and David Weir. 1994. The equivalence of four extensions of context free grammar formalisms. *Mathematical Systems Theory* 27:511–545.

Vikner, Sten. 2001. V^0-to-I^0 movement and *do*-insertion in optimality theory. In *Optimality-theoretic Syntax*, ed. Géraldine Legendre, Jane Grimshaw, and Sten Vikner. Cambridge, Massachusetts: MIT Press.

Weber, David John. 1989. *A Grammar of Huallaga (Huánuco) Quechua*. Los Angeles: University of California Press.

Weir, David. 1988. *Characterizing mildly context-sensitive grammar formalisms*. Doctoral dissertation, University of Pennsylvania, Philadelphia.

Weyl, Hermann. 1952. *Symmetry*. Princeton, New Jersey: Princeton University Press.

Wischer, Ilse, and Gabriele Diewald. 2002. *New Reflections on Grammaticalization*. Amsterdam: John Benjamins.

Wittgenstein, Ludwig. 1922. *Tractatus logico-philosophicus*. London, 1990: Routledge. Translated from the German by C.K. Ogden, with an Introduction by Bertrand Russell.

Zapeda, Ofelia. 1983. *A Papago Grammar*. Tucson: University of Arizona Press.

Zec, Draga, and Sharon Inkelas. 1990. Prosodically constrained syntax. In *The Phonology-Syntax Connection*, ed. Sharon Inkelas and Draga Zec. Stanford, California: CSLI Publications.

Zwicky, Arnold, and Geoffrey Pullum. 1983. Phonology in syntax: the Somali optional agreement rule. *Natural Language and Linguistic Theory* 1:385–402.

Index